MW00901223

"I'm Black and I'm Proud," wished the white girl.

"I'm Black and I'm Proud," wished the white girl.

◆

The Autobiography of Lynn Markovich Bryant

Lynn M. Bryant

iUniverse, Inc.
New York Lincoln Shanghai

"I'm Black and I'm Proud," wished the white girl.
The Autobiography of Lynn Markovich Bryant

All Rights Reserved © 2002, 2003 by Lynn M. Bryant

No part of this book may be reproduced or transmitted in any form or by any means, graphic, electronic, or mechanical, including photocopying, recording, taping, or by any information storage retrieval system, without the written permission of the publisher.

iUniverse, Inc.

For information address:
iUniverse, Inc.
2021 Pine Lake Road, Suite 100
Lincoln, NE 68512
www.iuniverse.com

To All My Former and Current Students:
Please disregard such a diversion from the fundamental conventions of standard grammar, mechanics, and structure, which I emphatically ingrained within you. This only being that this story is told entirely in my voice of total informality and "for-realness."

ISBN: 0-595-27466-8

Printed in the United States of America

Dedicated

To My Momma,
A deeply consecrated and sincere soul

and

To the Bahá'í Faith,
For with the laws of God, racism which is injurious to us all
Will assuredly be resolved

A Special Thanks

To my children Gregory, Jack, and Dee and
Particularly to my husband Bryant

For allowing me the time and attention away from them
To pursue this dream of sharing my story

A Special Note

This book was certainly not written to reveal and manifest a great "literary" piece of art. My true proposal and intent is to share my own very personal story with you, told straight from the heart.

Contents

Preface

Most white people would *never* dare speak or even think about the problem of racism in our dearly loved and cherished homeland of America. But I know this "thing," this dreadfully diminishing and annihilating disease affecting our entire country, has no hope of being eradicated and healed within the "body" of America until we admit that our body is sick, yield to permission for a total screening and examination, and begin following a prescriptive and healing remedy in the process of recovery. As long as we allow ourselves to remain in denial and stand by and do nothing, nothing will get better. And just because an illness may not be in full-fledged exposure does not mean that at any point it can not explode into a fully-blown and contagious epidemic beyond a point of medication and treatment.

If you look at a problem head on accompanied with a sincere heart, you can begin to comprehend and deal with it. This is the beginning in understanding and healing any dilemma.

No it's not always black and white. But sometimes it is, and it's vital that we stop pretending and deal with it. Once we know each other and can communicate, then we can attempt to understand each other. Thus resulting in the ability to finally move on.

And never in my life has something pressed upon me like this urgency to write this book. And soon. We got to affect some realistic attempts at change. We can't continue as business as usual. It's not. Let's be real. (Here's where I could quote undoubtedly hundreds of barbaric hate crimes that occurred recently in our "mature, civilized" nation embarking on the second millennium.)

"This question of the union of the white and black is very important for if it is not realized, erelong great difficulties will arise, and harmful results will follow," states 'Abdu'l-Bahá in the Bahá'í Writings. He further warns, "If this matter remaineth without change, enmity will be increased day by day, and the final result will be hardship and may end in bloodshed."

And I started not to mention God so as not to offend anyone, but that wouldn't be truthful in telling my story because He's such a tremendous part of my life.

So I sit in front of my computer (something I never try to touch during vacation) 8:30 in the morning, straight out of the shower still damp, during Christmas vacation when I'm supposed to be packing for a quick visit to family during the holidays.

This "thing," this book, is really weighing on me!

In fact here I am now, going about 80 miles per hour on I-95, in the northbound passing lane, jotting increasing ideas and thoughts on a post-it or two as my son lies asleep in the passenger seat.

I don't propose to be an authority on racism and race relations. (Though a few other folk may think so.) But I have had a lot experiences that both, fortunately and unfortunately, few people have dealt with and from several different perspectives and "worlds."

We can not allow ourselves to settle for things as is and chalk it up to, "That's just the way it is." We have to reevaluate ourselves and take responsibility for our beliefs, reactions, teaching toward the future, and ultimately responsibility for change.

My intent is hardly to offend anyone in any way. But I must be extremely candid and impart some harshness of reality in recounting just a glimpse into my story and how it has certainly affected me. That's the only way I know how to genuinely attempt to achieve that.

My story I realize has a slightly different outlook from a perspective that may be broader in some ranges than most people. But we all must remember that we are simply the end product of all our experiences. Therefore continued exposure and education to new ideas and concepts are essential in our progress, both as individuals and as a society in its entirety.

And if I can jog just one or two minds into actually thinking for themselves, instead of allowing ourselves to be hostage to society's mentality of complacency and unsubstantiated views of the past, then I've accomplished my purpose.

1

The Hyphenated and Blended Smalls-Markovich Family

.

Most people would think of the formation of my new family as rather unusual and quite intriguing, especially to have occurred during the throbbing heat of the Civil Rights Movement and amidst the hottest embers of the fire, the Deep South. South Carolina to be exact whose greatest claim to fame in the annals of history is its leadership role of the Confederate States in its civil rebellion against the United States. My mother's marriage to Elting Smalls was simply a few weeks following the assassination of Dr. Martin Luther King, Jr. As a mere sixth grader living still in a white world, I was so totally unaware of any of the significance of the current events of this time.

I can vividly recall my reaction to the news of Dr. King's death, for it had the same sensation of the country being under the threat of war. Though this was not Pearl Harbor and the beginning of a formal declaration of war by our executive office. It was a crystal clear statement of the continued and committed support for hatred that has existed in the on-going war of racism and discrimination that has always plagued our nation since its inception. After arriving home from school on April 5, 1968, I was ready to indulge myself in a little television viewing. But across every channel stabbed the news of Dr. King's murder. I cried and cried though I wasn't at all aware of the total implications of this senseless act. But I had a strong inkling and feeling of the magnitude of Dr. King's person and what his life stood for. All I knew at the time was simply that he was a great leader of people and was loved tremendously throughout our country.

And during this time of turmoil sprouted a young and quiet sapling in the groves of family trees down in the Lowcountry of South Carolina. The Markovich-Smalls Family! And oh, how people loved to introduce us, unfolding the tale of its uncanny formation and providing the statistical analysis of its racial composition. I assume it provided for so highly of an entertaining saga to be shared. So I

1

will make my meager attempt to introduce my newly formed family during this era of my life.

My mother met a gentleman the summer of 1965 at a Bahá'í Summer School in Frogmore, South Carolina after the passing of my father. This would be my new stepfather, Mr. Elting B. Smalls who had also shared in common with my mother the loss of a spouse. Another commonality was that they both had children they were raising alone. My mother had four children and Elting had six. But their most visible and noticeable difference was society's racial classifications. Mom was white, and my stepfather was black. Simple as that, but not so simple in terms of how society accepted or perceived a racial mixture, at this time, particularly when it came to marriage.

But as a child, I wasn't aware of its total ramifications. And I don't think things were as bad as they could have been due to several factors. First of all, our hometown was a little unique and different from the typical small Southern town in South Carolina. Whereas many of these hamlets and crossings were isolated and unexposed to the world at large, not to mention insistent on traditions and customs of the past, St. Helena Island or "Frogmore" (its nomenclature at the time), possessed several unique characteristics that afforded our new family a relatively non-threatening existence.

For one thing the racial climate of the coastal towns and cities is noticeably different from the norm of the inland burgs. I guess being on the coast affords a town more of an influx of people. Whether they're historic and scenic-seeking tourists, oceanfront retirees, or sojourning businessmen. Then coupled with this we have the personnel and families affiliated with the military installations of Parris Island Marine Corps Recruit Depot, the Marine Corps Air Station, and the Naval Hospital. So we definitely benefit from the mixture of mentalities that this diversity of people contributes to the community at large.

Also "The Island" had a majority black population in land ownership thanks to the "40 acres and a mule" compensation to former slaves following the Civil War. The blacks here, from the 1860's on, were always landowners and never sharecroppers. Possession of land has always provided people with a source of strength and pride. As such was the case with the people of St. Helena Island, a very strong, proud, and beautifully, dark-skinned black people that resided here. And immediately at this same time of land ownership was also the emergence of schools and advanced education.

Penn School was founded by the Quakers in the very heart and center of St. Helena Island in 1862 for the education of former slaves. One of only a few of its kind, it served as a boarding school for blacks in Beaufort and surrounding areas until the opening of "Separate but Equal" schools of 1954. This provided an even further source of strength to this community that I was now to call home and forever more. And through the years the Penn Campus was a beacon within the raging storm and fury of the darkness of segregation and discrimination. So it certainly wasn't surprising that many times Dr. King's presence would grace the Penn campus and grounds since he found it to be inspirational and strengthening during many of his planning and strategy sessions for his work with the Southern Christian Leadership Conference's fight for Civil Rights. So in other words, all this is to say that the people of St. Helena Island were a proud, educated, and strong people. And therefore, they didn't back down to "their place" that whites still attempted to insist upon in other secluded and remote areas of the South. Bottom line, the people of St. Helena didn't take no stuff.

And here was my stepfather, Mr. Elting B. Smalls, a graduate of Penn School and a property owner on St. Helena Island. Not to mention the fact that he stood 6 foot 6 inches and held an even greater enhanced stature from his 240-pound presence. It was just simply that no one, and I mean no one dare come to him incorrect or approach him "off the wall."

When my mother met Elting in the 1960's, he was a widower with six children, ranging in age from young teens to young adults. And to keep the record straight so that no one may get confused on a key component of my family's composition, Elting was black, his deceased wife Rosalee was black, and his six children were black. Or simply put at this point he had a black family.

(And let me diverge for a brief moment, but for anyone who may be uncomfortable with the term, "Black," I'm sorry. But I'm from definitely "old school." I don't go back as far as "Colored" and "Negro," but I never quite acclimatized myself to the new and improved phrase, "African American." I really try to be true to who I am, a very down to earth and for-real person, and "African American" is simply just too dog gone proper for me. And Lord knows I know how I feel about someone calling me European American. "White" is bad enough. I really don't want to be identified as anything other than "Lynn" so you can imagine how that sits with me. So bear with me if "Black" may have any negative connotations for anyone, for believe me I hold "Blackness" in a high regard just for knowing the strength and endurance that it symbolizes.) But as my students always tell me, "Back to the story."

The oldest of Elting's six children were two sons, Elting, Jr. (called simply "Junior") and Joenathan (nicknamed "Butch"). They were both young adults serving in the Army and the Air Force, towering tall men such as their father, but more lanky. Then there were four lovely daughters. Gloria and Omega were the oldest and quasi-mothers of the household, and were off at college, Bennett College in North Carolina and Benedict in Columbia, South Carolina. Then the two youngest daughters, Rosalyn, the outspoken, radical rebel and Maxine, the demure baby of the family, were still in Junior High.

My mother was a widow with four children. Mom, my deceased father, and their children were white. (And I'm only breaking this down like this because as society is now realizing we can't make the assumption that a family shares the same racial classification.) Her oldest children were the same age as Elting's youngest, two sons, Richard and Tom, both in junior high, as well. Then two daughters of elementary school age, my baby sister, Sally and myself. But Sally would soon have to step down from the lauded throne for the coveted position of the Family's Baby.

Then when Elting and my mother married in 1968, the merger brought his six black children and her four white children into one family. And soon to add to this new corporation would be four "Mixed" children. (Yes, and here again I'm going with the term I grew up with in my home. And for anyone who doesn't know that term, the old term is "Mulatto" and the new term is "Biracial." But let me continue to just be me and say "Mixed.") Well, their first son was Daniel, and then came two daughters, Felicia and Victoria, and the final baby of the family was now a son, Darrel.

And before I forget let me do share something that I always found rather amusing regarding my youngest siblings' births. The oldest of this last set of children, Daniel, was born in Massachusetts. You see Mom was rightfully-so frightened of giving birth to a bi-racial child in Beaufort, South Carolina in the 1960's and anywhere in the South for that matter. But what is so interesting with classifying people racially, you have to have a policy or formula to do this, for believe me, this is an impossible feat to accomplish. It's so antiquated and absurd. But they tried it then and they still do now. But here's a simple illustration of how inaccurate this policy can be. So in Massachusetts, where the race of a child is determined by the race of the mother, Daniel was classified as "White" on his birth certificate. Now his and my youngest siblings were all born in Beaufort, South Carolina. And they all have the same parents and share the exact same parental racial mixture as Daniel, the same black father and the same white mother. But they on the other hand are classified by the South's policy, and I quote for anyone who may not be familiar with it, "a drop of black blood and you're black." And sure enough Felicia, Victoria, and Darrel are all identified as "Black" on their birth certificates. Now isn't that a stone trip! Just never ceases to amaze me.

Now with fourteen offspring total, I know you're thinking how did we all fit in one house for believe me we "hardly" lived in a mansion. It was a very modest home with three bedrooms and only one bathroom! How did we ever make it? The Lord only knows, for sure. But with children becoming young adults and making their way out into the world and not all the family yet to be born, we averaged about six children in the house at one time. And then we did have an annex to our residence, which most people have in the "country." My grandmother's home (and though she was actually my step-grandmother, I can never "fix my mouth to say that" for she was always so much more of a grandmother to me than my "real" grandmother) was next door. And my stepsister, Maxine, lived with her to keep her company and to help her out. (Though it was probably Maxine that needed the help. Grammy was "totally" capable.)

And we were basically one big happy family. Back then you had too many chores around the house and too much work to do in the fields to have time for too much sibling rivalry or the problems that blended families today have. And we not only were two families uniting, but two families of different races converging. But I must truly say, it just never was an issue for us. Maybe for other folks, but definitely not us.

And it's so funny now as teachers and professors ask my niece or daughter to do a project in social sciences on our unique family and just "how was it?" It was just like any other family, they against us, the parents versus the children. As an illustration of this typical status, I divulge the following escapade.

One Saturday my parents had a special work project for us to complete. Our job was to paint the entire outside of our wooden-framed house before they returned from Savannah that afternoon. Luckily we had a lot of hands available. The littlest were too little to help and the oldest were away. Yet there still remained at least five of us for the task at hand: Tom, Richard, Rosalyn, Butch, and myself.

We had enough hands, but the problem was having enough ladders to reach the upper portions of the house. We only had one ladder. My brothers came up with the bright idea of using our large, flatbed truck that we normally used for hauling tomatoes to the packinghouse. My brother, Tom who was about 14, begged and convinced my stepbrother Butch, who was home visiting from the Air Force, to allow him to drive the truck.

Little did Butch know how bad Tom's driving really was which included an episode of driving one of the family cars into the ditch. So when Tom backed our big, old truck up to the house for us to stand on, we were in for a not-so-good surprise. Instead of pushing in the clutch pedal to switch gears, Tom mashed the gas pedal. As you might have guessed, the truck hit the front of our house. Fortunately for us, the wall did not collapse, but it did slide in by six inches. My bedroom and our TV room in the front of the house now had a gaping view from the outdoors.

There was much alarm and panic amongst all of us, especially the older brothers who were responsible. I was merely a helper so "My name was gnat, and I was out of that!" They were the ones that were in charge and would have to answer to our huge, towering, and stern stepfather, as he loomed over them almost as tall as one of the room doors.

My brothers came to the conclusion that if the wall could be pushed in by the truck, then it probably could be pulled out by the truck as well. So they tied a rope around the wall and fastened the other end to the truck. This time Butch was the designated driver. He ever so gingerly and slowly drove the truck forward, as we watched to signal when the wall had reached its exact location. We hurriedly completed the painting, and added extra coats to the area of the crack in the wall. You couldn't even see it, after it was painted.

We cleaned up all the painting supplies, stored them, and Butch parked the truck back under the oak tree by the old shed. Then we washed up, retired to the TV room to chill out, and pretend that nothing unusual had happened during the paint job. As we were relaxing, our parents' green, Chevrolet station wagon ambushed us through our one-way-in, one-way-out dusty driveway.

Everyone tried to remain cool and calm, as our stepfather inspected the work. He appeared pleased, as he paced around the house, but when he came inside the house he had a puzzled expression on his face. "Did anything happen while you were painting today?" he asked us all.

"No, nothing happened," we all timidly replied in unison. Though we all wondered how he had caught on to us.

"Are you certain?" he asked again, as if giving us one last chance to plea guilty before sentencing.

"Yes," we replied firmly, standing our ground in a united front.

"Well, why is the floor in the front room scraped up so badly?" he continued to interrogate us.

Finally my brothers had to confess to the horrible mistake made that day and prepare to suffer the consequences. To their unbelievable relief, there were no beatings given out that day, but I don't believe Tom was allowed to drive for almost an entire year!

Some other "fun" times were traveling as a rather eye-opening and attention-getting family around the community, into "town", and "on the road." We were always a source of entertainment, fascination, and intrigue to passersby and onlookers. And boy did my momma seem to enjoy "testing" people's comfort zones that the "good ole" ways of the South had afforded them. Since the Civil Rights Bill of 1964 had been passed and was now beginning to be enforced in most of the South, Momma insisted on testing out whether it was rightfully being adhered to. But of course, when I think of it, she had no alternative unless she divided the family in half. So though Segregation had been legally outlawed, it certainly had not left the hearts, minds, and practices of many people.

When Momma took us to see the doctor, Dr. Keyserling's office, still had two separate waiting rooms. The divisive placards indicating your proper place for "Colored" and for "Whites" had been discarded. But patients were still adhering to the old custom and comfort level of continuing to sit in separate waiting areas. So being the "fight-for-what's-right" momma that my momma has always been, she marched us right into whichever waiting room, she felt like that day. In fact she may have even been on a rotation schedule, knowing Momma. One visit you'd find her at home and at ease chit chatting with the other mothers or the ailing elderly folks in the "black" waiting room. And then for the next appointment, she would be quietly standing her ground under close scrutiny and surveillance of the alarmed and unsettled occupants in the "white" waiting room.

But it was always too cute. Here was Momma usually with Sally and I (her two youngest "white" complexioned children), and Daniel, Felicia, Victoria, and Darrel (toddlers and hand babies of the "brown" complexion). You'd see her marching into the "what once was" and "continued to be practiced" as the "white" waiting room, with head held high, most confidently and self-assured.

And as she barraged into the room, for you couldn't miss the throng of noise that accompanied my younger siblings, all eyes raised from the magazines that had occupied their moments of waiting, as they became enthralled with our family. "Who were we?" "Were we lost?" "Didn't we know we were supposed to be in the 'other' waiting room?" All these questions rambled through their minds, I'm sure. But no one dare question my momma and the stand and statement she was demanding.

We must have stuck to the same alternating cycle for our beach visitations, as well. Hunting Island State Park, today has two separate parks, the entrance for the campground and the entrance for beach access and the lighthouse. But historically this was not the original purpose of these separate entrances. Yes! Even the beach was segregated. You had the black beach, and you had the white beach. And yes I know segregation was now illegal, but people still clung to the old ways and believed in either "staying in their place" or "keeping people in their place."

Now at the black beach, it was never a problem with our "rainbow coalition" of a family. Black people evidently just found us harmless, yet so interesting because we were probably "one of" or "thee only" interracial family in Beaufort at the time. But never were we shown or felt contempt or resentment. At the white beach, never were we approached with hostility, though there were a few there I am sure, battling with a strong urge to. But it was just the stares of disgust and the trances that some became engaged in, with mouths open and hanging to the ground, when they realized that yes I'm seeing what I think I'm seeing. So I always found that slightly uncomfortable, and therefore enjoyed the comfort and "open arms" of the black beach. Plus they had a restaurant with piccolos. Any place there was some good ole Soul Music, that's the place I wanted to be. I liked nothing better.

Or then there was the time, one my older stepsisters, Rosalyn (who if you're following this, you realize that all my stepfamily were of a "black" complexion), was hospitalized in Beaufort Memorial for a night or two. And you know how mommas are. So of course, Momma was right there in a flash. But the clerk on the reception desk unknowingly informed my mother that only family was allowed to visit. And boy I thought Momma was going to knock the man out if he didn't soon understand or at least pretend to understand the concept she was attempting to drill into his skull that this white momma was indeed the mother of this black teenage patient. By the look on his face he pretended to "get it," but I feel it was probably more the tone of urgency and insistence in my mother's voice.

Throughout my book, you'll notice that I reference my newly acquired siblings as "stepsisters" and "stepbrothers," but this is merely for the reader's clarity-sake. For I always thought of my new sisters as simply "sisters," certainly not "stepsisters." For from the onset they treated me as their own younger sister. So don't let the referencing mechanisms throw you off. We had a close relationship growing up. That reference is only for your assistance in following along more fluidly.

Growing up in Beaufort was certainly a walk in the park due to its mental setting and racial climate. But when we ventured out, that was a slightly different story. Like the time Momma drove a station wagon full of teenagers of every color, shape, and form to a Bahá'í Youth Conference in Birmingham, Alabama. The year was probably 1969. And believe me, Alabama was not catching on well to this new concept called Civil Rights and the abolishment of their dearly loved system of Segregation. So many service stations graciously offered their policy that they couldn't serve us, until at times we weren't even certain as to whether we'd have enough gas to continue the trip.

And there was a point in the trip down to Alabama that our old Chevy suffered from a flat tire and Momma was in desperate need of a mechanic's assistance or merely an individual who could perform a tire change. And as you probably can readily predict, we sat on that country road for hours and hours, as people purposely passed us by, before a policeman showed up on the scene and begrudgingly offered assistance. Now mind you this is the neck of the woods where people always offer their neighbor and even a stranger a helping hand. But not if it's the wrong color or one is found guilty of "mixing" colors. Heaven forbid.

For believe me, one thing that an individual impaired in racial acceptance hates more than a black person is what they reference a "Nigger Lover." They can't handle that. In their minds you can be nothing more than a traitor. And believe me the thought totally enrages them and basically creates instant and total rage and insanity. Not that this was necessarily the total case here. For people do fear the unknown or unexpected. But needless to say the fact remains, we did sit stranded for hours upon hours, a lone woman and a station wagon full of kids. And why? For the sole reason of being guilty of being an integrated family in segregated times.

2

From 506 West Jefferson to Route 1, Box 209

To say it was merely a change of address and residence would be a gross understatement. It was a move into a whole different world. And as a child, I took it so much simpler than the years that followed in creating "me." Of course, the emotional, psychological, and social realms were so different. But this was even evident in reminiscing the sensory environments.

And what wonderful memories and delicious delights! The kitchen at Route 1, Box 209 on Tom Fripp Plantation is my first thought. And why wouldn't it be, the kitchen is certainly the true heart of most homes, especially in my new world. Fried chicken, collard greens with smoked neck bone, white long-grain rice, and yellow, melt-in-your-mouth morsels of buttery, soft cornbread. And certainly I would be remiss if I did not end this with good ole grape KoolAid, complete with quartered pieces of lemon. This was a typical dinner, but mostly a typical "Sunday" dinner. And for breakfast, what about some white hominy grits with shrimp and gravy or perhaps some whiting fish fried whole, I mean complete from head to tail, eyeballs and all. And don't forget the hot sauce for the fried chicken and the fried fish. Of course carefully crafted with the key tools: a Piggly Wiggly brown paper grocery bag holding well-seasoned flour or cornmeal, the big black cast iron skillet, cooked over a medium-high flame on the gas pilot stove, always lit with match sticks from a small box of the Diamond brand. This all really takes me back. You can't believe. Though do you think for a minute that this was my immediate idea of mouth-watering meals when I first made my transition between worlds? It was definitely a growing process, and now it's a down right battle to resist such meals.

This was such a new world to me. For one thing I had never eaten rice for dinner, and in the Lowcountry of South Carolina, rice is eaten nearly with every dinner. I had only eaten rice for breakfast as a cereal-type food, and usually with butter, cinnamon, and sugar. So when I transferred this habit to my new dinners in my new world, believe me it was observed just as oddly as I viewed "rice for dinner." Thank goodness I eventually learned to eat rice the Lowcountry's proper way. And as for collard greens, the closest experience I had ever had to them was spinach, which I wasn't too thrilled about either. And how about fish being fried whole and sitting just as pretty as you please on the platter with their bulging eyes staring up at you and their tails still holding a slight wave of a swim. What a difference from the breaded fish sticks served at 506 West Jefferson. And I'll never forget my first encounter with grits. Yes, I did think it was a little odd that the cafeteria lady at Penn Center had served them sitting on a tray with eggs and (I started to say bacon, but I'm sure it was most likely my new favorite—smoked sausage.) So when I first laid eyes on this white breakfast substance, I proceeded my usual breakfast ritual of adding the finishing ingredients: milk, sugar, and butter. And I couldn't figure out why it wasn't in a bowl to begin with, but already on my first day or two in the South I was quickly catching on that things were not quite the same here, and it wasn't business as usual. So I began eating my "cereal," but the taste was so off the mark, I couldn't handle it. I ran to my mother to inquire as to what was wrong with the "cream of wheat." And there I was, off and running in a new world.

So please excuse me as I attempt to compare my new world of Route 1, Box 209 to my old world of 506 West Jefferson. But you see my new world has continued to grow with me to this day, and my old world died long ago, and is now such a distant world to me.

The next stop I remember so well were the wonderful aromas of all the toiletries and grooming products housed in the bathroom and bedroom. When going back in my mind to these scents and smells, I couldn't resist running out to Wal-Mart to find some good ole Jergens lotion. I just had to have that scent. I didn't even know whether they still made it. It seems that every other fragrance under the sun is now the rage in our world of Victoria Secrets and Bath and Body Works lotions. But after searching through five or six different scents of Jergens lotion, there it was—the Original Scent. But the words *"Cherry-Almond Scent"* completely threw me off. Yet when in doubt, the nose knows. All these years, and I never knew that scent had an actual name, except the name "Jergens lotion." Well, I opened that cap, and talk about time travel. There I was immediately sent back so many years ago, to that bathroom at Route 1, Box 209 in Tom Fripp. (I thought I had died and gone to heaven. And if you haven't ever smelled some good ole-fashioned Jergens lotion or haven't smelled it in awhile, indulge yourself. It really takes you back to the good ole days. Thank God that they still make it. What a true delight!) But here I am in the bathroom with the plastic bottle of wintergreen isopropyl rubbing alcohol and the blue bergamot hair dressing. I don't know why, but I still adore the memories of those smells. The smell of the wintergreen alcohol as we rubbed it on our many mosquito, sand gnat, or chigger bites. And the smell of that blue-colored bergamot hair grease, as my stepsisters conditioned their scalps. Of course amid all these bottles and jars, I still remember the jar of the green-colored Ultra Sheen hair dressing and the red cardboard can with a tin top that housed the all-time favorite, Royal Crown hair grease. There were always a lot of hair products. But the most intriguing item to me, always was—the straightening comb. At the time, being a young white girl with minimal experiences with black people, this was most definitely a very new and interesting journey of learning for me. You see at my new home at Route 1, Box 209, I had many new sisters that lived there. And part of the beauty and pride of my black stepsisters was their long, lovely, well-kept hair. And back in the 1960's in my new world, perms were not the thing. So what a fascination and love I had of watching my older stepsisters sitting in the kitchen straightening each other's hair. You had to be close to the gas stove where you had two hot combs in use. One sat on the eye of the stove in the flame heating up, while the other one worked its magic of straightening coarser hair into long sleek locks that could easily be managed and styled. Then the two ironing combs were interchanged, as the one in use eventually lost its heat. This was a whole evening affair, but what a pleasure of sitting around watching, learning, listening to stories, and talking about the latest news with my new sisters in my new world. And here I was taking it all in and enjoying every moment.

3

The Bahá'í Faith's Impact on My World

I had been born into what I imagined was a rather common middle-class white family. That's me, Lynn Carol Markovich, born on April 12, 1956 in Petoskey, Michigan to the proud parents, Robert and Laura Markovich. Here the Markovich family resided at 506 West Jefferson Street. I had two older brothers, Richard and Thomas. And in 1960, "baby" Sally was born. (Yes, she was named straight out of my brother Tom's first grade basal reading book. Remember the one about Dick, Jane, Baby Sally, and Spot, the dog?) My dad was the manager of the cable television station. My mother was a typical housewife. It was the typical "Leave It to Beaver"-type family of the 1950's and 1960's.

Petoskey was a small resort town because of the beautiful scenery of Little Travers Bay and became known for its "million-dollar sunset," not to mention the numerous ski lodges in that area. It is located at the northern most part of the Lower Peninsula on Lake Michigan close to the Mackinaw Bridge that connects the Lower Peninsula to the Upper Peninsula. In other words, it was located amidst a lot of snow and a lot of cold. (Even on the "warmest" day of summer, the water was still ice cold at the lake. And you could find a clump of white snow, even during the mid of summer, hidden in the shadows of one of the pines in the woods where we picked Mozzarella mushrooms and blackberries.)

I enjoyed growing up in northern Michigan because there was so much snow. I enjoyed all the winter sports such as ice-skating, snow skiing, and sledding. I also watched my brothers play ice hockey, but that sport was way too rough for me. Sometimes it would snow so much that I couldn't even see my next-door neighbor's house. Then my brothers would dig tunnels and make igloos in the huge snowdrifts in our yard. They also liked to have snowball fights, but they hit too hard. I loved to make snow angels in the freshly fallen snow or build snowmen complete with carrot noses and real scarves. Probably the worst part was when I'd walk to school in the snow, climb a huge snowdrift, get stuck in the snow, call to be pulled out, and have to dig out my lost boot.

My dad was the most important person to me in the world. He was a wonderful father! He did everything with us. We went skiing, skating, tobogganing, swimming, to watch my brothers' baseball games, to the library, to the park, to the movies, picking mushrooms or berries, and driving just to see the scenery. Every night we would watch TV together. His favorite show was "The Twilight Zone" which terrified me, but I watched it anyway just so I could be with him. Then when it was bedtime, I'd crawl up in his lap and he'd read aloud to me story after story. I could never get enough of him.

One of my most memorable occasions as a child was with my father and older brothers. I was only about five or six years old at the time. Well, in my hometown we did indeed have a lot of snow! One winter, my father wanted to give his children the thrill of our lives. So he got his new snowmobile from the cable company where he was the manager. Then he informed our mom that he would be taking us on a little trip across the Little Travers Bay. My mom was not too happy because she felt it was too dangerous, but dad insisted on the adventure! So we made the five-mile journey on a toboggan sled tied to the snowmobile traveling over the thick ice on the frozen bay. Well, as you can see I must have made it because here I am today alive and well. I'll never forget that day!

But growing up in Petoskey, one huge observance I never thought of then, that I now see is that there were a lot of white people that lived in Petoskey, Michigan, and only one black family in the whole town, I learned later. Even though, the schools were not segregated, Petoskey's only little elementary school, Lincoln Elementary, was an all-white school. This was because the one black family that lived in Petoskey only had high school-aged children. So this was the world I emerged from as a child.

But there was one extremely large factor and experience in my early childhood that made my world a little bit different from the typical resident of Petoskey. I was not a White Anglo-Saxon Protestant, or WASP as they term it. I was born and raised in the Bahá'í Faith. This had and has had an extremely deep influence on me during that time and throughout my life. The Bahá'í Faith is totally responsible for the whole turn of events in my life and how I was able to handle such radical changes.

Though during my early years, I grew up in an all-white environment that was not my total experience, as a young child. I was reared in the Bahá'í Faith, and our family was the only Bahá'í family in Petoskey. So our family attended many Bahá'í meetings, conferences, schools, and gatherings throughout the state of

Michigan and in particular, at Davidson Bahá'í School in Flint, Michigan (which is now known as Louhelen Bahá'í School.) In fact, Flint was where my parents were born, raised, and later met through the Bahá'í Faith. They both came into the Faith through Davidson Bahá'í School. When we visited the Bahá'í School in the Flint area, actually in the small town of Davidson, it was always such a beautiful blend of peoples, their colors and their cultures: Whites, Blacks, Persians, Asians, etc.

The Markovich family had also become close friends with the Martin Family of Adrian, Michigan while visiting Davidson for summer school sessions. Many times our family would go spend a weekend with "Uncle Bob," "Aunt Elizabeth," and their two daughters, Debbie and Cathy. Uncle Bob and Aunt Elizabeth soon became so close that they were like another mom and dad to us. (A close relationship that exists to this day—forty some years later. Luckily the Martins too, happened to relocate to Winnsboro, South Carolina about the same time we moved to the state's Lowcountry.) We had so many enjoyable times together, just talking, playing board games like Monopoly and the like, and cooking and eating. Our favorite dish and specialty that became a tradition for our families was "Sloppy Joes." And I always found the Martins' dining table in the kitchen where we shared all these happy meals to be so fascinating. It was an all-glass tabletop, and such a marvel and impression to me as a young child that the first piece of furniture I purchased as a newlywed, many years later, was a glass dining room set which we still twenty years later enjoy eating at. But it just extends such fond memories of the friendship my family shared with the Martin family. And sometimes I forget because it's so insignificant to me, but during the early 1960's, it was indeed rather significant. The Martin family happened to be a black family.

At the time, I quite took this multi-cultural experience for granted. The Bahá'í Faith was always this way, this beautiful mixture of peoples, and I never thought anything about it that it might actually be out of the ordinary at the time.

You see the primary foundation of the Bahá'í Faith is the unity of all God's children, unity in spite of all of mankind's divisive categories. The Bahá'í Faith insists on the unity of religion, the unity of races, and the unity of countries. There is one God, and we must be united as one to realize the full strength and potentials of mankind during this era in civilization.

"Close your eyes to racial differences, and welcome all with the light of oneness," Bahá'u'lláh, prophet-founder of the Bahá'í Faith proclaimed to the world while imprisoned in the mid-East during the 1860's for his religious beliefs and convictions. His son, 'Abdu'l-Bahá further stated, "God did not make these divisions; these divisions have had their origin in man himself. Therefore, as they are against the plan and purpose of God they are false and imaginary."

The Bahá'í teachings were what was and has been second nature to me since I was a small child. Needless to say, I was very sheltered in my birthplace of Petoskey and the Bahá'í community of Michigan.

It's all very interesting how the Bahá'í Faith played such a pivotal role in the turn of fate in my life that was soon to unfold. Each summer, it was rather common for our family to take a two-week vacation at the Davidson Bahá'í School in Flint, attending a two-week long summer school session. Well, our family's last attendance at this summer school was the summer of 1964. And for the next year's summer vacation, my father had already promised with my mother that we would attend the Bahá'í Summer School for the Southern States that was held at Penn Center in Frogmore, South Carolina. But our two weeks at Davidson were as usual, a normally fun-filled family experience, and at the close of the session, my family returned home to Petoskey. I stayed in Flint for a few days with my Aunt Marge to visit with my cousins. Upon my family's return to Petoskey, my father was scheduled for a short fishing trip with other fathers from my brothers' little league baseball team. They were going out fishing on Lake Michigan for a few days.

One morning while I was visiting at my Aunt Marge's, I heard the telephone ring and heard my aunt talking about someone missing. When the conversation ended, she suddenly appeared in my presence, explaining to me that my father and the other three men had drowned. That one of Lake Michigan's unmerciful storms had descended upon them, demolishing their 28-foot boat to shreds. (One of the men's bodies never was found.) My mother and two brothers were now on their way to Charlevoix to identify his body. My whole being immediately seemed to go into comatose, warding off and shielding the piercing attacks of my aunt's news. I just couldn't fathom it. Here I was but an eight-year-old, returning home at the end of the summer of 1964 to attend my father's funeral, adjust to my father having passed, and attempting to begin my third grade school year as normal. How could that be?

The funeral went well; if that's something you can actually say. My "Uncle" Bob and "Aunt" Elizabeth brought their family up to spend the week to assist my mother with any and everything she may have needed. And of course my "blood relatives" all arrived as well. (Sorry for such a referencing, but I'll explain my feelings later. That's a whole chapter by itself.) Mom, my brothers, sister, and I all took my father's passing as well as could be expected. Or at least I can speak for my mother and I. She is a very staunch and strong believer in the Bahá'í Faith and in her reliance on God, trusting in Him to take care of my father in passing to the next world. She truly had faith and confidence so she was not in a total shroud of misery and agony. My father's family and my mother's family all Christians, did not take my father's death quite as well. But I fortunately followed mom's lead so it wasn't so overwhelming. The Christian and Bahá'í Faith both teach that death is a time to rejoice, and my mother truly believed in this. My sister Sally was only four years old. My brothers, Richard and Tom, were adolescents, eleven and twelve. It definitely had the most impact on them.

The following summer, the summer of 1965, my mother carried through with my father's final plans and wishes that our family attend the Bahá'í Summer School for the Southern States to be held in Frogmore, South Carolina.

This was the beginning stage of embarking toward a whole new world and life. This Bahá'í Summer School was being held at Penn Center in Frogmore, South Carolina, one of the only locations where integrated groups could meet during the 1960's in the Southeastern states. The location then known as Frogmore has in recent years been more accurately named St. Helena Island. St. Helena Island is a large coastal sea island, which was divided into plantations during slavery. One of the plantations was Frogmore Plantation. Even after the abolishment of slavery, these areas were identified for many years as the original plantation names to assist in naming communities. Frogmore referred to one small area of the island, and later residents of the Island demanded that the entire island and its postal office be accurately named St. Helena Island.

Immediately following slavery, much of the South Carolina coastline, and particularly St. Helena Island and its now more affluent neighboring island, Hilton Head, and surrounding coastal sea islands were all black-owned land. In fact when one of my college friends, whom was black himself, once visited my home, he incredibly remarked, "I've never seen so many black people in one place!" And yes the Lowcountry of South Carolina is definitely black-dominated.

And all of this is to simply say-St. Helena Island was and is a very strong black community, both historically and currently. This is to give you a further understanding of the strong foundation of the new world I was about to step into. I stepped so simply and naively, and had no idea of the implications and impact this would have on my life and the "me" I was yet to be.

Being a child at the time, for me, nothing transpired out of the ordinary during the Bahá'í Summer School session at Frogmore. It was the usual attendance of children's classes, meeting new friends, going on carefree child excursions during free time to explore the natural wonders of the saltwater creek, the huge giant oaks that were draped with Spanish moss, and all the secret paths that we either made or discovered. The normal Summer School experience, be it in Davidson, Michigan or Frogmore, South Carolina. Only the natural surroundings differed, for we were in our safe cocoon of the sheltered Bahá'í environment.

But little to my knowledge, still being truly a child and out of "grown folks business," something did transpire during that brief visit to Frogmore. My mother became romantically interested in a fellow Bahá'í gentleman and resident of Frogmore. Also little to my knowledge, in the weeks and few months remaining that summer, they corresponded quite regularly and seriously. And by the early fall, my mother had become so serious in her interests of this gentleman that she decided to pack up and move herself and her four children to Frogmore, South Carolina to become better acquainted with him.

And so the huge move and first great step toward my new world.

4

The Initiation, Indoctrination, and Education Into the White World—Southern Style

Upon my mother's announcement of this upcoming move to South Carolina, there was mixed emotion in the Markovich household at 506 West Jefferson. I myself being only nine at the time, didn't know what to think, but it sounded like another childlike excursion or exploration, just on a slightly larger version. Little did I know how much larger a version. My brothers, Tom and Richard, now twelve and thirteen, were the reluctant ones, leaving their junior high, friends, familiar surroundings, and basically all that had remained normal in their life after the loss of a large part of theirs and my life—our father. But I mostly emphasize their loss because of the impact it had on them at that age. But what could they say? We were the children; mom was our infallible authority. So we looked at the positive prospects of the move that we could predict from our present knowledge of South Carolina, and the focus was living on the Atlantic Ocean and indulging ourselves in the beach. In other words we envisioned living the life of "Surf's Up" and all the wonderful visions of the movies that Frankie Avalon and Annette Funicello brought to mind, not to mention all the Beach Boy music that was the rage at the time.

The fall of 1965, Laura Markovich arrived in Frogmore, South Carolina with her four children: Richard, Tom, Lynn, and Sally. Arrangements had already been made in procuring a suitable house to rent. So we soon arrived, unpacked, became slightly acquainted with our new surroundings, and even frequented the beach several times as we settled in. Being new to the area, mother was immediately informed by well-meaning and helpful welcomers what school we would attend. And I was soon registered to attend school at Beaufort Elementary and my brothers, Beaufort Junior High, in the neighboring town of Beaufort, ten miles in on the mainland. Sally was five, but I don't believe kindergartens had been established quite yet in the public schools of South Carolina. So she remained in Mom's charge at home.

And this is where it all truly began for me-at a two-story, massive, forbearing, redbrick institution on Carteret Street of Beaufort, South Carolina—Beaufort Elementary. This was my initiation, indoctrination, and education into the "Two-World System" that I never had an inkling existed. But immediately there was no denying it, and it was soon being bombed upon me, like I were a target in a war zone under siege and constant air strikes. Here I was, Lynn Carol Markovich. Welcome to the White and Black Worlds and all the regulations, policies, and procedures that pertain to each, their minimal allowable interaction among them, and their tremendously enforced non-interaction among them, both in written, non-written, and mostly "just understood" terms. And here I was learning a double whammy-that I was now not only a "Yankee", but more important that I must now have a full knowledge and remember at all times and under all conditions and situations that I was a "White" person. What a sad and rude awakening for a completely "uneducated" child in these new worlds with all their new rules attached thereof.

I was in fourth grade and assigned to Miss Beaty's class. I also soon learned that I as a Yankee was not so warmly welcomed by the large majority of these little white Beaufortonians. So I mostly stayed to myself until one girl felt sorry for me and took me under her wing. We had the most fun during recess when she would include me with other friends from the remaining homeroom classes, when we met on the playground. But soon here, the missile launches began. "You're not supposed to play with *them*!" (Oh yes, this was the first time I heard this word in this new context and intonation—"THEM!")

"Why not?"

"Because *they're* Black!"

And they had me actually believing that this was a genuine, authentic school rule. I didn't find it hard to believe for I was aware that I was now unequivocally in a totally new world. Though I wasn't yet "well aware" of the exact boundaries and limitations of this world. But this was my initiation into the "Two-World System" of our country, particularly in the South. It was now beginning to unfold in my mind, the actualization of their being a "White World" and a "Black World," and of the underlying implications and understandings within and between those worlds. Oh, what an eye opening for a nine-year-old child.

Well sir! I liked their nerve. They didn't want anything to do with me, nor did they allow anyone else to befriend me. I look back at this to this day, and it still sets up a burning flame within my chest. And as I'm looking back at school memories, old class pictures and report cards, I am still yet discovering the actual effects this had on me that I wasn't aware of. You see they put a complete halt to my friendship with that black girl in my class, for as they truly had me believing that was an actual school rule. (Later though, I must confess, there was one white girl that I became friends with that year, Marian Martin. She was such a warm and friendly girl, so unlike the others. And in fact, I even spent the night over once or twice.)

But as I'm looking back at that class photo, I'm truly hurt inside for I don't even remember what my friend's name was that reached out to me and extended that life preserver of a much needed friendship. A few names of students I remembered were etched on the back of the photograph, but hers was not one of them. That's very sad, but that's how well my new world enforced their rules, even down to the children. And I'm sure it was only second nature to them, without even a thought. Also what's interesting, looking back at my report cards, that year I missed nine days of school during the final semester, and never preceding that year or following that year had I ever missed more than one or two days at the very most. Needless to say, I soon grew to hate that school and the system of this new world.

Fortunately at the close of that school year, the school district sent forms home to parents to indicate their school of choice for the following school year. You see to attempt to comply with the Brown vs. the Board of Education decision; many school districts had invented this policy called "Freedom of Choice." That simply meant any student was free to choose the school they would like to attend, meaning on the record that there was no legally enforced segregation of schools. Of course, the underlying current of separation still remained. Now you did have a few black families that chose to send their children to the predominantly white schools for they knew these schools were allocated much better funding and provisions than the black schools. In Miss Beaty's fourth grade class that year, out of 32 students, there were only three black children, two boys (Kerwin Felix and Calvin Coaxum) and one girl (the only girl that had befriended me as "the new kid on the block.")

Well, as I sat on the bus on my normal ten-mile ride home, I studied over that "Freedom of Choice" form. On it were listed all the elementary, junior, and high schools of Beaufort County, both black and white schools. Parents were simply to complete the requested data, check the appropriate school, and return to the school prior to closing of the school year. Well, as I read down the list, I excitedly read the name St. Helena Elementary. Wow, that was right down the road from my house. Actually only about one mile. And taking into account my total distaste and disgruntlement with Beaufort Elementary, my immediate and only recourse was to choose St. Helena Elementary. There's no way it could be worse. It just had to be an improvement.

5

"Gal, who you tink you is?"

Well, as I presented my mother with this infamous "Freedom of Choice" form that evening, I also informed her of my wishes and my choice of schools for the upcoming year. I don't recall any resistance, and I'm sure there wasn't, for why would there be. My mom was definitely not a conspirator nor a contributor in this "White World"—"Black World" system I had now been thrown into. Now there may have been some discussion amongst the adults (my mom, her fiancé, and some of her Bahá'í friends in the community) concerning my choice, but in a proactive and supportive response. In fact they must have thought that my choice was an excellent idea for in August of 1966 I began school at St. Helena School, along with my little sister Sally, my brother Tom and two white Bahá'í friends new to the area from California, Allen and Duska. Sally was beginning first grade that year, I was in fifth grade, and Tom, Allen, and Duska were older though and were enrolled in the Junior High section of St. Helena School.

St. Helena School was an all-black school for elementary through high school-aged students. With the Freedom of Choice policy, you had some blacks that elected to attend white schools for what they felt would be improved educational offerings. But I don't seriously believe there had ever been any whites that pre-ferred and chose to attend a black school. And believe me, I wasn't out to make a stand on racism or race relations in the segregated South of the 1960's. I was still a neophyte in the "White World—Black World" existence. This choice was sim-ply made from being totally "unwelcomed" and unwanted at Beaufort Elemen-tary, which happened to be the white school. So as I said, why not try the black school. It had to be better. It would be impossible to be worse.

And boy ole boy, *was it* better! I was totally welcomed, accepted, and embraced into the Black World and into St. Helena School from the moment I stepped within its walls. What a safe, warm, loving, and happy haven I found within. What a totally opposite feeling. How could two worlds such as these exist side by side, yet be so different. (Believe me, I now understand why these rules of a Two World System are brainwashed within children from an infantile age. How else, can one swallow it? I certainly wasn't able to comprehend segregation, not coming from the Bahá'í perspective and education that I had been privileged to receive as a young child.) And after a brief encounter and assault with one new world, the White World; here I began my journey into another new, but completely different world, the Black World via the route of St. Helena School.

So here I found myself in 1966, one of this little group of white children who took Freedom of Choice in a view that had never been taken before, choosing to attend an all-black school prior to forced integration (that didn't come to some areas of the South until the 1970–1971 school year). Again I stress, I at the time did not know the significance of such a choice. Yet it's so funny when friends today that knew me since then, make comments on my choice of schools. Marie Gibbs claims, "Yeah, Lynn broke the Color Barrier." Or David Evans professes how I was a "Legend."

The following year we returned to Michigan temporarily, and the other family returned to California. But after a year, we returned permanently to South Carolina. And Tom decided to attend Beaufort High. (But my stepsisters, Rosalyn and Maxine, who had left to attend Beaufort Junior High, soon actually returned to St. Helena High due to such mistreatment and discrimination.) But now, Sally and I were the only two little white faces that remained at St. Helena. Not that it ever mattered. Being in a totally black school was hardly an issue.

All I knew was that I was merely going to school closer to my home and in hopes that I may have a better chance of making friends. What a great chance I had ended up taking. I was assigned to Mrs. Keith's fifth grade homeroom. All the girls in the class welcomed me, and we quickly became friends with no underlying rules, restrictions, or regulations. I was happy and school was great! (A new feeling at school, as well as a whole new opinion toward school in general.) No one treated me any differently and especially not as a stranger or an outcast. They warmly included me into their circle of friendship. The only distinction that I did recall because it has impacted on my life to this day—the question and comment, "Gal, why you speak so proper? Who you 'tink' you is?" (Or closely to that effect.)

Now for anyone that may need me to translate—for you are only getting the written words, and believe me, you are certainly missing a lot in the body language, the facial expression, and the entire feeling of the spoken statement. Not to mention the strong Gullah dialect of a coastal sea island. (I might have caught onto the speech of my classmates rather quickly, but the true Gullah language spoken by the older residents of the islands took me years to understand. And some things I am yet to understand for it is truly a language directly from the West Coast of Africa and the days of slavery.) Well in translated form, my fellow classmate was telling me I was talking too proper and that I evidently thought I was better than others.

Well! I certainly wanted that misunderstanding quickly cleared up. I certainly wasn't a snooty or uppity type person. I definitely wanted to fit in to the scheme of things and the circle of friends. And unconsciously I proceeded to do that quite well. My mid-west Yankee accent and standard of speech was quickly yielding in exchange for the language of my new classmates, Southern black dialect with a *strong* mixture of the Gullah language. (I later learned during graduate studies while writing a research paper entitled "The Relationship Between Reading and Black Dialect" that linguists refer to this language as "Nonstandard English." Hmmm!! And what exactly do they mean by that?)

This language thing I have dealt with to this day. And believe me, I certainly have some strong viewpoints in this area. For when I adopted my new language during elementary school, I held on to it for dear life and never let go. I look back at it now and realize that it represented a newfound happiness and bonding that I love to this day.

I've received a lot attention drawn to my "accent" and voice for its unusualness, as well as a lot of flack. Actually the dialect is not unusual. When I'm on the phone, people automatically assume I'm black because that's what they hear—a black voice.

It's funny too, when I'm walking about running errands or shopping in my hometown, I can pass right by many black acquaintances without being recognized. If I'm by myself and unaccompanied by any black friends or family, I blend right in with the appearance of an ordinary white woman. And it is quite funny because not until I open my mouth and say, "Hey, how ya' been doin'?" and they've caught my voice and accent, do I get a response.

"Oh, hey girl! I didn't know that was you, Lynn." And I know exactly what's transpired, the Case of the Transparent White Woman. Not 'til that voice registers, am I Lynn, Our Home Girl from the Island.

What really messes people up is that my skin tone does not match up to the voice. And believe me, that does mess them up. I have had a Frenchman ask me if I were French, Puerto Ricans ask if I were Puerto Rican, even if I were Portuguese, and the inquiries go on and on.

One extremely hilarious and an amusing event of a gross misinterpretation of me by a dear Bahá'í friend from Savannah, Georgia, Mike O'Neal, I'd known through numerous functions through the years. Oh and it's important to say, he's black. Well, Mike was contacting me to inform me about one of the upcoming Bahá'í events in his area so I could spread the word in my community. During the conversation he inquires, "By the way are you going to the Black Women's Gathering at Louis Gregory Institute?" Of course I know of the affair for it's an annual event for African American Bahá'í women. I mean, my sisters who are mixed, have received invitations on numerous occasions.

So I respond jokingly, "Well yes I guess, as an honorary guest."

And Mike's asks hugely puzzled, "What???"

"Well, Mike I *am* white!"

"You're what!" he screeches in a total state of shock and confusion.

So I proceed to break down my whole family by specific racial identification. And he responds that he just never knew. He always thought I was black, but just light-skinned. And further explains to me the wide range in complexions in his family, a black family, from skin as light as mine all the way to rather dark complexioned members. From his family experience, he just assumed I fit that same description. So we both laughed and laughed about it. That's why this whole race thing really can be quite absurd and confusing.

While in college, one of my somewhat narrow-minded professors, inquired with his little nasty intonation, "Either you're a Yankee!!! or you're from the Low-country." Bingo! He actually calculated an accurate inference based on his marginal reference of schema. Yes, I was definitely from the "Lowcountry" referring to the lowly elevated marshland and sea islands in "southern" South Carolina, but by way of my birthplace, Michigan.

Through my lifetime, especially during college and upon graduating from college, I received the most negativity concerning my language. That really got next to me because your language is "you." It is a major ingredient of what comprises the "you-ness" of "you." And an attack against your language gets to be rather personal for it registers as an assault against you in your entirety.

I even believe that subconsciously I had built up a complex about my language that even reflected in my English grades during college. Though being a straight A student in all other subjects, I always found it difficult to squeeze out a B and many times my best was only a C. Through the years of my teaching career, I have had to build up a confidence in my ability of written expression in order to effectively teach it and pass it on to my students at St. Helena Elementary. While working on two master degrees and a few years in an administrative role in education, my competency in writing was further strengthened. And never in my wildest dreams could I ever have envisioned now teaching composition writing and actually writing a book for publication. (Even though I must say the style and voice of this book I've tried to stay pretty much true to my spoken voice and personal side of me, rather than my academic and professional side.)

In college I got a lot of hazing at a predominantly white southern institution, Clemson University, for having what they called a "Geechie" or "Gullah" accent. Fortunately by this time in life, I had established a rather strong pride in my language and didn't allow criticisms to affect me as much.

Even my husband, a former marine drill instructor, and always in full command of "Proper English"—he couldn't understand how a schoolteacher could speak so remotely distant from Standard English. But I always reminded him that he did not get to listen to me speak in a classroom setting. So I assured him that I "rose" to the occasion (though I resent that phrasing for it insinuates that one language is on a higher level), but rather I "transferred" to the appropriate language for the appropriate setting. For when in an informal setting among friends and family, I have always dearly loved the language dear to my heart-that cozy sanctuary afforded by the language from my childhood and school years at St. Helena with the warmth and beauty of the Gullah and black dialects.

I also recall with spite, as a newlywed in southern California, the time when I couldn't find a teaching position, and was working as a clerk typist and receptionist for Compugraphics, a manufacturer of computers for newspaper production. The Office Manager, Shelia—a New Yorker in every sense of her diction (surely a preliminary druid), evaluated me on my work performance in the office. She rated me exceptional and satisfactory in all areas with exception to one. And she had the audacity to mark me unsatisfactory and needed improvement in "Telephone Diction." Now you know I truly took offense to this, for in a professional setting, I always speak in "Proper English," (or as linguists say "Standard English.") But I couldn't change my accent now, and didn't intend to try either. And I certainly had never been graded on my accent. But that's all right, little did she know that many of our clients across the country and abroad, always requested to speak to none other than me, the receptionist with the smooth and mellow accent from South Carolina. There's just something a little warmer and appealing in such a voice than one that is cold and robotic. I don't mean to brag, but it was the first time that I can recall that despite some narrow-minded people, the world at large truly valued the richness and warmth of my dialect.

Thus I certainly commend and praise all proponents and supporters of diverse dialects. For years and years, the Gullah language and dialect were viewed as representing a language spoken by ignorant and uneducated people. Many a person's level of intelligence and knowledge has been grossly misperceived based on their speech, vocabulary, and articulation.

Consequently parents, teachers, and community frowned upon and discouraged its use for they felt it would greatly impede one's progress and success in the world. And I do see their point due to the stigma attached and the prejudices it receives. But the richness in culture and heritage that the Gullah language preserves is so vital. I can't thank the speakers of Gullah, its researchers, educators, and overall supporters enough or it would have become an extinct and forgotten language.

There are many such proponents, but I mention only a few that I have had a more personal connection with. People such as my dear friend and classmate, Ronald Daise and his wife Natalie, have done so much to keep the Gullah language and culture alive and appreciated—through their seminars, presentations, books, music, and award-winning children's television show that aired on Nickelodeon, "Gullah Gullah Island."

Other huge contributors that keep the Gullah language and culture alive and well have been Reverend Irvin Greene, Sharon Simmons, and Natasha Robinson. Marquetta Goodwine is phenomenal in her knowledge, research, performances, and educating others in Gullah. And a special tremendous shout out to my dear friend and classmate, Anita Singleton Prather, also known by her stage name, Aunt Pearlie Sue. She is a sensationally gifted and hugely humorous storyteller of the history and tales of the Gullah experience. Oh, you name it; she's done it: audiotapes, CD's, videotapes, films, and live performances from coast to coast, including the sell out crowds at the House of Blues in News Orleans and traveling to film nominations in Hollywood and the Caribbean.

Another contributor to the Gullah language and culture is Rosalee Pazant (an educator) and the Pazant family (also many of which include several educators and several fine musicians) whose hometown is Beaufort, South Carolina. They are the family that founded the annual Gullah Festival, dedicated to the celebration of the entire Gullah culture: its people, language, stories, customs, music, dance, art, cuisine, and attire.) It is one of the largest black festivals in the nation. (And here I point out the long-time attached stigma attached to the Gullah language. When I asked one of my girlfriends about accompanying me to attend some of the events at the Gullah Festival, she admitted that she really didn't have much to do with it because it represented a negative concept of local black people. Well, sir! You see what I'm talking about with this language thing. It's really something. So of course, the two of us being very strong-minded and that being my tight friend, but never knowing her view on this topic, I certainly had to leave that alone.) But you see my point. Right? Totally brainwashed.

So I continue to thank all the educators in this area of language. And therefore I am quite compelled and obligated to recognize Dr. Evelyn Dandy of Savannah, Georgia. In the field of teacher education, she has spent a tremendous amount of work and efforts in the area of dialectal education. Her focus has been teaching teachers the importance of its acceptance, but yet too teaching them to teach children when to maneuver between "speech registers" to fit the appropriate setting. I remember taking one of her classes through Georgia Southern University. And during that class, I shared with the class the Gullah language by reading aloud Ronald Daise's first book, *De Gullah Storybook*. A pretty funny sight, a white woman reading in Gullah to a predominantly white audience studying about dialectal acceptance, with particular emphasis on black dialects. But I "briefly" shared my background. (Don't worry. By now I know you're clearly on to me that I love to talk and ramble on. But I was good that day. I kept it short and sweet. It wasn't the full autobiographical version. Okay.) But Dr. Dandy is the one that urged me to write my autobiography for she felt I had a rather usual story to tell. And so you can clearly thank or blame her for her encouragement for it stuck with me from that day forward.

In concluding this chapter, I reiterate, for I can't say it enough—language has been a large part of my identity and it is vitally significant in my life. So you see how Mrs. Keith's homeroom class of section 5-B has "hugely" impacted on my life at that time and throughout the duration of my life. I'm proud of and love my language.

6

Racism Raises its Ugly Head Within What Once was Family

After my first semester of attending St. Helena Elementary in 1966, Mom informed us that her courtship to Mr. Elting B. Smalls had proven to be a success and that they were now pursuing marriage. So we were moving back to Michigan temporarily to make preparations for her marriage. This would include the sale of our house and property, which resulted in a rather easy transaction. But immensely difficult, would be the preparation for marriage. For as my mother was and is a firm believer and member in the Bahá'í Faith, one of the laws of marriage requires that the two individuals venturing into the bond of marriage, obtain written consent of all living natural parents, regardless of the age of the children. And my mom at this time, was a 36-year-old widow with four children. (And it's interesting to note to myself that while I still had my white Northern influence I referred to my mother as Mom, but later under my black Southern exposure I then and now call her Momma. For awhile I couldn't figure that out myself why I was switching throughout the chapters. I had to think a minute on that one. Just a change with my language, including even my momma's name!)

Well, let me tell you—"her" family was certainly in cahoots long before her arrival home to Michigan. (Sorry for the reference of "her family," but from that day forward, they were never any longer "our" family, and actually barely "hers.") For shortly upon our return to Petoskey, Michigan, they all converged on our house there, and swarmed down like a mob of vultures on a small bird of prey, none other than my mother. They thereupon were intent on truly setting this wayward soul back on the straight and narrow path.

Here I was ten years old at the time, and I so vividly recall their unified offensive strike upon my mother. The "meeting" was held in the large kitchen at the rear of our home, I guess as to be out of the range of innocent ears. Though it was evident that they soon lost sight of any consideration of children. During the attack they pounded relentlessly against my mother. "How dare she consider marrying a black man" and "She must be totally crazy!" were the essence of the conviction by the jury. And one of my uncles, oh the profanity that yielded from his mouth. I was never raised with cursing in the home, and believe me I took this assault against my sweet, defenseless mother very seriously. My mother's youngest brother and sister, I don't believe they were in on the attack, and my oldest uncle was a Bahá'í and had lived in California for years. So the main violators were my mother's middle brother and oldest sister. (My one uncle with the foul language and my one aunt with the emotional assailment.) Now her oldest sister would never have condoned the profanity, for she was such a strongly convicted "Christian." (You sure got to excuse me, but some things really set me off. Not necessarily by themselves because I have become slightly more tolerant of people that exhibit racism, ignorance, and hypocrisy as I've grown older. But when in conjunction with my mom, I'm sorry, I kind of lose it!) And here is a strong point in case.

Fortunately my mother was not in need of consent of marriage from all her brothers and sisters, but merely her parents, though this would prove to be a tall order by itself. And as far as Elting's parents, his mother had already given her consent and his father was deceased. Now as for my grandmother, she was rather wishy-washy. First she gave her consent, but then she reneged and took it back. (Probably through the manipulation of the fine work and influence of my mother's siblings.) And later she did in the end yield permission again. But as for my grandfather, he was quite a tougher cookie, more like an old rock-hard, stale, biscuit.

My mother's plan of strategy for him would have to be much more intense. For one thing, her parents had divorced during her childhood, and so she felt she needed to get reacquainted with him. So after selling our house to our close friends and neighbors down the street, my mother made the decision to move closer to her father and be able to spend some quality time with him. Her intention was to re-educate him at this point in his life, and at the same time allow him to acquaint himself with the adult version of his daughter. She needed to convince him in spite of the popular opinion of her siblings that she indeed was not crazy and that surely he would reconsider allowing her to act upon the marriage proposal she had received. (Looking at this now as an adult, I'm thinking boy, my mom really wanted this man bad! She certainly went through a lot for them to get married.) And eventually, after purchasing a home in southern Michigan, in the small town of Erie, five miles north of my grandfather's home, Toledo,

Ohio and residing for a little less than a year, my mother finally received consent for marriage.

Thereon my mother and Elting quickly finalized wedding plans. (I guess before anyone had time to rescind his or her consent.) And they were married at the Bahá'í Center in Adrian, Michigan on May 3, 1968 with their reception held at none other than our dear friends' home, Bob and Elizabeth Martin's. For one thing, at the time, the state of South Carolina would not acknowledge such a marriage. (It's really amazing how the Martin Family has always been there in my life. Friends while my dad was living, comforters during my dad's funeral, hosts for my mom's remarriage, new residents to South Carolina at the same time when we moved too, and so much an integral part of my life up to this day. Deborah in fact ended up recently taking a position as the media specialist or librarian at our school and relocating on Lady's Island. We are close hanging buddies. And even have adjoining doors between her library and my computer room. Pretty uncanny. We've come so far and through so many years in and out of each other's lives.) Sometimes we chalk things up to coincidence. But I don't know if there's a such thing as that much coincidence. It's experiences in life like these when we have to admit that it must be a part of a much larger plan than our little meager attempts.

Well it was from this very point in my life, my mother's remarriage, that my extended family ceased to exist to me or my new world. They themselves and the times we spent together would now only become virtually vague and almost non-existent memories of my early childhood years in Michigan. As their offense blocked us out of the family, I too countered with my own defense, successfully blocking them out as well. How else could I have survived this pain of excommunication they had sentenced upon us?

7

Adjusting, Adapting, and Adopting to Black Beauty

There was an immensity of learning to acquire in this new world in which I had been thrust into. On the surface, business as usual, but the minor details, yes the "little things" proved to provide quite an abundance of educational experiences.

As an adolescent, beauty maintenance appears to become a strong focal point of a young lady's youth and throughout her lifetime hopefully. This was an age where I was truly watching and listening to every move of my older stepsisters to acquire any special tips of beautification possible. But in the black world versus the white world, there are quite contrasting techniques and methods involved in this area of expertise.

My first lesson was with hair. Of course I had to learn that perms for blacks were also called relaxers and that they straighten the hair. Whereas, perms for whites are usually permanents that add a curl to the hair. Complete opposites, right? Though my stepsisters usually straightened their hair with hot combs.

Also whereas whites try to wash their hair frequently, almost every day to rid themselves of oily or greasy hair, blacks add hair grease to condition the scalp so that it won't be too dry. And as far as washing hair, that's about once every two weeks and most black women will go to a hairdresser for this service or have a friend wash their hair. It is rare that most black women would wash their own hair. A lot more care and attention is given to black women's hair than that of white women's. For a black woman, the hair is definitely to be worn as a crown. No such thing as wash and wear, unless you have dreadlocks, braids, or a short natural which in itself still must be conditioned and shaped.

One amusing incident with the hair thing, was when I was an adult and was teaching remedial reading to fourth, fifth and sixth graders at St. Helena Elementary. Most of my students would begin coming to the Reading Lab for assistance in third grade and continue through sixth grade so I would have contact with the same set of kids for three consecutive years. And I would get to know them quite well and just as well, they would get to know me.

Well, one day I was reading aloud to my sixth graders which was quite usual for I am personally committed to providing this enrichment for my students on a daily basis. But what was quite unusual this particular day, out of the clear blue and totally off the wall, a boy named Jabbar interrupted the story with quite a perplexing inquiry of myself, "Miz Bryant, don't you have a perm in your hair?"

Now I certainly didn't know what triggered this question and still don't 'til this day. But all the other kids quickly responded in unison and strong authority in rectifying this statement, "No boy, Miz Bryant is white! Her hair's already straight."

To which Jabbar countered with a bewildered expression but emphatic response, "Miz Bryant ain't white!" Which he had went on to explain that he knew my father and he was in fact black so I too was black. (I guess my language, my mannerisms, and the way I interacted with my students, coupled with a black stepfather, added up to the sum perception of me being black.) But I found this most incredible for this was a student I had worked with for three years on a daily basis. Was my "whiteness" virtually nonexistent now? Jabbar certainly thought so and it took much explanation to demonstrate that I indeed was white rather than black.

(Though it made me "no-never-mind" what color Jabbar thought I was. My primary concern that day as Jabbar's teacher was that his assignments still remained to be completed. And that's what really was of utmost importance, though we didn't want anyone teasing or ridiculing Jabbar for calling Miz Bryant black. Innocent mistake. I could have quite easily have done it myself.)

Now when it comes to the length of one's hair, this is almost a totally different topic on its own. Hair length was a huge thing back in the Black World during the 1960's. The longer a black girl or woman's hair, the more beautiful she was. A young lady that had shoulder length hair and was of a "light-skinned" complexion or what is just simply referred to as "light-skinned" had it totally "going on!" (But the skin color thing is a whole other issue, as well.) Now my stepsisters had long hair, but they were dark-complexioned. (So one out of two wasn't bad.)

Afros or naturals hadn't quite yet hit our small remote and rural community. If fact, we once saw a girl from Africa in the audience of an event on the Penn Center campus who had a very short natural. I recall how we were all staring and whispering trying to figure out if she were a male or female. Never had we seen a "natural." But by the 1970's, our community was catching up with the rest of the nation with Afros, dashikis, and "Black Power."

So when my stepsister, Rosalyn, defiantly cut her dark, lovely, and flowing locks of hair from shoulder length to a short natural, the remainder of the family suffered from extreme shock and horror. They scolded her, "It won't grow back!" Like this was a sentence for life. But frankly I don't believe she ever chose to grow it back. Of course, Rosalyn, has always been an extremely strong-minded and independent woman so this was a natural recourse in making a statement of rebellion to the present system and status quo. Personally, I thought it was super cool and admired her for having such a "don't-care-what-ya'll-think" attitude.

As I watched my older stepsisters, I did have enough sense to realize that I could not do the hot comb thing or the relaxer, but I did figure I could do the roller set for curls in my hair. Mom had done this through the years so I equated the roller setting to be a simple replication of what I had seen. Wrong! I proceeded to roll my hair up in several of these pink rollers which enclosed a built-in brush. Hopefully, I could now have lovely body and styles such as my stepsisters. But when I attempted to uncurl and remove these rollers, one of those pesky varmints would not budge. It had become unrelentingly entrapped and entangled in my hair and after several unsuccessful efforts to remove it, mom actually had to resort to cutting the curler out of my head.

My hair was pretty long at this time and actually for the large majority of my life. In fact I was known as "the white girl at the black school with the long hair down past her hips." That was my descriptor. And once that was given, everyone knew precisely who was being referenced. I never really thought about it before, but I guess I had this thing for hair length, straight out my new learning in my new world that "longer was lovelier." And the long hair thing held with me probably until I was well in my mid-30's.

My girlfriend, Beverly, tried time and time again to get me to replace it with a short and updated style to no avail. Another factor was that I just hadn't ever learned to manage and groom white people's hair, which was what I was stuck with, but didn't have enough knowledge of. I never did learn to roll, mousse, or blow dry hair. I just never had the exposure to these elements of the White World. Like when you see white girls in the movies having sleepovers, makeovers, and practicing styling each other's hair. So for over 20 years, it was long, straight hair down to my hips or many times for a tidier appearance that resembled actual grooming or styling, I would pull it straight back into a pony tail and plait or braid it straight down my back.

So when I finally decided to go with Beverly's promptings to obtain a more stylish and up-to-date look with a haircut and style, my husband, Bryant was shocked and felt violated. Let me tell you, my husband is definitely, definitely undeniably "old school" so when the hair went, so did his mind. And when I returned home from Calvin's Cheveaux Company of Columbia with my long plait in my hand and hair above my shoulders, he wasn't too pleased. But being "totally grown" and to prove my rights of womanhood, I had got him where it really makes a point, the hair thing. And after many frowns, much disdain, and several unsupportive comments, I proceeded to haul back and throw the braided plait of hair straight at him. "Here, this is what you love. (The hair) So take it to bed tonight and ya'll have a great time together!" Then and there was the end of my long hair days, and the beginning of my short hair days. And believe me there's something about the symbolism of independence and strength with short hair. It's certainly an attitude and I definitely like what it represents and how it makes me feel. Strong, yet sassy.

(Funny though, once I cut that hair, I had lost my most identifying feature. So many black people in my community no longer recognized me. I now blended right in with the large group of whites out in public. We now "all looked alike." Heard that phrase before? Maybe on the flip side. Huh?)

I've covered the hair thing pretty much with exception to a minor detail—shaving hair. Particularly shaving one's legs. That was not a part of a black woman's beauty habits during this era. So by the time I reached adolescence, being of Polish, German, Irish, and English descent, my legs had become engulfed in hairy underbrush almost resembling a small forest. At St. Helena Junior High and High, I knew of *no one* who shaved their legs. But of course on the most part, black people don't have an abundance of hair on their legs anyway so they never appeared as bear-like a figure as I had become. And shaving under the armpits hadn't even been totally established at the time as a beauty regime. For many girls in gym class were being snickered about for having furry armpits.

So when I began attending Beaufort High, of course my hairy legs were another source of ridicule to new white classmates. At least for the bold, rude ones that didn't mind pointing out to me their "professed authority on proper hair etiquette." And from a black prospective, black guys told me that my hairy legs were sexy. Now of course, this may have been a line for at this time in my life I was still rather naïve, but I have a feeling that this was totally acceptable and preferred. Of course, it might be going back to that obsession with the hair thing.

And I started to say that this custom of shaving was clearly a European tradition, but when I really think about it, many European women do not hold this habit of shaving legs and underarms. I don't know its roots, but it is more commonly a white American woman's ritual. So being the independent thinker that I've had no other choice to be in life, I responded to them with "Who *says* women must shave their legs? Men don't shave their legs! It certainly isn't a necessity of life or serves any valuable purpose. Why should I let society dictate to me what I must do with the hair on my legs!" And that was the end of that. But of course, as I went off to college and began living with white girls, I decided that I did like the smooth, chic look of my legs, minus the hair. But this had to be on my terms. Being the radical and different one, I wasn't about to give in to those tyrants at Beaufort High! I guess when you're raised different and in a different world, you totally learn to question why. Why do we do what we do? Not because we've always done it that way, but truly for what purpose?

And let me close this chapter with an equally indispensable beauty habit with skin care. One thing a white girl in a black world soon discovers is the meaning of "ash" and "ghost." And I'm not talking about the remains from a fire or a phantom. But I was soon to find out why we always had plenty of Jergen's and Vaseline lotion on hand. And for anyone who might be as uninformed and unexposed as I was at the time let me clue you in. (For always remember, ignorance is simply a lack of exposure, not a lack of intelligence. If you've never been exposed, you just don't know. And of course, that's going from any known situation to an unknown situation.)

"Ash" and "ghost" are references to dry skin. We all have it. But on darker-complexioned people, it is so much more noticeable. A black person's skin may actually appear white-like. Hence the terms "ash" or "ghost." And that is definitely a gross sign for a lack of grooming in the black world. So lotion don't go any place without it! And—believe me, my youngest son has fully adapted this rule of thumb. That child has to go through a minimum of a least one 24-ounce bottle of lotion per week. I kid you not.

But probably my most comical incident with beauty habits has to be with my new acquaintance and encounter with the jar of Nadinola. Ninety-nine point 9999999% of white people, I am *positive*, have no idea what Nadinola is. And even young black people today remain among the very same statistical data. Not that it's a tremendously big deal for a white person to know what Nadinola is, *unless* they try to apply it to their skin.

Well, being a young teenager at the time of this occurrence, naturally I was battling the #1 battle that most teenagers of any color fight, acne or what we simply called "bumps." So having a terrible case of acne, I was desperate. I tried the alcohol, the Clearasil, the Noxema-you name it! All to no avail. So when I came across a jar of Nadinola next to the jar of Noxema on my stepsister's vanity, I thought let's try this.

And oh boy! The result was a terrible red, burning and blaring rash and irritation to erupt across my entire face. I ran with my face glowering and the culprit, a jar of Nadinola in tow, to my oldest, wisest, and calmest stepsister, Gloria. (Though I myself certainly was not the least bit calm at the moment.) But I certainly was in need of her infinite and limitless wisdom. "Gloria! Look at my face. I put some of this on my bumps and look what it's done!"

Well, Gloria responded cool as a cucumber and just as nonchalant as ever, "Nadinola isn't for acne. Didn't you read the jar? It's a bleaching cream. It's designed for black skin. It's definitely not for white people's skin."

My young, feeble, and unexposed mind could only relate to Clorox bleach that I used to wash the family's laundry each Saturday morning. Bleaching clothes to make them white was clearly my only frame of reference here. "Well, why on earth would any black person want to be white?" was my bewilderment, especially amidst a world of black pride.

"Girl, it's to smooth out the dark spots and blemishes that may appear in a black woman's skin and make the tone even. It is definitely too strong for your skin. Go wash it off with some cold water, put some Noxema on it to cool it down, and don't ever mess with that Nadinola bleaching cream again!"

"Yes, Gloria," I muffled out almost inaudibly in a low, low hush with my head hanging down in pure humility and shame for my stupidity. But as I still say, "When you don't know. You just don't know." And that goes for white people knowing the total intricacies of a black person's world or black people knowing all the ins and outs of a white person's world, or anyone's world for that matter.

And so went my newly acquainted knowledge of the powers that be in a little unsuspecting, "Noxema-perpetrating" jar of Nadinola.

8

Additional Lessons in Black 101

A lot of these lessons and rules in Blackness, which as I learned as a child and adolescent were probably, not as well known within the white world as they are today. Black comedians I would credit as some of the greatest educators in Black 101 for those progressive whites who are open-minded, daring, and brave enough to venture within their audiences at comedy shows or within the refuge of their padded and worn La-Z-Boys at home. They have brought a lot of Black 101 Rules to the forefront. And when I say "The Rules of Black 101," (for my white-complexioned readers) don't be as gullible as myself when I believed that the "White Southern Rules" at Beaufort Elementary were publicly recorded rules that legally governed and dictated my social interactions with my black classmates and other black children. No, these are simply common "understandings" within the black world.

BLK 101 Rule #1: "Never, never, never under any uncertain terms call a black person the 'N-word, if you're of the white persuasion!" (In other words any "genetically" white person, including myself.) I don't care how tight you may be with a black person or how down you are with a black person, or that you may even have amnesia at times like me and "think you're black" because you may hang with a lot of black people; *do not* and I strongly and emphatically plea, *"do not"* ever under any uncertain terms call a black person the "N-word," even if you're joking or attempting to use it as a hip slang word of endearment. It just is *not* going to work coming out of the mouth of a white person. And believe me, unfortunately, I know this from personal experience learned the hard way, by almost getting slapped down to the ground by my ninth grade boyfriend.

Lance and I were sitting out in his car in my driveway, goofing around while just talking and laughing about any and everything. (And actually it wasn't exactly a driveway, but more of a dusty, dirt section of the yard under a huge oak that served as a "driveway" and "carport" on our small farm out in the country.) Now I must have been about 14 at the time, and Lance was somewhat older. So his knowledge base was slightly broader, though I was soon to rapidly widen my grasp of a new and vital concept. With Black 101, this rule is taught almost upon the first day a black baby leaves the warmth and protection of his or her mother's womb to enter this, at times, very cold and malice world.

As we continued to laugh and joke around, for some unmemorable reason, Lance called me a "Cracker." Well, having lived in the South at the time for about five years and having begun to learn the rules within the black world and the white world, I had already been educated enough to know that this was not an acceptable word and was only used in a way to either demean or display complete and undeniable contempt for a white person. So searching for a way to redeem myself against this attack of nomenclature warfare, I retaliated with what I felt would be the rightfully weighted bombshell of the "N-word." And boy had I made an extremely poor comparison of equivalency between the degrading words, "Cracker" and the "N-word." The weighing tables went completely awry and the balance scale had come swiftly tumbling down, as Lance began to slap me across the face in a firm, swift reflex, the split-second the word had traveled through his outer ear, inner ear, and had landed within his mind. The receipt was immediately transferred to his arm and hand.

I proceeded to defend and explain myself for the use of this word in response to his choice in an extremely poor and distasteful labeling of me with what I felt was an equally offensive word, "Cracker." Oh I thought I knew so much about this black world and this white world thing, but yet little, oh so little, was I yet to know up to this point. Though within the course of less than a second's worth lapse in time, Lance had undeniably informed me of this tightly upheld and bound rule and regulation. A lesson indelibly inscribed within and throughout my total consciousness forever more.

BLK 101 Rule #2: "Don't mess with anyone's money, food, or their man." (Or whatever may best apply here). And a particularly helpful addendum to this rule is "Don't mess with anyone's family," as well. This rule I feel would hold true in all the varying worlds of cultures. This was a very basic rule, which I heard time and time again as soon as I became a member of Mrs. Keith's fifth grade class at St. Helena Elementary. A very simple and fundamental concept, but if not complied with caused serious ramifications. Usually in some form of physical assault, no matter how small the fight or shuffle. But property was to be respected and if not, one must assuredly save face. Don't get me wrong, my peers were extremely more sharing than I was accustomed to. If you were in need, they'd either give entirely or share their last. But under no uncertain terms were you to make the assumption to take without either asking permission or preferably being asked.

For example, if you were to go visiting at someone's home, never were you to dare even think about asking for something to eat or drink. And even if you were offered something, your momma really didn't want you to accept. (Also she didn't want people to think she hadn't fed her children.) I guess everyone had so little then, that if you did accept that might put them out of part of their dinner. And of course you *would* always be offered something no matter how minute the portion. These were the universal rules of sharing. And then again in some households you would have to eat to spare someone's feelings. If you reject someone's offer, they feel that their food isn't good enough. So all the way around it was always a tricky situation.

Now talking about or messing with someone's family that was an outright declaration of war. Particularly "talking about someone's momma." We all know that's fighting words amongst children and child-like adults, at times as well. Trust me as a teacher, this still holds true. Want to start a raucous amongst black children in a classroom, just softly utter the words "Your momma." As kids get older and are able to discern the varying intents and purposes, they enjoy the sport of "Playin' the Dozens" or "Momma Jokes." Both of these are for mere pleasure and showcasing the skill of quick thinking and wit. Simply a recreational activity. But the appreciation for this art form does not arrive until an age of maturity is reached, certainly not for the early school-aged years.

BLK 101 Rule #3: "You've got to be ten times better than a white person to make it." If a black parent has been competent in parenting a black child, he or she must instill this critical concept to properly prepare them for success in a white dominated society and for the harsh reality that things are not fair in the real world. Discrimination and racism still run rampant. So yes a black person must be all the much more prepared to even begin to compete out here.

BLK 101 Rule #4: And closely aligned to the previous topic, *"Don't call someone out of their name"* which is simply name-calling. Particularly, something like "your black self," "your big head," or the like. Always call someone by his or her name. And please, my white-complexioned people, *do not* refer to a group of black people as "them," "they," or "those people." Big no, no when referencing black people or really any other group of people for that much. It's like you're distinctly distancing yourself as far as possible when referencing a group of people, like they have some dreadfully contagious disease such as leprosy or the like. It comes across as if whoever you are speaking of is of a lower level or unworthy of being included in your group. And there's a lot that goes with the intonation as well.

On this same note, when conversing with blacks in a professional or formal setting, white people should be mindful of addressing adults with their title attached, such as *"Dr.* Davis," *"Mrs.* Gibbs," *"Mr.* Pringle," or the like. Unless of course someone offers the invitation to call them by their first name. A lot of this goes back to times when whites would *only* refer to a black by their first name or use the all-time degrading terms of "boy" or "girl." The power of words is so many times over-looked, but these types of references were all purposely used by whites to attempt to put blacks "in their place" and place themselves at a level of superiority. And it just doesn't fly any more. Therefore any semblance of a flash back to those times is a grossly huge mistake.

BLK 101 Rule #5: "Black women don't play." And now I'm not talking about "playing" sports or "playing" out at recess. I mean most black women don't take being mistreated, pushed over, or trampled upon. Black women are extremely assertive and can stand their own ground. This is one trait I never quite acquired which I hugely admire. Though at times I do try my hardest to fake it. I say, "Fake it 'til you make it."

BLK 101 Rule #6: "Speak when you see people." And I'm sure my southern people know about this rule for it's part of the entire southern culture, both black and white. But I don't think it transfers to northern culture as a whole. A lot of people don't know this rule and if they did, it would help them tremendously. But it's very important in black culture to recognize and acknowledge each other. As you enter a room or walk down the street and pass someone, it's your obligation and a general courtesy to speak. A simple "Good mornin'," or "Hey how ya doin'?" are crucial. Otherwise it indicates that I mean nothing to you to the point that you don't really even see or acknowledge my presence. Now back in the day, old folks, would chastise children and even grown folk, if they didn't "speak" to people. That was a very important part of teaching manners or just plain good ole "home training." It is just as important as "Please" and "Thank you," or in the south when speaking to elders the almighty "Yes, sir" and "Yes, Ma'am."

What I have discovered to be quite fascinating is that black people will "speak" and acknowledge another black person anywhere on the face of this planet. And I never picked up on this totally until during a trip to Okinawa, Japan to visit my husband while he was stationed there a year with the Marine Corps. We had been sightseeing quite a bit while I visited and one day we had been gone all day to a rather remote area of the island. In fact, I teased my husband because he had been the only black person, in fact probably the only American, I had seen all day. Yet when we did finally come across a black man that day, Bryant's "Hey man, how ya doin'?" really jumped out at me and got my full attention.

"Do you know him?" I inquired of Bryant.

"No, I was just speaking," Bryant replied.

"Oh." And that's when it really clicked. Black people always speak to each other. But don't think that includes white people. Not typically. And I really hate that when I'm walking out of the grocery store and distant acquaintances will pass right by me without even speaking unless I speak first. And the reason being, if they don't hear my voice and realize it's me Lynn, they take me as just another white woman in passing and simply tune me out. Oh I really despised that until I truly learned what was going on. I remember Maya Angelou speaking of this in one of her autobiographies of the fact that black people don't speak to whites purposely because they don't have to, like they were required to in the years of the past. So now it's a point *not* to speak because they have that choice and freedom not to acknowledge whites. They truly don't even "see" whites. In passing they automatically "tune out" a person when they see the color "white." And so I've now learned first hand at times what it is to become "invisible." Not a great feeling, but it's an important feeling to feel and understand what others have felt and experienced for centuries.

BLK 101 Rule #7: "Nothing's wrong with CPT." Colored People Time is acceptable under most situations, except when trying to catch a flight out at the airport or the like. Now it can cause some complications otherwise, as well as a lot of misunderstandings. And for my white readers, if you're unclear on the CPT thing, it usually runs about an hour late to the white world which I would refer to as standard time, but I never did like the term "standard," like an alternative is of a lesser value or unacceptable. And don't hold me to the precise minute on that hour calculation. (That's part of the whole point. Flexibility versus rigidity. You see the whole point in this concept is that time does not rule your life. From this viewpoint, situations and people are the major players that dictate your day, not the clock on the wall.)

Having been raised and even being employed for the most part of my life in the black world, I didn't know that this time issue was such a divisive element between the two worlds of black and white. But it's really a biggie I've learned when one collides with the other. Being a little late to work or to a meeting was never a big deal. But during recent years, I've learned from white colleagues and meeting-goers that the white world looks at being late as being inconsiderate and discourteous. Hmm, I had no idea. Yet at the same time, I've always understood in blacks that helping a family member or neighbor in distress or even offering a friendly conversation was more important than being prompt or (heaven forbid this concept) being early to an engagement or meeting. It's all about that caring and people-oriented focus and element. And it doesn't necessarily make one world bad and the other good, in either way. It's just that the two worlds' concepts on this take are totally different. So this is where an understanding of each other's cultures and customs really comes into play. It can eliminate a whole lot of misunderstandings.

And studying under Dr. Dandy at Armstrong College in Savannah, Georgia as we studied black culture and language, it really was an eye-opener to whites and even to me which I thought I had all the insight on black culture. But it really taught me the history and how far back some of these concepts originated which can not help but be ingrained and embedded in the black world. The whole time concept goes back to African beliefs, customs, and philosophies that an occasion begins at the moment when everyone is in assemblage, not at a specific time of a timepiece, such as a mere clock or watch.

In fact, when my dear friends, Todd Ewing and Mike O'Neal, share stories of their visits to the villages of different African countries, they always include the story and song that the village people share each time a person enters the gathering, "Welcome, brother welcome. And with your love…" And this goes on and on throughout the gathering. There isn't any "eye-cutting," "grimaces," or "hushed comments," but a true and genuine greeting that this person's presence is welcomed and the time factor doesn't even concern them. So this I felt really explained a custom and tradition that we make light of in jest, as we tease people about Colored People Time. But it's not about being late. That's not the focus. It's about being together no matter what one has to go through to be there. It's walking in someone else's shoes and being considerate and appreciative of what they've been through to reach their destination. And it is critical that we attempt to become familiar with other cultures' customs, instead of quickly pointing an accusing finger because we don't understand. And for me now that I understand the White World's point of view on lateness, I myself will try to do better with the time thing. Though I must say it is hard to teach an old dog new tricks. But at least now I am cognizant and will bear these feelings in mind.

BLK 101 Rule #8: "The light-skinned girl with the long hair gets the man." (And no I don't mean "weave.") Of course color should not matter, but it has in the past and even continues to this day amongst some black people. And I realize this is a stigma that White society has subconsciously brainwashed throughout the Black community. Take for example the noted psychological studies of black girls that chose a white doll baby over a black doll. Though I must say the stigma has greatly diminished. And as usual I can always rely heavily on my Black comedians as a most worthy and reliable source on the "State of the Black Union." They have even taken note and commented about the light-skinned brother losing "play" (or that's "action" in some lingoes) and that now it's the dark-skinned, black brothers who get all the attention of the women.

This antiquated concept of "light skinned-ness prevailing" is something that always really got next to me during my adolescent years, and still does 'til this day. And I vividly recall like it may have happened this very morning, students who had self-appointed themselves in authority and vehemently proclaimed to other black students, "She can't win Miss St. Helena! She's too dark."

You know I was enraged, feeling here I must have gone deep undercover to infiltrate the KKK activities and was now engaged with one of their affiliates. And I'm like, "Whatever happened to 'Say it loud. I'm black and I'm proud?'" I wanted to know. But I never got an adequate response. There wasn't one. It was still business as usual, beauty means to be light-skinned with long hair. Doesn't matter if you have anything else going for you. And this little skin rule went for the guys as well. Though I must say women have greatly thrown away this misconception for there are far more noteworthy qualities that are in need of identification for a successful relationship.

Another played-out rule strongly linked with this rule #6 is that "the white girl" always gets the guy. And *again* my unfailing barometers, our comedians. (Believe me there's a reason why jokes come to fruition and you laugh when you recognize the truth of them.) We always hear about a black guy that selects the most out-of-shape, ugliest, and trashiest white woman he can find to bring home and flaunt as his prize. Well, maybe back in the day when they were forbidden fruit or maybe just as a form of revenge against the white man for all the thousands and thousands and hundreds of thousands of black women they had raped and exploited.

And how I hated this on a very personal level. For back in the late 60's and early 70's I was usually the only white girl (and sometimes still am the only white girl or woman) in a black nightclub or black gathering. And who did the guys used to make a straight beeline for. None other than, little flat-chested, white as a sheet, homely, four-eyed visioned Lynn. The only really pretty thing was my waist-length hair. Fortunately I look a little better now on most days. At least I truly believe I wouldn't be considered trailer trash. Many times guys would directly by-pass one of my lovely black stepsisters to get to me. It was flattering at first, the attention, before I really realized what was happening. But after that I grew to resent it for I knew I was hardly competition and despised the actual reason I was sought out of a crowd. Luckily I can say that today that habit is almost totally taboo and rightfully so. Good riddance. For let me tell you it's no picnic being the only "white only on the outside" white girl. (Yeah, read that again if you don't get it the first time. I had to reread it my "ownself.")

9

My Grammy and Bread Puddin'

The most invincible strength of Black culture is its firm foundation built on a steadfast faith and commitment to God and family. My grandmother, who we all dearly called "Grammy," was a living symbol that embodied both these elements. And though Grammy was actually my "step" grandmother, we were a million times closer than my paternal and maternal grandmothers, and probably more bonded and connected than any of my friends on my age level.

Immediately when I view Grammy, my file's default opens up in Grammy's extremely clean and cozy little living room. Or the very next site would be that tiny, sweet kitchen that wreaked with sunshine until it looked like it couldn't hold any more and always, always wafted the most scrumptious, mouth-watering aromas throughout her humble, little home, out the front door, and down the path to our house. Talk about the warmest, safest memories held so dear. It was right here.

We would sit in her warm and darkened living room, soaking in the warmth of her old-timey brick fireplace. And in the corner behind the front door always stood a cane that I remember Grammy never using. (Story was that when her dear friend Nellie passed on she had left it there for Grammy.) And she'd sit and rock back and forth ever so softly in her blue vinyl upholstered rocking chair, and I'd be on the couch (she called it the "davenport") which matched her chair in a blue vinyl. Of course it didn't match anything else, but that wasn't the point. Each and every inch of her living room and entire house was always neat as a pin. The saying, "Cleanliness is next to Godliness," Grammy genuinely practiced. Grammy's house simply emulated cleanliness. In fact one of her greatest desires was that one of her granddaughters would one day become a nurse because she said she "loved the whiteness and cleanliness of their uniforms." (Which most of us did go into service careers as educators, counselors, and the like, though none were in the field of medicine.)

There we'd sit ever so contentedly, wrapped and smothered in total tranquillity and sheer bliss. We'd both sip on orange pekoe hot tea as we dipped in and completely soaked our favorite snack, large Nabisco milk crackers or old-fashioned gingersnaps. Grammy taught me so many of her fine dining delights of the Lowcountry. And I even taught her a trick or two that I had come to specialize in. Like eating smoked sausage cold, straight out of the "ice box" (or refrigerator) along with her favorite, a slice of either Captain John Derst raisin or yellow bread. And though at first she was opposed totally to this crazed concept, trusting me as a true confident and companion, and observing that I hadn't been hospitalized as of yet, she yielded and actually enjoyed my silly and childish practice. We always enjoyed a thorough exchange of ideas and thoughts. Though there really wasn't much of a comparison in our capacities and capabilities. Here you had a wise and worldly woman paired with an unexposed and still-yet-to-be-educated adolescent.

Grammy's introduction to food for the soul with a coastal sea island twist was the most sensational and incredible experiences. First and foremost, she initiated me into a world of pure ecstasy with her shrimp and gravy abundantly drenched and engulfing a mound of hot, white steamy grits. What a delight! Or then again, about tied with this parcel of paradise, was her shrimp, okra, and tomatoes soaking over some fluffy, long-grained rice. And Grammy loved to add a sprinkle or so of curry powder to all her seafood and even to her flour coating in her brown Piggly Wiggly bag used for succulently fried chicken to a simply-to-die-for gorgeous golden brown. Grammy even cooked stewed liver and onions with gravy that not only made your mouth melt and beg, but melted in your mouth as well, as you bit every bite. And to think that I had actually believed that I hated liver. (Of course, that was my momma's rubbery and tasteless nightmare. Excuse me Momma, but you just couldn't cook liver.) Then there was Grammy's stewed chicken that she would cook down so tender until we would both eat up and suck up every little morsel, including each drop of gravy and flavor, even down to and beyond the bone, for she taught me to chew up the marrow, bone, and all. It was so tender and yummy you just couldn't get enough; you even about ate your fingers off! (Hey, can you remotely tell that I miss my grandmother's cooking? Just nothing like it on the face of this planet. My only hope is that perhaps on the other side, He'll extend us that mercy in His house.)

But I have to confess that my most "favoritest," favoritest (yeah, I know those aren't real words) memories of my Grammy's delightfully and divinely prepared dishes had to be her phenomenally and incredibly delightful bread puddin'. I mean every time I see bread puddin', my heart and mind does a hop, skip, and dive back into Grammy's sunshiny and radiating kitchen with a pan of bread puddin' just out of her gas-burning oven, sitting on top of one of the eyes on the stove, cooling down enough so that I can pop a piece into my mouth and savor every little ingredient of flavor against every taste bud of existence. I mean that stuff was moist and yummy! How incredibly good it was. And every time I see some that appears to halfway measure up to my expectations of hers, I try a piece so I can take that delightful journey back home to her. Sometime back, I did run across some in Mom's Restaurant in Port Royal, an out-of-this-world soul food dispensary. And lo and behold I got hold of some of their bread puddin'. Pretty good I must say and the lady always cut you the biggest piece that could last you the whole evening through to breakfast if practiced a hint of self-control. Of course, it never was quite as yummy, though it made for a satisfactory substitution. And through the years I've finally mastered and refined my own replication to the point that I can actually survive in this world until I get to the next to taste hers again.

With all this fabulous food Grammy was always cooking up, of course, she needed to restock her kitchen on a regular basis. So none other than her #1 sampler, eater, and buddy in general would either chauffeur her or run the errands for her to old faithful, Piggly Wiggly grocery store, and go wherever else she may need, be it Edwards five and dime department store, or Prince Street to pay her telephone bill. At this time, I had just gotten my driver's license, and I *loved* to drive into Beaufort to shop for Grammy. I didn't even mind pulling out her large-folded green Food Stamps certification card and the stapled booklet of Food Stamps of varying monetary denominations that the cashier would have to painstakingly tear out while the line behind me grew exceedingly longer and longer, and they grew more and more impatient with me. (You see back then, there weren't those fancy Food Stamp credit cards that the cashier can swipe through the computer in a matter of a split second.) And don't let Grammy start up with talking about Food Stamps and how they were meant for the elderly and sickly, "But now you have these young girls having babies and sitting up collecting welfare and food stamps!" She said how in her day having babies out of wedlock was not condoned and tolerated. In fact, you got the boot out the door; you were a disgrace to the family. Now we as a society all coddle, condone, and reinforce this negative behavior saying it's alright and actually aiding and embedding its perpetuation. Those old ways, ideals, and values worked, but we didn't appreciate them. But our new and improved ways certainly ain't getting' it.

I'm amazed though that for me I didn't chicken out for some of these errands, for I was painfully shy at this time and easily and readily able to be embarrassed.

But it didn't matter. It was all good because I can truthfully say I *never* had a problem doing anything for my Grammy!

Many a night, wielding a flashlight in hand, I ferociously braved the dirt path that had been drudged into the grass between our house and Grammy's house. (For I was truly afraid of the dark and believe I still am to this day.) I'd be headed to Grammy's to either watch TV with her, talk on her phone "unlimited" minutes to my boyfriend (grandmothers are too sweet when it comes to telephone time), or to spend the night with her and enjoy a myriad of astonishing and fascinating stories of her days gone passed. At night, we'd watch the TV show, "Julia," starring Diahann Carroll with all the lights in the house turned off to ensure an affordable electric bill at the end of the month. ("Julia" was one of the very first black sitcoms that had come on TV.) Then on Saturday mornings, after chores, we'd never miss "Soul Train." That was totally my cup of tea, listening to all that great soul music and watching Don Cornelius, the performers, and the audience "get down" and "get off."

At night, if it was wintertime, we'd pile up a zillion hand-made cozy quilts on top of the highly perched bed, turn off the gas heaters, then jump into the middle of this hot thermos of a sandwich in utter comfy-ness. Then we'd begin our sojourn of the past through her many personal stories. She'd tell of the miles she'd walk to a little one-room schoolhouse or to the praise house for song and worship service. This was right in the Tom Fripp community in the area that had once been a slave plantation owned by a Mr. Tom Fripp. And even until just a couple years ago, out of a bad habit and tradition, it was still called Tom Fripp Plantation. Then Grammy would also tell me about walking the six or seven miles from St. Helena Island to shop in Beaufort. They would have to catch a ferryboat across the river for there were no bridges to connect many of these coastal islands back during her youth.

And I knew I had to be genuinely one of her best buddies, the evening she shared with me the tale of her wedding night with her husband, Adam. Unbelievable as it may be, she told me how the two of them had to sleep in the same bedroom as her mother on her wedding night. I'm sure times were incredibly hard, and it wasn't like people during her time and circumstances could just take a honeymoon cruise to the Bahamas or spend a night at the Hilton or Hyatt. So I found that to be one of her most intriguing and captivating stories. You should have seen me. You know my lower jaw had dropped to its lowest depth and was dragging the floor when it came to this story.

I think one of my favorite and most cherished memories of Grammy's words of wisdom and advisement came whenever a thunder storm would pass through, and with living on the coastal Sea Islands they frequented us on a rather regular and routinely basis. As we watched the bolts of lightning thrashing out in the nearby fields, and heard the pounding hammering of the thunder, Grammy would issue her appropriate and timely warning to accompany the weather report. "Be quiet, children. No talking while the Lord is talking." In fact, like a regularly scheduled fire drill at school, we'd all get up under the covers of the bed and repose in complete silence. And believe me that was hard to do as much as my stepsister, Maxine or my Grammy and I loved to chatter the day, evening, and night away.

Grammy was firmly rooted in God and in the House of the Lord, the church. She in fact was, I believe, to have been one of the founding mothers of her church, Ebenezer Baptist Church. She attended church service every Sunday without fail. And all along with my other relished moments of chauffeuring my grandmother, I loved to drive her to church on Sunday mornings. Then picking her up after church was even more enjoyable. I'd get to be her sounding board as I listened intently and understandingly to all her fussing about the goings-on in the church.

First she would lecture about how the women come to church just to dress and be seen, don't even have their mind on the message of the sermon that day. Out to catch a man, one of those no count deacons or even eyeballing the preacher himself. She said that all that there was, was an over emphasis on one's outside and what you wear to church and that the Lord looked inside and within (though your clothes should be clean and in good repair.) Anything else was unimportant in the eyes of the Lord. Then she'd go on to rumble about the over-zealous passing of baskets. "Why did they have three and four offerings in one service! Whenever and whatever they had to offer should be shared on the first go round. What were they doing with all that money anyway?" Sometimes, I wondered why she continued to attend church with all its gross shortcomings. Apparently she overlooked them or perhaps she wanted to take every opportunity to enjoy her most dearly loved spiritual, "Amazing Grace." Oh, how she loved that song and now I can feel why.

I think many times her greatest inspiration from church was right in her very home, sitting in her rocking chair soaking up and basking in every word delivered during Oral Roberts' words of upliftment and encouragement. Grammy *adored* Oral Roberts and his television outreach ministry. Then at nights or on a Saturday or Sunday afternoon, we'd sit either at the table in her bright, cheery kitchen or relax at the table on her little, screened in front porch. And she would dictate her message that she wished that I neatly would scribe out on a neat and delicate sheet of stationary. After addressing the envelope, she'd have me enclose either two dollars or sometimes a five-dollar bill to be her offering to help Oral Roberts and also to be thanked in return with the receipt of a prayer cloth. She watched Oral Roberts and had me write to him so frequently that you would have sworn they were madly crazed lovers. But that was Grammy. She just loved the Lord and anything and anyone that represented Him in the right light.

She always strongly instilled in me, "Remember, Lynn, the church is not a building. Your true church is in your heart. So always carry it with you." And as Grammy's health and vision began to fail her, she had to hold on to that advisement with an even fiercer tenacity. For now on many Sundays, it became a necessity that she stay home and attend church within her heart for those days. She would call on me to read to her from that tremendously huge white Bible trimmed in gold that my sister-in-law had once gifted her. And that was one of my greatest loves, to sit at Grammy's side and read the Bible to her. What beautiful and sweet moments those were.

Grammy believed strongly in a strong work ethic and that idleness was truly the devil's workshop. She was *always* working! She kept a small garden and raised chickens as well. Almost every morning or evening you'd see her tending those tender green plants of corn, okra, tomatoes, sweet potatoes, and any sundry of vegetables with a hoe in hand. As well as honeydew melon and cantaloupe. (Oh how Grammy and I loved a slice or two with some smoked sausage and hot tea for our breakfast.) You'd even see Grammy on many occasion toting and slinging an ax as she chopped up wood in the yard to set one of those comfy and homey blazes in her little fireplace.

Oh and she'd fuss about a white and somewhat wealthy neighbor, Mr. Charles Henry, who owned and operated a dairy farm in Tom Fripp. She'd rant and rave about him inching his way at stealing her land, by plowing his hay fields over the property line by an additional half-a-foot each year. Then he'd chain off their mutually shared extra entry road. And the last straw was when one of his sons broke off the stone property marker the recently hired surveyors had just made placement of. For she was certain the boys had been intentionally informed with specific instructions from their father and had purposely carried those out. And rightfully so for her concern, for through the years many a black landowner had property down right stolen from them! Many a white man had acquired wealth at the expense of black people. It started with slavery and the former slave masters always resented its abolition and were hell bent on regaining what they had lost, free labor.

Even with her own son, she had issues as well. He drove her plum crazy with his yard dogs that had complete and free reign of the farm. And they had killed several of her hens and they remained in a state of fear to the point that many a day they were unable to lay eggs. So you and I know how things really nag at and aggravate old folks. Such was her case, too.

And you'd see her in her chicken coop gathering the light brown eggs the hens had recently delivered. And what was her reward to them? Well, periodically, let me say we'd savor the flavor of one of those tender and delicately stewed-down hens after she had wrung their necks, gingerly plucked each and every feather, and cut it down into edible portions. How many people even have a concept of this process? Kids just think you go to KFC and that's how fried chicken comes to pass.

Oh, and she'd keep us children straight with other values as well. Which my guilt continues to haunt me to this day, for she always preached to us the evils of using paper plates and paper products. "Lazy and nasty people use paper plates! They're just too lazy and trifflin' to wash their dishes." So you know a slight cringe goes through me whenever I reach for the Dixie paper or Styrofoam plates. "But Grammy—you have no idea how crazed and hectic this world is today! Please forgive me."

Grammy had many insights into the comings and goings of this world. And one insight I found so silly at the time was that she truly believed that man had not walked on the moon and that it was all a staged act. Well, I thought, "Grammy, it had to be real. It was on the news." But now I'm thinking whoever really knows for sure. None of us were there. I certainly wouldn't bet my mama's life on its certainty of existence. And along with her disbelief in "the system" I'm sure because it had failed her so often, between the times of living through the dreadful Depression and blatant and daily inequities of more modern times. Grammy did not believe in the banking system. Simple as that. And after her passing, I learned to what extent she did not believe in it. For she had buried her entire lifesaving's (no matter how meager was not the point) in a mason-canning jar under the bottom bricks of her homey, little fireplace.

As Grammy grew elderly along came sickness. And when she finally had to go for a stay in the hospital, she ever so calmly and peacefully told me, "I'm pretty tired now. I'm ready to go home." So when she did let go and return home to the Lord, I was truly happy for her because that was her most ardent wish and heart's desire. But to this day I so greatly miss her. Her tenderness and her strength, both housed within the same temple was to always be adored and admired.

Upon Grammy's passing, as her things were put in order and the contents of her mason jar savings was bequeathed according to her elicit instructions, lo and behold she had remembered me. I was virtually blown away to another place and time, when my oldest stepsister, Gloria, had informed me that Grammy had left ten dollars that she wanted me to have. I thought long and hard about how I could best utilize this money so as to always remember her through a special purchase. Well I decided upon a delicate, dainty, and fragile little pair of brilliantly shining sandstone earrings that glazed within the turnstile case at Modern Jewelers on Bay Street. Earrings I would cherish and treasure for a lifetime. They were perfect! The sunrays danced in and out and all around those earrings just as they had within Grammy's bright and cheery kitchen filled with the ever-present appealing aromas, but more so, always filled with love.

(You know I soon after actually lost those special earrings, diving under the incoming rage of surf at Hunting Island Beach. But I never lost the love I had for Grammy or all my fond memories of her.)

Grammy, known to the outside world, as Elizabeth Smalls, was born September 14, 1898 and she died a month before I graduated from Beaufort High School on April 9, 1974. And I look at the time of her passing now as a blessing in many ways because I would have hated her to be exposed to my most trying and turbulent times during my college days at Clemson. Though clearly my greatest strength was no longer at my side, but oh what a strength she had rooted within me. An added strength and reliance on His strength. For you see Grammy was the grandmother I never really had. Remember, we (my mother and siblings) had been virtually excommunicated from the family when she had moved to South Carolina from Michigan for my mother had defied them by marrying a black man. (Oh well, you don't miss what you don't know. What can I say?) And in fact, people get confused when I speak of her. "You mean your mother's mother or your father's mother?" "No, I mean my stepfather's mother." Though she was *never* a *"step"*-grandmother to me, simply and endearingly, just Grammy.

And now I'm hoping, we as her grandchildren have continued to succeed in bringing that soft, kind smile upon her face as she looks down upon us from heaven. My heart's desire is that she's happy with us and proud of whom we've become.

Thank you, Grammy for your bread puddin' and for all your love. I'll always hold you within my heart for I so dearly love you too!

10

Exposure, Transformation, and Infusion into Soul

Where does one begin to explain the transformation and processes of change in going from "being white" to "being black"? (And for anyone not following me totally, I'm clearly speaking in terms of culture, not physical features. For my experience was purely cultural. No, I did not change my pigmentation as did John Howard Griffin, the author of Black Like Me, in order to do first-hand research into discrimination against blacks.) The language transformation was definitely a significant component of this change process, which I have already attempted to explain rather fully.

Another *huge* transition was the internalization, appreciation, and just tremendous *love* of black music and bond that holds with the black dance. Now my reference here is to what was now to become my cherished childhood, teenage, and young adult music—"soul music" of the late 60's and 70's. Now days, it's classified in the record stores as "rhythm and blues" or on the radio as "old school." At any rate, this is the music that became my whole world and the musical thirst I acquired as a youth, and can't and don't want to let go of to this day. In fact, each morning, I can't wait to listen to the Tom Joyner Show radio show on Savannah, Georgia's Love 101.1, as I get dressed, ready myself for the day, and drive on into work. What a great way to start the day!

You see during the mid 60's, when I moved to St. Helena Island into virtually a total black environment, between my home, neighborhood, and school, every music I encountered was soul music, and it was definitely "Love at first hear!"

And what was probably my greatest influence upon me as I was thrust as a projectile and quickly and completely infused into this music, new-to-me was my adoption, inclusion, and immersion into the St. Helena High School Marching Band. It was in 1966 that Gary Sterling, the drum major for the SHHS Band and a very close Bahá'í friend of the family asked if I could try out for the band, as a

55

mascot majorette. Somehow, our band director, Mr. Felix, agreed. For there were numerous reasons that the St. Helena High School Band was one of the best in the Southeast at this time. And one of those reasons was the gorgeous figures of the SHHS majorettes.

Yet Mr. Felix afforded me the opportunity, and most times that's what any of us need in life-a chance. So I gave it my best shot. Here I was a scrawny, little white girl from northern Michigan with absolutely no, and I repeat, "No rhythm," trying out for one of the best, jammin'est high school marching bands ever. I was in fifth grade at the time and the other junior majorette, Shelia Toomer, was a sixth grader from a neighboring black school that fed into our high school, Lady's Island Elementary.

Somehow Mr. Felix gave me the benefit of a doubt and accepted me into the band. The other majorettes all had a lot of pity for me, and took me on as a little sister and an extremely challenging project, "Teaching the White Girl to Dance on Beat with Some Soul." And they actually, I don't know how, succeeded. They taught me how to dance, after *a lot* of patience, all the latest dances at the time: "The Cha Cha Cha," "The Tighten Up," even "The Four Corners" and all. For that was definitely a prerequisite for being a St. Helena majorette.

I'll never forget asking the older majorettes when I first began practicing and trying out for the band as a majorette, all who were either juniors or seniors in high school, the question that continuously perplexed my mind, "How do you move 'that'?" As I stood pointing to the girls' lower pelvic regions. And they all laughed, but proceeded to show me step by step what to move, how to move, and in what sequence to arrive at the final outcome of the "Four Corners." And after much, much practice, reviewing, and encouragement to "loosen up", "loosen up, Lynn," time and time again, I got the stiff-as-a-board out of me and could actually hang as we moved and grooved to all that great soul music the band played for us. For they all had the music rocking, from Arthur Lynard and Moses Mouzone on the drums (the heart of any band) to Eleanor Smalls on clarinet, Freda Porter on flute, Julius "Faggy" Pringle and Rufus "Chug a Mug" Fripp on the tubas, Arthur Smalls on coronet, and my sister Ros on tenor sax.

We were one big family and also had a lot fun together outside of practice, like on our adventures to the infamous Mr. A.J. Brown's corner store. That was a ball! We'd joke and play around about Mr. A.J. Brown (and we'd always say his full name just like that) putting his nasty looking hand, the large remaining scar of a bad burn, on our treasures and booty of snacks for afternoon practice. The Ne-Hi sodas, Tom's barbecued potato chips, the two for a penny butter cookies and coconut bar cookies, Mary Jane and Now Later candies, orange sherbet Push

Ups, all the way down to the pickled pig feet—for these would have to hold us until we finished practice well after dark and made it on home to dinner. Not to mention the baton beatings you'd receive if you had been courting, goofing, or gallivanting and were late on returning from A.J. Brown's to practice. Courtesy of none other than us, the majorette's wands of stainless steel. Not that we happily parted from our batons for this blasphemy meted out to fellow friends.

The majorettes also shielded and protected me during many turbulent ordeals. There was our first drum majorette Cheryl Grant, followed by Patricia Smalls. Then some of the other majorettes I recall were Betty Jean Holmes, Cherry Smalls, and LoLo Atkins. And they all were like big sisters to me. For remember, here I was a little white girl in an all black high school band during the heat and hostility of the 1960's in the South. A lot of change was going down with their Jim Crow laws, and some folk were not too happy. Schools were very meagerly integrated through their policy called, "Freedom of Choice."

One time as we traveled to a neighboring town called Ridgeland for a Christmas parade, I later learned that several of the majorettes and band members had to actually defend me with their batons against some rather prejudiced people in the crowd that didn't appreciate seeing a little white girl performing with an all black band. But oh well for them, I'm ever grateful of how all the band members always took up for and protected me—they always had my back. And all the while, Mr. Felix was there as well, sheltering and looking over me, just like a father.

And I truly thank Mr. Felix to this day for what he gave me as a child. The gift to experience and appreciate totally the awesome richness of music and movement within Black Culture. Indeed, this is a priceless gift that I have treasured and enjoyed throughout my lifetime. And still to this very day, you can barely get me to leave a dance floor—I simply would "dance 'til the break of dawn." I love it so!

My addiction I can blame and hold totally accountable to the music that Mr. Felix translated and drafted late into the wee hours from songs that he would listen to over and over again recorded on 45's to sheet music for each and every instrument and part for the entire St. Helena High School Marching Band. And what a gold mine he did unearth to allow us to razzle and dazzle the fans at the fabulous football half times and show-stopping parades. Junior Walker and the All Stars' "What Does It Take," and "Shotgun," Etta James' "Tell Mama," Booker T. and the MGs' "Green Onions," Archie Bell and the Drells' "Tighten Up," the Barkays' "Soulfinger," Cliff Nobles' "The Horse," Hugh Masekela's

"Grazin' in the Grass," and Stevie Wonder's "My Cherie Amour," as the list goes on and on, just like my craze of dance, "'Til the break of dawn."

There the St. Helena High School Marching Band would be prestigiously high stepping in the Christmas or Memorial Day parades through the streets of Beaufort. And we'd always be led by an additional and unofficial drum major, none other than, Mr. Tuitty Fruitty himself. (A legend in his own right who may have been limited in intellect, but was hardly limited when it came to an appreciation of people, pleasure, and music. He would always lead his favorite band down the street with his small whop-sided, tin baton. And we were always honored that we were the recipients of this honor for we knew it was genuine, unbiased, and true.) Oh, but when we rounded the corner of Carteret and Bay Streets, this was the real spotlight for an intense finale of our performance, amongst the throngs of hundreds of gawking eyes and wailing and screeching voices. And we'd give 'em what they wanted-a show that would simply rock and sock it to them. We'd light into one of the #1 tunes at the top of the soul charts on the radio, coupled with the latest dance moves choreographed concisely to the confines of our time, space, and the rector scale we wanted to elicit—always at least a 10 plus. And there we'd stop dead center in the middle of Bay Street, with brass horns wailing and hollering, the bass drum pacing out the rhythm, and majorette hips bouncing to the beat—to put on a show that would start a party with the entire parade crowd in the middle of downtown Beaufort.

And never will I forget the teaching and preaching of the Godfather of Soul, none other than Mr. James Brown himself, in the lyrics of his soulful songs such as "Say It Loud, I'm Black and I'm Proud." Oh the St. Helena Marching Band proudly-so and rightfully-so emitted this declaration to the world, both in music and word, as the lyrics were shot out by the band members and majorettes at our numerous performances and engagements. I basked in this pride for them as well, though I always felt a hint of sadness that I couldn't rightfully share in allowing this same phrase to be enunciated and parted from the lips of my white-self. "Say It Loud, I'm Black and I'm Proud" wasn't exactly in congruence with my appearance. So I simply settled for a subtle and hushed, lip-synced addendum.

As junior high students, we listened to all the latest soul music at St. Helena School, under the massive oak trees in the front yard, with a portable record player on 45's during recess. (And young people, I know you have no idea here about "45's," but those are small album-looking vinyl disks, with only one single title on each side.) The Jackson Five had just exploded into the music world, and we were in love with they themselves and all their songs such as, "Stop the Love You Save" and "A-B-C, 1-2-3." But then in cars, were there cassettes or CD's?

Not! Only eight-track tapes! (Don't ask. All I can say, they were audiotapes almost as large as videotapes for movies.) Or we simply listened to WPAL out of Charleston (the only local black radio station within our reception area) after school and on Saturdays while doing morning chores.

And of course, we rose early Saturday mornings with our eye on the prize; working through Saturday chores (washing clothes, hanging out line after line, cleaning the bathroom, dusting, sweeping, mopping, and waxing the entire wood flooring of our house) all with lightning speed. Our end reward, finish in time to watch "S-o-o-o-o-o-o-o-u-l Train" at noon with none other than the renowned, Mr. Don Cornelius himself who we thought was as "chill as ice." Then here would come the Tempts with "Just My Imagination" to totally blow us away, the Supremes dispersing so divinely the ultimate pledge of "Someday We'll be Together," or the "never-to-be-seen-again" union of commitment and capabilities of Marvin Gaye and Tammy Terrell, witnessed in the loving lyrics and musical miracle of a song such as "You're All I Need to Get By." That was pure and unadulterated music and showmanship in its total and all-prevailing glory. Often to be imitated, but never able to be duplicated in the course of time or world of existence.

Gosh, my whole world was music! And summers added even further brilliance and glory to this splendid pastime, obsession, and addiction. For the Fourth of July, the entire family would either pile into our Chevy station wagon or on a more adventurous and daring odyssey, our stepfather would take the large, flatbed truck he used for hauling our tomatoes and cucumbers for sale to the packinghouses. Our destination, none other than the "then-famed" Singleton Beach on Hilton Head Island. (When Hilton Head was still "in the country" and predominantly black-owned land, which was also the case with basically all the property of the coastal Sea Islands.)

Now there were some serious nightclubs right on the beach (or should I say "dayclubs") for they were open all day to the entire public (both young and old). And luckily the ID system was null and void. But young people knew their place. We could order sandwiches (pork chop, chicken, or fried fish), chips, and soda or hit the dance floor. (But no one even dared to think of ordering an alcoholic beverage.) And boy was the club jumping! In broad daylight, too! There we'd be weaving in and out, bopping about, amongst a sea of bodies moving and grooving ever so succinctly to the sounds of the piccolo, which we endlessly fed with silver. And out they rolled, with Wilson Pickett's "Funky Broadway," Mel and Tim's "Backfield in Motion," James Brown with "Popcorn," Chairman of the Board's "You Got Me Dangling on a String,"—as we continued to bounce and sway the rest of the day away. Or the heavy-tear-jerking love ballads of The Moments' "I Found Love on a Two-Way Street," The Originals' "I'll Never Hear the Bells," Freda Payne with "Band of Gold," Otis Reddings with "Sittin' on the Dock of the Bay," Smokey Robinson with "The Tears of a Clown," and just-take-me-away with the Tempts' "Just My Imagination (Runnin' Away with Me)."

And when we weren't playing at the beach during the summer, we'd be working at the tomato packinghouses or sheds. Which was definitely the bomb! Not the work in itself for I had reoccurring and nightmaring visions of zillions of hard, apple-green tomatoes rolling by endlessly on the conveyor belt in my head as it thrashed about my pillow throughout the night. But the dinner breaks at the packinghouse made the torturous, mundane task all more than worth its while. For we would truck on down Highway 21, making a quick jaunt around the corner, and there we'd be at the Sugar Bowl within a flash. And this was definitely my idea of a small paradise here on earth. (Never has taken much to make me deliriously happy; just give me some soul-stirring or get-up-and-dance music and I'm beyond satisfied and content.) For superficially, the Sugar Bowl, was nothing more than a small and very humble "hole-in-the-wall" that served dinners to the seasonal workers of the packing sheds and migrant workers that toiled in the tomato fields. But if you looked within the heart and soul of the Sugar Bowl, it was surely a diamond in the rough, yeah and pretty rough it was.

First and foremost, they had a jukebox in the front serving room amidst several small dining tables clad in traditional kitchen couture for that era, oil cloth with large red and white checkerboard. Then there was the actual cooking kitchen at the rear with a counter and stools where you'd place your much awaited dinner order. And for kids that had already worked a seven or eight-hour day and still had several hours in sight after dinner, the menu seemed like lobster and champagne for all we knew. We definitely had our heart's desire available: fried pork chop, fried chicken, or fried fish sandwiches which would be comprised of a big piece of meat, bone and all, slapped between two pieces of plain white bread, a scoop of potato salad on the side, and a bottle of orange or grape Ne-Hi soda to slosh it all down. (And yes, everything was always fried. No one even had a concept of something as bland as, baked or broiled. Of course, no one had heard of cholesterol then either. Now maybe at your grandma's house you'd encounter and enjoy something that had been stewed, but if you were paying cash money that would have to be something that had been fried to a succulent and tantalizing golden brown.) And one summer, I especially gloated in the fact that one of my older stepsisters, Rosalyn, was one of the cooks preparing all this luscious, mouth-watering cuisine. Thus I felt as if I had some kind of special connection by actually residing with a celebrity employed there.

Yet the ultimate joy was assigned to that jukebox in the corner of the dining room. Oh how we'd ensure that we could get our little pocket change together to feed its soul, even if we had to slacken up on our dinner order. For we knew it was in a state of starvation, and we were desperately starving for what it had to offer, even more so than those sandwiches Ros was serving up. So we'd load it up in a glutinous manner so we could bop and swing our dinner hour away. And in between being reunited with all our best friends and best times that the piccolo wielded out, we'd grab a bite or two of our sandwiches. This was the moment frozen in time forever in my mind when I fell deeply in love. Not with a boy, though I did have my little crushes going with our little dance partners, but rather with my enrapture in my lifelong love affairs with Jackie Wilson's "Your Love is Lifting Me Higher" and Tyrone Davis' "Turn Back the Hands of Time" or my most, most favorite of Junior Walker and the All Stars' "What Does it Take?" I had fallen helplessly in love with these melodies. They had reaffirmed my unfailing and unshaken commitment and addiction to rhythm and blues. I could not breathe without it. In fact to this very day, when I hear either of these songs, I'm lifted away completely to another plane and level of existence and all-embracing ecstasy.

People really have never gotten it with me. Most folk that really know me, know I love to go out to a club and dance the night away. And people that don't know me personally, but only from a distance, you can only imagine their views and thoughts. They are certain that I'm an extremely loose woman, out man hunting, a pathetic alcoholic, or simply a drug-enthralled addict. Though I've never drunk a drop of beer or wine or smoked any type ingredient, legal or illegal, during my entire lifetime. Never needed it. Dancing, like I love to dance, is the high of highest heights in itself. And I do believe in making love, but firmly within the confines of a lengthy, confirmed, and committed relationship; most preferably marriage, in keeping with God's divinely established institutions. (Though some may reference this activity as "sex," I have a strong aversion for that type of terminology for it represents to me a casual encounter and a void of spirit.) I've simply always had my own personal relationship with God seeped in love, fear, appreciation, and adoration throughout all the many sojourns on the hills and in the valleys of my life.

But let me tell you dancing has kept me out of "trouble," rather than gotten me into it. I mean I certainly wasn't going to waste my time talking to a guy in a club, when I'm wasting valuable dance music. That would totally be insane for me. So while other teenagers were engaged in promiscuity and sexual explorations and experiments, that was the furthest thing from my mind. I was going to be dancing!!! Now I'm sure this does not work this way with all teenagers, especially with some of the new and improved versions of "dirty dancing," but for me that was and still is how it clicks with me. Not that I didn't have to learn how to put a young man quickly in his place. Yes that went with the territory. But I definitely learned to handle myself so that I could have a great night of dancing.

Because of my maturity and responsibility participating in the Bahá'í Faith and in assisting in the care of my younger brothers and sisters and the household duties, my mother had a huge confidence and placed total trust in me to always basically just do the right thing, regardless of place or time. So she allowed me at the age of fourteen to go out dancing with my older stepsisters, Rosalyn and Maxine, who were then about seventeen and eighteen. And boy did we have a ball!

We'd head out in the suave and hip forest green 1968 Chevrolet station wagon to one of the military clubs for we had quite an abundance of them in our small, itty bitty town of Beaufort, South Carolina. We actually had and still have three military installations: the Parris Island Marine Corps Recruit Depot, the Beaufort Marine Corps Air Station, and the Beaufort Naval Hospital. Many a night we'd hit the E-Club on the Air Station or the Quarterdeck Club at the Naval Hospital for we wanted a change from what we knew was in the local population at the civilian clubs. But of course, you always got to see what's going on with your own peoples, so we always rotated in our visits to the local clubs as well. There was a club on Bladen Street that we'd step off into from time to time. Once we even peeped into the Silver Slipper on Greene Street, which now has become one of favorite artsy stores. But one of our favorites was the Boatman Club, later to become Donaldsons', and now Studio 7, out in the back woods of Burton. And I think on occasion we might have frequented Soul Shack down in Scott Plantation a time or two. But that wasn't really a good dance spot for us, for in the rear of the club was a little dark hole of a room, walls plastered with fluorescent, black light, velvety posters. And that room always reeked heavily of marijuana smoke. So that definitely wasn't our type of place.

Of course, we had our little hole in the walls in each neighborhood. That was so if you didn't have transportation, the few coins to put gas in your ride, or even be old enough to drive, you still had nearby access to a little fun. We had a little "juke joint" on the second road in Tom Fripp called Psychedelic Shack owned by Mr. S. B. Wright. It appeared to be nothing more than a slightly oversized block pump house. Maximum occupancy was probably no more than 20. It housed a jukebox and small counter where they sold soda, beer, and chips. But boy the fun you could have in there as a teenager dancing to all the latest hits that the piccolo belted out. And where did the name come from? None other than the Tempting Temptations' hit song at the time, also entitled, "Psychedelic Shack." It was about this same time that I can't help but replay the eight-track tapes and juke-box selections to another of the Tempts' songs, "Ball of Confusion" and Curtis Mayfield's "If You Had a Choice of Colors."

And what a great era in time this was for going out clubbing. These were the ultimate partying days, for the Disco Virus hadn't even erupted yet. And this was definitely a sweet time when it came to gentlemen. I know girls and young women today wouldn't even be able to grasp the concept. But back in the day, guys would ever so politely come up to your table and ask you to dance, they would buy you a soda or drink (whatever your pleasure) and usually the whole table, he would escort you back to your seat and thank you, he would actually pull the seat out for you, and you never heard a man use profanity in a young lady's presence. But young ladies didn't use that language either. Men respected women because they carried themselves in a respectful manner. What an extreme change today is all I can say.

We had a lot of good times in going out, just the three of us, Rosalyn, Maxine, and I or sometimes an additional one or two sisters or friends. These were defi-nitely the best of times. For my stepsisters were beautiful girls with beautiful fig-ures, and then there was me too. I couldn't add to the beauty much, but at least I added a hint of intrigue to our entrance into the clubs with my little white out-of-place face. Though I never felt out of place. We'd find a table and immediately hit the dance floor. And if the party hadn't started yet, we jumped out onto the floor and got it started.

Boy those were definitely the great days! And we did that all through junior high and high school days until Maxine and Rosalyn headed out to college at Wilberforce University in Ohio. Then when my younger sister Sally became old enough, I took her under my wing, and shared my dancing world with her, just as my older sisters had afforded me. And a glorious era that was with Eddie Ken-dricks, the Commodores, Earth Wind, and Fire, the Isley Brothers, the Emo-tions, Denise Williams, LTD, Heatwave, Peabo, SOS Band, Bootsy and Parliament, Brothers Johnson and the like. Though I'll have to say one of my all time favorite "get-up-and-move-something" songs had to be hands down, Johnny Taylor's "Disco Lady." Just listen to that song. You just got to move; no doubt about it. Oh, what pure and clean fun.

Yet how many people do you know, if any, that would go out to a club every night of the week, if their schedule and circumstances allowed it, purely for the love of dancing all night, and I mean literally all night until the lights come on, the last note flees from the speakers, and the DJ emphatically announces at the wee hours of the morn, "You don't have to go home, but you've gotta leave here!" Oh I've done it so many times for I simply crave it! I mean in the beginning of my teaching career, I don't know how I ever did it, but I went out every night of the week. And I'd dance 'til the lights came on and my blouse would be drenched in sweat to the point where I could actually wring sweat out of it. Which I loved nothing better for that was a true badge for a night well spent dancing. Then I'd fall into bed about 3:00 or 4:00 am and jump up at 7:00 am to bound into school, ready and rejuvenated for another day absorbed within my second love, teaching!

Though it didn't take my husband, and at the time still a boyfriend, too much time to figure it all out. So since he's always been for the most part a homebody and huge hostage of the almighty TV, he'd simply call the club whenever he wanted to see me or talk to me because I guess that was the one place he was certain he could find me during "dancing hours." And through the years, he's attempted to slow me down with this passion and obsession of mine with dance to no avail. I mean we've gone through the "Four o'clock in the morning is no time for a married woman to be coming home" to a compromise of him either bearing the torture of sacrificing to be my dance partner all night or of me simply coming home at a more respectable time of maybe one-thirty or two-ish. (Though all confirmed and certified club-goers know full well that the party doesn't start until well after twelve and actually closer to one. Anyone that thinks otherwise, is merely an amateur partier or serious imposture.)

Through the years it is rather amusing to reflect on how my musical knowledge and preference totally flipped from an exclusive adoration of the groups such as the Beatles, the Turtles, and even Sam the Shams, and the Pharaohs—to come around a 360 degree turn to the complete Motown Sound of the Temptations, the Supremes, Smokey Robinson and the Miracles, the Four Tops, and list goes on and on. Not to say I don't have an appreciation still for the Beatles for I love and respect any source of music that is truly and totally infused with heart and soul. But it can't come any other way.

Here I just wanted to share my "Favorites List" for it further explains who I am, even though I never had compiled it until I went through the process of writing this book.

Favorite Song: "What Does It Take" by Junior Walker and the All Stars

Favorite Male Vocalists: Eddie Kendricks, Babyface, Brian McKnight Tony Rich, and Luther

Favorite Female Vocalists: Patti LaBelle, Carol King, Alicia Keys, and Macy Gray

Favorite Comedians: Steve Harvey and Chris Rock (Thanks for always keeping it real and so true.) Gary Owens is pretty good too. (One of the only white persons I totally relate to.)

Favorite Dancers: Debbie Allen, Gregory Hines, Mikhail Barishnakov, and Gene Kelly (Why can't white men dance like that any more?)

Favorite Foods: Bread Puddin' and Shrimp of every style and variety

Favorite Soda: Diet Coke (That's my white side coming through, though now I am trying to kick caffeine. Ever try to find Diet Coke in a black nightclub? The two rarely coexist.)

Favorite Teacher: Mr. Joseph S. Sherman (My high school Chemistry teacher)

Favorite All-time Educator: Mary McLeod Bethune

Favorite Poet: Langston Hughes

Favorite Authors: Terry McMillan and Maya Angelou

Favorite Actress: Angela Bassett

Favorite Actors: Denzel Washington and Sean Connery

Favorite Colors: Orange and Purple (Not together as in Clemson colors, but separate. I'm definitely not a die-hard Clemson Tiger fan. Back in the day, but not this day. Just happens to be a coincidence as I'm noticing here as I actually identified and wrote them side by side.)

Favorite TV Shows: "A Different World," "Soul Food," and "The Bernie Mack Show" (which I hugely, hugely adore)

Favorite Movie: "Malcolm X"

Favorite Card Games: Bid Whist and Spades

Favorite Dance: The Bus Stop and the Swing

And looking back at this transformation into soul, I find it rather interesting. You see some people try to "be black" which I guess is fine if that's their dream and aspiration. But it was never truly a choice for me. It just naturally transpired within the course and confines of my experiences. Maybe I could have fought it, but why would you fight something that was so good to you. I mean I could attempt to "be white," but that would be a fake front and why and for what purpose? So I've settled to be content with just being me. And I'm fully aware it's a little on the black side (rather quite a lot), but I make no excuses. I'm being true to myself, who I am within, and therefore what makes me most happy. Take it or leave it, it makes me no difference. I'm just satisfied.

11

Give Me that Ole Time Religion

So you may begin to see why people do have some difficulty grasping the concept of me correctly. But to put it in a nutshell, I'm simply a girl that was raised up being black, that happens to have developed a torrid absorption and addiction to dancing, and fortunately remains guided in life by her undying love and fear of the Lord.

Some church folk have really judged me about this whole enrapture of mine with secular music, even though I love spiritual music just as ardently. They're like, "If you're going to be 'saved' you can't go out dancing because that's not serving the Lord." But my thing is this, first and foremost who is my judge as to whether I am saved or not? Who on this earth and within the arena of our limited existence here, knows and understands my personal relationship with God? Evidently the Lord has invested a lot of power in these individuals and has forgotten to serve me with a notification of change in the Hands of truest authority.

Second of all, who is to say the Lord has a problem with secular dancing done in moderation, respect, and guarding not to degrade the temple of one's soul? Every activity we participate in I wouldn't say is directly serving the Lord. When guys get together to play a game of basketball in the church leagues or even in the neighborhood recreation center, is that serving the Lord? Dancing and basketball, I see as both being leisure and recreational activities. What's the problem here?

Though I do see their point of view as far as the nightclub scene presently stands, for there's a lot of tasteless and degrading dancing, totally inappropriate attire, oblivious drinking, excessive smoking, womanizing, man-hunting, and the like. Okay I give them that; the environment is not conducive to rectified character and strengthening of spirit. But here I'm in a dilemma because I love to dance. I love dancing more than the greatest love making I've ever had. Well maybe tied. Don't want to tell a bold face lie. In fact, I can't live without dancing. I need dancing before I need food and oxygen. So you see my problem here.

I once in fact met a fine specimen of a young man at the Image Nightclub in Beaufort, back in the day. We were dancing, talking, laughing, enjoying the music, and having a harmlessly good time. We exchanged phone numbers and we saw each other on a few occasions and grew to like each other's personalities and interests. Well soon after, during one of our telephone conversations, I wanted to meet him out at the Image Nightclub again. And he informed me that instead he'd like me to have the experience of attending church with him. Of course, I immediately agreed because I love sharing with others in their praise and worship of God. And additionally so because I find this quality of spirituality within a man as rather attractive to the spiritual element of my being.

So therefore, I found myself forsaking my love of dancing on the best dance night of the week, a Friday night. Not that I would forsake the Lord for dancing, but I always saw the Christian Sabbath on Sunday as the height of public worship and fellowship at church. (Of course, you have to also bear in mind that Sabbaths of varying religions fall on a host of weekdays. But he was definitely into the church and how far into the church, I was now about to find out.) Here we were on a Friday night headed to a small Holiness church in the backwoods of Burton, South Carolina, which is country with a capital C.

Now bare in mind I've never attended a Holiness church in my life. I was in for quite an experience, to put it rather mildly. They had a traveling female evangelist visiting for their revival that week from Florida. Well she preached with a rather strong and forceful delivery, as well as a plenitude of "hallelujahs," but I don't recall any quoting of scripture or reading of the Word, just the raised volume and magnitude of her voice. Then the musical renditions were heavily reinforced, accompanied, and practically taken over by the amplifiers connected to the bass guitar and the mikes in close proximity of the snare drums and tambourines. Throughout the program, women were dancing, jumping, jabbing, attired in disarray, falling out, and basically out of control for as far as my little feeble and unexposed mind could comprehend. In fact as I stood clapping to the beat and enjoying the music, I had to be mindful of my surroundings because those women in their frenzy could have unintentionally knocked you out before even realizing they had hit you with such force during their shout. For one did catch me off guard at first, and I definitely got hold of a right elbow from the row to the front of me.

Now following these segments of the program, the service came to a culmination of the evening's events with laying on of the hands. The evangelist requested that the entire congregation present in the House of the Lord gather at the front and surround her. And we diligently obeyed. But as I observed her laying on of her hand on each person, one by one as she prayed for them, several fell completely out to be attended by the ushers with a lot of fanning to resuscitate. Then one person even went into what appeared to be an uncontrollable epileptic seizure as a direct response to her praying and laying on of her hands. When she reached me in the circle and asked if I'd like her to pray for me, I meekly and ignorantly allowed a faint whisper of response, "No thank you, Ma'am. I'll pass tonight." Later on I learned that that the Holy Ghost had entered that person's being and they were "talking in tongues." But at the time I was purely scared to death of the end effects of that type of worship, which I had never before witnessed.

So after the benediction and as we walked down the narrow dirt church drive to my parked car, my fellow friend asked how I had enjoyed the service and whether I would like to return. Well I told him it was definitely a new experience for me and that I respect all of the unique and diverse forms of worshipping the Lord, but that under no uncertain terms did I possess any intentions of returning with him. I certainly wanted to remain true to myself in spite of a very strong attraction to him as a man, to always remain as frank and candid as possible.

Well, a few days passed and we set up a date to go walking at the Waterfront Park to talk, but really it was for him to dump me totally and rapidly like a hot, rotten potato. He informed me that as much as he cared for me that if his right arm were offensive unto the Lord, he must cut it off so that he may enter heaven. In other words he was saying, "I was not saved." Hold the horses! Here we go again. How does this man know my "Saved Status" with the Lord? Oooh, that burns me up! Hold me back. Therefore I concluded the conversation by going through my entire rebuttal of setting him straight, and we parted and went our separate ways.

And whom do you think I would bump into several months later, down at that same Image Nightclub? None other than Mr. Saved Holiness himself. Well sir, all I can say, with saving like that I rather stick with my form of a more consistent and daily on-going relationship with the Lord. Let me stick with what I know. And God bless him that he had gotten himself together spiritually. But what had that all really been about? And I certainly would never profess to be the judge of that and just set me straight when I do have amnesia and try to be someone else's judge. For with human nature we love to do it. All I can say is let's clean up our own backyards before we become so overzealous in cleaning our neighbor's, while ours is still reeking of so much hazardous waste that we have the entire neighborhood in a quagmire of putrid stench.

Now most people would not follow a chapter on the music "of the world" with one on "music of the church." And I started not to, then I thought about it, and thought, actually why not? For they both have evolved from the same source and are interwoven and entwined within each other. People attempt to separate them, but really there is no true separation. There are clearly more commonalties than differences. They both elicit movement in a profound way. They both rouse people's souls to a height of delight. They both simply evoke happiness.

I fell in love with gospel music and spirituals when I became a part of the St. Helena community. At small Bahá'í gatherings where we would meet for devotions or what some folk would refer to as old-timey praise meetings, I immediately became hooked. We'd gather together for worship through sharing prayers, Holy Scripture, and spirituals. There we'd be jammed like sardines into the living room of dearly beloved Mrs. Louise Williams or Mrs. Gracie Reddicks. And the songs would begin to fall down from heaven like soft and warm summer rain. From Mr. Abraham Brown with his specialty and always requested rendition of "Trampin'." "Oh, I'm trampin', trampin', tryin' to make heaven my home." And that right foot would just be tapping. And Mr. Abraham Brown didn't by any means possess a professional or even close to a gifted voice, but as for his heart that was a different story. He had a heart as pure as gold. And that purity and steadfastness in the Lord was infused thoroughly into each and every word of every hymn he shared and diffused throughout the room to us.

But my very most favorite spiritual was one that my dear family friend, Gary Sterling would mesmerize and hold each and everyone hostage and helplessly spellbound with. For whatever Mr. Abraham Brown may have lacked in vocal capabilities, Gary made up for above and beyond. There he'd always be with his trusty companion, his acoustic guitar, and his other most faithful instrument, that God-given gifted voice that testified of God's power, greatness, and glory.

Then he'd light right into my nearest exposure and experience to heaven on earth, singing straight from his soul: "There are some things that I may not know. There are some places I may not go. But in my heart, there's one thing I know. Yes, God is real for I can feel Him in my soul. Yes, God is real. Real in my soul. Yes, God real for He has washed and made me whole. His love for me is like pure gold. Yes God is real for I can feel Him in my soul." And I'd been transported on a direct ascent and flight to paradise. Oh how I loved to hear Gary sing that spiritual. And I've never since heard anyone sing that song like I've felt it through his voice, spirit, and sharing.

Gary was a Bahá'í friend that was very close to my family. In fact so close that he traveled all the way from Scott Plantation on St. Helena Island to Adrian,

Michigan to sing at my mom and stepfather's wedding. This was the same guy that had been a drum major of the band and had gotten me involved in the St. Helena High School Band as a majorette. Outside our small world of St. Helena Island, this was the era or period of the war they referred to at the time as the Vietnam Conflict so Gary was immediately drafted at age 18 straight out of high school to serve his country. Fortunately under Bahá'í law he was allowed to serve in a noncombatant status as a medic, not that it was any safer for they sent him to the front line just as they did all the other thousands of young American youth. In fact, I'm sure it was almost more of a risk, trudging through swamps and jungles of a strange and foreign land with a medical kit in tote rather than at least armed with an M-16 for some illusion of protection.

But the one positive factor about his three-year drafting with the Army, he was able to begin performing professionally with a band and further practice which strengthened his musical and performing talents. After completing his indentured service to the U.S. Army, he moved to Hawaii and lived there many years performing in the nightclubs, dance studios, and even recording studios as an entertainer, dance instructor, and solo artist. He recorded albums and even had videos that made it on the Hawaiian television broadcast. Last I saw Gary, he was en route to produce and choreograph a mega-show down under in the world of Australia. So far he's gone from whence he's came. What a beautiful feeling to see a gifted person such as he to actually be able to share his talent with so many people throughout the world.

This love of gospel music that developed in my early years has continued to ride along with me throughout my life. It's the most vital and identifiable spiritual substance that I connect with within church. Yet it's the greatest element that I miss within the Bahá'í Faith and find lacking within the majority of predominantly white churches. Oh, I get a taste now and then of spirituals. In fact the Bahá'ís have and are becoming much better at including music and ways of worship from all the diverse populations of its membership. For that's one of its most fundamental principles, "Unity through Diversity." And luckily for me, that includes what my soul has acquired a strong ferocious thirst for most: downhome, good old-fashioned, gospel music.

And I certainly would be remiss to continue without sharing a soul-stirring, yet somewhat very comical episode. Several years ago, I was in attendance as a delegate to the National Convention at the National Bahá'í Center in Wilmette, Illinois on the outskirts of Chicago. I had been there for three days already transcending time and place, subsisting on the sheer spirit that emanated from the hearts and souls that had bonded at this gathering. With their sole purpose of electing the National Spiritual Assembly and making formal recommendations to that incoming newly elected body.

So there I was, as a new delegate and a total neophyte, in this great assemblage of wisdom and mature spirituality. It was the fourth day and final day for consultation of the delegates; I would be flying out of O'Hare airport that very afternoon. But that morning I sat upstairs in undiminished silence within the sanctuary of the Bahá'í House of Worship in prayer and mediation. And as I finished my offering up of silent prayer, and I was quietly and timidly arising from my seat, I looked to the right of me. And there on the pews sat both, Van Gilmer and Dell Campbell, huge musicians, particularly renown within the national Bahá'í community. And in that instance of a glance of them, I vowed, for I then knew why I had been called upon to serve as a delegate, that I would share with the entire American Bahá'í community what was and had been, for sometime, weighing heavily upon my heart.

After the final session was called to order that morning by Dorothy Nelson, the Chairman of the Convention, and two lengthy lines were forming at the mikes at the front of Foundation Hall with delegates awaiting to share their recommendations to the Convention, I mustered up the courage and strength to join their ranks, praying all the while that I could find the words to convey adequately the message within my heart. After much waiting and much praying standing in that line, they called on me, Delegate #23. I can only share with you a glimpse into the missive relayed from my heart for I must say the words were indeed not verbalized very well, but my spirit rose emphatically to the occasion to impart ever so succinctly the contents of my heart. And I could never entirely express this here in words for it certainly was not a word thing. But to give you an idea, this was the jest of its composition and intent.

"Hi! I'm Lynn Bryant and I bring you greetings from the Sea Islands of South Carolina. My concern for the Bahá'í community regards music. As we all know from the Sacred Writings of our beloved Faith, 'We have made music a ladder by which souls may ascend to the realm on high.' But I find myself and others are starving for this food. I was raised within the Black Community including the Black Church, and my spirit can not survive or soar without music. (And here I also interjected the brief story, so very sad to me, of a dear friend who severed her membership and fellowship in the Bahá'í Faith because she so sorely was hurting for food for her soul—Music.) I would like to recommend to the National Spiritual Assembly that they appoint immediately a task force for the sole purpose of finding a way of immersing the American Bahá'í Community within music. I love music. I need music. I'm starving!" This was the essence of my heart-felt message, coupled with an influx of a hot and heavy downpour of tears and an uncontrollably shaking and trembling voice from the onset and throughout the course of my recommendation. And from the initial tear that flowed, my dear "adopted" mother, Mrs. Elizabeth Martin, rescued me, by running up and standing with her arms warmly and strongly wrapped around me that gave me the strength to speak from my heart without giving into my knees and completely passing out. Which was definitely a thought for a moment.

I didn't know how the assembly of delegates had received this complete eruption of total heart and emotion. Through all the tears, hysterics, and drama, had they grasped my intention clearly enough? Well my answer soon enough came. As I meandered back to my seat, all energy entirely drained from my entire being, a rather Bohemianly-clad gentleman made his way from the rear of the auditorium to the seat at my side. He quickly thrust a rather large wad of bills into the palm of my hand with a brief and sincere utterance of "I hope this helps." (Even though it certainly appeared as though he truly needed it much more than me.) But what a sweet spirit and soul. I couldn't believe it.

I was in a total state of confusion. No, my message had not been conveyed; it had evidently been too mired with emotion. I asked him what the money was for. He said so I could buy food because I must have traveled some distance without eating and hoped that would help. I thanked him for such genuine kindness, but explained my need for music, as food for the soul, not literally food itself. Evidently he hadn't heard my message in its entirety. Otherwise, I don't think he would have been so far from the mark. My desperation had certainly been perceived by him, just not the clear and complete content of the message. So I was a little disappointed that I cried so much throughout the delivery until I had allowed my emotions to completely shroud its meaning. But I had to laugh at myself, in spite of being seeped in all this deepness of emotion, that this man had actually given me money. It was rather amusing and helped to calm my shaking and trembling body.

At the close of the final session, as I began to exit Foundation Hall, my spirits were uplifted instantly for I knew that many people had "gotten it." Delegate after delegate, embraced me with a warm hug and their response was that they too felt greatly just as what I had been feeling. Never had I felt so unconditionally loved, unjudged, and wrapped completely in love. Many of these delegates were black for they knew immediately the place and thought I was coming from and several were white for we all need the spirit that gospel music feeds us. Some of us just might not be accustomed to that style of music, but we can all definitely benefit and appreciate it.

So let me tell you the message I shared must have sent a clear and vital message. When the Highlights audiotape was distributed by National to all Local Spiritual Assemblies throughout the United States, there my ever so humble plea had been captured and recorded. And my request has been ever so handsomely answered by the National Spiritual Assembly of the Bahá'ís of the United States. In fact at the last Regional Conference for the Southern States in Nashville and a National Conference held recently in Milwaukee, gospel music was ever present and shared a large portion of the program. And the National Bahá'í Gospel Choir led by Eric Dozier has really been doing it and continues to do it for the American community, as well as the world at large, through their on-going concert tours, at home and abroad. (Eric has developed and is now even expanding with local chapters of his One Human Family Workshop Choirs throughout the country. What a true service and blessing!)

Thank you for hearing my plea. So you see, the heart can be successful in communicating for those who always say, "Don't be so emotional, Lynn." Though I no longer make excuses for talking through my heart. It's the only way I know and the only way I want to know. Even though at times it can be a little shaky, it definitely prevails.

12

No Cousins, No Kin

The firmest foundation and building block for society is the basic unity of the family. And therefore, one of the greatest strengths of black culture and any other culture in the world is the strong bond of family. A black family is there for each other through thick and thin, regardless of the transgression or situation. They have each other's back unconditionally. This has been the traditional black family, as I have known it growing up in a black world. And it has really proven to be the greatest asset and power of black people. (That coupled with a deep and strongly rooted faith in God and the supreme power of His almighty Hands.)

The manifestation of this reality is depicted in a multitude of vast and varied scenarios and situations. Some are displayed during times of crisis. An elderly grandmother struggling to raise grandchildren while the parent is furthering an education, away in the military, or unfortunately those sad situations of a parent incarcerated or strung out on drugs. A mother agonizing in every feasible attempt possible to raise bail money or to make a way for visitation of a child behind bars. Or other times when every family member in a position to do so pitches in whatever contribution they can to forge together for a tuition payment, a delinquent property tax, or payments to prevent a foreclosure or repossession. Or then still yet, a daughter or son that has taken in an aging or handicapped parent to an already full to capacity home and full to capacity work schedule. But the words "nursing home" don't even exist in the black language.

Yet today the strength of the black family is under attack by numerous weapons and tactics. Though one alarming trend I've observed as blacks that have battled the upward economic mobility is a change in traditional black family. Some blacks equate being successful or "having made it" by acquiescing and assimilating the culture and values of modern, mainstream society. And some of these belief systems are not too favorable. Through my intimate engagement and inclusion in the black world, I've so sadly acknowledged a decline in the strength of the black family affecting and influencing a large segment. Though I'm unequivocally compelled to believe that this also merely parallels and mirrors the downward spiral in the morality and standards of society at large. Yet still remains the stronghold of the black culture, the black family, which is sustaining relentless and assailing attacks.

This is why I'm emphatic about black folk being weary of having to be measured and accepted merely by white standards "to make it" in white society. "You've got to speak Standard English" (with crisp diction and pronunciation.) "You've got to dress professionally" (and be sure not to include any ethnicity.) "Your hair grooming can not be ethnic." "You must be a graduate of one of 'their' acclaimed 'ivory' towers." "You must ride in one of 'their' symbols of success." "You must reside in one of their affluent and gated communities." The list of requirements goes on and on. And that's just acknowledging the superficial. Let's go to a deeper level of beliefs and morals.

And let me stop right here and preface these preceding paragraphs. Though all these observations apply to society as a whole, I particularly note black families. Why? Because their families have been the only saving grace and source of power and strength when there were no other. And that has allowed black people to endure the pain and countless calamities and still arrive at a destination from whence they've continued to come. It is crucial that this great source of power, the family, always be acknowledged and remembered in the black community. Without it where would blacks be?

You see I've also taught for twenty-three years in the same school in my community. In fact the school that I attended as a child. I've watched how education has ceased from being of the utmost importance and significance. Now it's all about what brand name sneakers, designer clothing, or latest hair style that is emphasized. (This is just one example of acquiring the standards of mainstream America.) It used to be back in the day, "Child, you get that lesson! And don't worry about what you're wearing as long as it's clean, in good repair, and ironed." But now parents try to give their children all that they were deprived of while growing up. (Down to the Nintendo, Sega 64, and now the Box. Remember when we just had a stick to play with and sometimes a ball, if we were lucky?)

And some of what we do for our children is all well and good. But bear in mind how those trials, tribulations, and adversities strengthened you. Let's hold on to that and continue to make our children strong and resilient for life's challenges.

Also, I would be grossly negligent if I did not address the school and home relationship. (Which I later will devote an entire chapter.) But remember how parents had teachers' backs all the way! It'd be like, "Child, don't let that teacher call the house." You knew it was all over then. No questions asked. No explanations tolerated. Parents would go to "whooping" you until they couldn't "whoop" no more. And that's a time when behavior problems were unheard of in the schools. Parents had control of their children within their eyesight and out of their eyesight. And parents and teachers were on the same team, not on opposing sides in knockdown, drag-out battles to the end. And this is when students really acquired a much vaster amount of knowledge in the classroom for there was no time or energy wasted in or after school with "foolishness." Old folks would always say, "Chile, don't follow no foolishness. You hear!"

But what have we done for our children? No we're into the child's rights, the child's side of the story, and not to mention "time out" intervention. (Oprah, I dearly love you, but please accept that there are varied choices in rearing children. And time out is not always the best option. Believe me I've learned the hard way. But that's definitely a whole other story.) And these new ideas that some blacks are now adopting as they are included into society as a whole, what I call "white," are all well and good, but in moderation and with using just plain old common sense. For unfortunately, as the adults are battling, who do you think is winning? And do we truly believe a child knows what's best for him? And if you do believe that, you certainly haven't reared children. (They might have been residents in your home, but you undoubtedly didn't rear them.)

Another crack in the stronghold of the black family, is the acceptance of out of wedlock parenting and/or "shacking up." And I'm not attempting to pass judgment on anyone. But God's law is God's law whether we turn our heads from it or not. Fornication and sexual relationships outside the stronghold of matrimony are strongly forbidden in God's sight. And we are feeling the consequences and ramifications for not adhering to the Lord's guidelines for healthy living. And who again suffers? The children. It is difficult and next to impossible for single and oftentimes young parents to provide the support to their children comparable to a healthy, functioning, two-parent family.

But the most heinous and fatal incorporation of mainstream America into Black America is Drugs. This has begun and will continue to be an annihilation of a people. Some children are born into this world already being sentenced to drug addiction, drug withdrawals, and permanent physical and mental disabilities. They never were even afforded the opportunity to "Just Say No." And each time I look at who is to incur the greatest harm, in each incident without fail, it's our children. For the composition and execution of our families is the greatest refuge for children. And when mom or dad is strung out on Crack, what happens to that safe haven? It's out the window.

Fortunately, symbols of family strength within the black community remain and continue to be prominent, in spite of these untiring sabotages. These times when the bond of family still continues to radiate and shine through brilliantly are during celebratory or commemorative occasions. Long standing, firmly established, and greatly anticipated family reunions that are bulging at the seams with every kinfolk and cousin to an unimaginable and infinite power from every corner of the world. Huge weddings squished into any size church as long as it's at home and in the family church, with receptions where young and old, electric slide the night away out on the dance floor. But only after indulging in some down-home-style soul food.

Then funerals are tremendous gatherings of family and what I call the extended family in black culture, which is "the entire community." Family members arrive by plane, train, bus, or caravan from every nook and cranny of the world. They might not have made it to the reunion in centuries, but they're not going to miss a funeral, especially if it's "Big Momma" (that's grandma) or another equally significant pillar of the family. And food! There certainly is gobs of food. Everyone in the community brings dish upon dish of delicious and tantalizing soul food so the family does not have to cook during this time of grieving, but also to feed the never-ending flood of well-meaning folk that come to just "sit" and keep the family company. (Though some never seem to leave.)

Graduations are certainly momentous, as well. Accomplishments and milestones in education are definitely not taken lightly, and rightfully so. A typical black graduate, whether it be from preschool, high school, undergraduate college, law school, or medical school—the throng of family fans and well-wishers in attendance always averages right around a dozen, give or take a few. And many a black mother can't possibly restrain herself from calling out, "That's my baby!" as her child strides across the stage in cap and gown with outstretched hand to receive that rolled up parchment or certificate and the ultimate handshake of "job well done." Everyone in the family is present for this occasion, particularly "Big Momma" though she may have had to amble in quite gingerly with well-measured steps in her walker or have been escorted in in her wheelchair. Even the youngest of hand babies have not been left out, as their periodic wailing out evidences throughout the commencement. Nevertheless, it's of no alarm or nuisance to anyone in the family, as long as the entire family is united there to witness with awe and pride the continued and cherished climbing of the family unit to higher rungs of life.

Holidays of course are big-time family time. You name it. Be it Thanksgiving, Christmas, News Year's Eve, Fourth of July, or even Memorial Day. These occasions always involve a gathering of as many family members as feasible, and of course it's always coupled with food and most times prayer and invocation of the Lord with praise and thanksgiving of all that He has made possible.

I never knew how important New Year's Eve was in the Black World, until I was a young lady of the ripe old age of 18 and dating my first hard love, a young black man nicknamed "Fuzzy." Well, as you know, one of my foremost loves is dancing, then and still now. Fuzzy and I would be out getting into the groove, dancing at Soul Shack, Soul Palace, Ike's, Donaldson's, etc. etc. (Yes, everything definitely had "Soul.") And Fuzzy, wasn't much of a churchgoer, but at about five minutes before midnight on New Year's Eve, we had to make a mad dash to his mother's home to get down on our knees and pray the New Year in. Then of course, you ate some collard greens to bring you money, hop and johns which is field peas and rice to bring you good luck, and chittlins with hot sauce to crown the midnight meal.

You see this tradition of holy supplication and the breaking of bread has always been such an integral component and tradition in black culture. It is no mistake that this cuisine has earned the endearingly title of simply "soul food." It's no such thing as finger sandwiches, chips, snacks, hors d'oeuvres or other finger foods at any of the above-mentioned black family gatherings. You're most definitely going to need a fork and plate and hopefully some place to sit down so you can get your grub on. And don't worry about being cute and seditty because the cooks won't take kindly to that. You see each morsel has been prepared with generous helpings of love and for your ultimate enjoyment. So dig right into that fried chicken, barbecued ribs, fried fish, stewed pig feet, chittlins', shrimp and gravy, macaroni and cheese, red rice, potato salad, white rice with collard greens, fresh green beans, okra and tomatoes, butter beans and smoked neck bone, buttery corn bread, sour cream pound cake, and sweet potato pie. (Ohhh, I'm getting hungry.) But that's what you call "Soul Food," and it's the heart and soul of any black family gathering.

Now for my non-black readers or my black readers who want to reminisce the good old days for they may unfortunately be pursing their career away from family or have just gotten a little too uppity, be sure to watch either the movie or the television series, "Soul Food." It will give you a pretty accurate depiction of what a good strong black family looks like and goes through. From the felon that's been released and seeking employment (and as the comedians say and is so true, every family has one so don't ever feel by your lonesome), to the successful professional who is called upon a little too often for monetary assistance, down to the huge (and I mean huge) Sunday dinners of all that delicious and scrumptiously mouth-watering soul food. That's just a few of the visions and symbols of what a traditionally strong black family is. But the main point here, coupled with this emphasis on food is the love that binds each other through it all, the good and the bad. Always there for each other.

Yet having been exiled from my mother's family as a child when she dared to marry a black man, I have always possessed such a void and longing for family. And my father's family cut us loose even before that. The last time I saw or communicated with any of them was at his funeral when I was eight years old. (This wasn't even a racial thing here for my mother didn't remarry until four years after my father's death. But then every family has their baggage and skeletons, and they always felt dad had married below them. Whatever!) But when I saw that neither my mother's or my father's family wanted to be bothered with me, I'm like this, "I don't want to be bothered with you either." I in fact, have really developed almost contempt for them. Of course I don't even know if they're dead or alive, sick or well, in desperate poverty or perhaps wealth, homeless or where they may reside. Really, neither my family, nor I have ever been contacted in regards to my father's family. I assume my paternal grandparents have passed on by now and probably some of my aunts and uncles. But I truly have no idea. And what's really sad is that at a young age, I had to settle for the fact that I could no longer even care. (I was just thinking, would they even perhaps get a little misty-eyed if they read this book and realized how wrong they had done me. But of course, why would they even pick up a book such as this to read and therefore even realize that I'm their long lost niece or cousin.)

I did see my mother's mother once or twice after my mother's remarriage, as well as my Aunt Caroline a couple times. And they have been the only members that have attempted to maintain a relationship. Aunt Caroline sends a Christmas card with a letter every couple of years. (She probably would correspond more, but Momma has this phobia of letter writing and never responds.) And Grandma Thurlow used to stay in touch with letters and cards until she passed. She even once sent me a birthday card my freshman year in college. Enclosed was a five-dollar bill that I cherished as if it were an entire gold mine. Oh and then there is Uncle Dan that visited once and has called two or three times in the past forty some years. And he actually did take in one of my brothers for a while during Richard's turbulent teenage years. Now for my Uncle Chuck, last time I saw him was when he was busy wielding profanity at my mother when she informed her family of her wedding plans. Though he did have the audacity to call once or twice to borrow money from Momma. And being the forgiving and kind-spirited woman she is, she actually sent it. I was hot, as you may well imagine. And of course he never repaid her with his "sorry" shiftless self. And then there is my mother's oldest brother, Uncle Bob, who made his home and entire life in California at an early age. It's like when he left, he closed those chapters of his life growing up in a dysfunctional and impoverished home behind forever. For he really never communicated with my mother, though in this case it was not due to her marriage. Unfortunately, I feel as though they just weren't raised to be that close to each other.

Then we come to Aunt Marge and her husband Uncle Jay. (And I'm amazing myself that I can even remember these names for Lord knows I've tried to block them entirely out of my life.) Now those two, they're almost a book in themselves. First of all let me point out a critical factor to me. Aunt Marge and Uncle Jay are what people in the black community would refer to as strict and devout "holiness" or "saved" individuals. I mean they are truly orthodox "religious" fanatics. They didn't believe in doing anything, barely even breathing. My cousins couldn't wear slacks. They couldn't wear make up, at any age. Definitely no sinful jewelry. They couldn't listen to the radio. Of course, dancing was out of the question. They weren't even allowed to watch TV programs, and believe me back in the 1960's the regulations hardly even allowed a kiss on the cheek. (They only had shows like "Leave It to Beaver" and "Bonanza" at the time. Certainly videos and MTV did not exist.) So I could see at an early age that this family went a little overboard with their religious convictions. Yet be weary of "so-called-religious" folk that are always professing and trying to convince you that they're "saved" while they judge and throw stones at you. Well with all this so-called religion, these were the ones that "acted up" the very worst! Total estrangement from our family once Momma told them she was in love with someone that happened to be of a darker hue than theirs was. (Now that's what I truly call "religious" and "saved!")

Well years later these saintly souls did out of the mercy of their hearts write to my mother to invite her to a family reunion in Michigan. But as an afterthought they added a P.S. "Please understand. Just bring Richard, Tom, Lynn, and Sally." That was no afterthought. That was the main point of the letter. And the true translation was "Bring only your white children. Don't embarrass us or cause trouble by bringing your racially mixed children or black stepchildren." At the time I was home from college for the summer working. Boy was I livid! That went through me. I liked Aunt Marge's nerve. She didn't beat around the bush. Well, neither did I! As you have caught on, my mother is way too kind-hearted for a task like this at hand. And don't get me wrong, I've acquired a lot of her qualities and virtues. And I'm pretty sweet until you take me too far past a limit.

Then I'm through with you. Well Aunt Marge had undoubtedly exceeded the maximum limit with me. How dare she request that of my momma? And how dare she even begin to think in her wildest dreams that any of us were going to roll up in there with only a portion of the family while the rest of my family remained at home following their bidding of "Whites Only! No Colored Allowed." (Don't ever let Yankees fool you. Blacks know this. But I'm sure many whites may be in denial of this. Just acknowledging the good ole boy Southern crackers riding in pickup trucks with Confederate flag license plates as the only racists in society is a gross underestimate of the far-reaching plague of this illness. Unfortunately it crosses all appearances, classifications, and even the Mason-Dixon Line.)

Therefore in response to my aunt's so-called "invitation," I typed a very direct, no nonsense letter addressed to Mrs. Thomas in most stringent of business-style formats. (She once had been Aunt Marge, but was hardly an aunt to me any longer.) And I proceeded to give her every piece of my mind, but in only the most matter-of-fact and in only the most prestigious vocabulary. Grammar, mechanics, and structure impeccable. The basic message was "You certainly got your nerve. And you can forget it! If you don't want our entire family there, you don't want any of us there." That was about thirty years ago. No acknowledgment since. Then about five years ago who pops up on my mother's front steps? None other than Mr. and Mrs. Thomas headed to Florida for retirement. For when folk get old, they start to truly evaluate the lives they've lived and their rapidly approaching afterlife, and they begin to examine and scrutinize the wrongs they've done. And now they wanted to make amends for they feared that they may be soon engulfed in the raging flames of Hades. And quite fortunately for them, it is not my call, for I don't forgive and forget for wrongs of such magnitude blatantly and purposefully meted out against me, my family, and particularly to my momma. If there's nothing else that I've internalized from being raised black, it's "You don't mess with someone's family" and most emphatically "You don't mess with a person's momma." And they were guilty of a double jeopardy of transgression. So when they offered their feeble words of forgiveness to my momma after all of these years of hurt and pain, I'm like no I'm not impressed and I'm not hardly interested. I've always held the fierce conviction that deeds are far mightier than words. And you don't intentionally harm and mangle those you truly love.

Therefore as far as family, I have my mother, brothers and sisters, and now in recent years my nieces and nephews. Everyone has an instinctive and natural need for family. Grandparents (except fortunately Grammy), aunts, uncles, and cousins I have no true concept of what that is to possess. So now as my son Jack, at the age of 18, inquires in a true perplexity, "Mom, don't I have some white cousins somewhere? Grandma's white. You're white. I should have some more white family." And I'm left in a complete stupor. For my response is so senseless, yet stirring up long forgotten pain, as I give him a mature motherly answer, but still feeling the unwanted child within, I'm thinking, "No they didn't want us." And I've played hard like it didn't matter all these years, but yes it certainly would have been nice to have these family members in my life.

13

Beverly and the Dore Family

My thirst for family has always been there, but just lying under the surface, totally oblivious of one of my basic life needs, simply "family." So when I came in contact with and to experience what a truly strong, united family is, it brought tears to my eyes then and still does to this day.

My first and always most memorable concept of a truly empowered family through unity, love, and faith in the Almighty will always be the Dore Family. This was my first very personal and in-depth experience with such a strongly bonded family. This is a real-life "Soul Food" family.

(And let me get this straight for the record right this moment, no they're not a perfect family. I certainly realize there's no such entity. But they're a heroically and genuinely unified family that works together through the ups and downs of life. And I unceasingly admire and commend their accomplishments. Yes, there are certainly so many examples of these types of family in my community. That's why I emphasize the strength of traditional black families. (And fortunately this was a family that embraced me on such a personal level almost as one of their own.) The Dore Family had such an initial impact on me years ago and still does to this day.

I met Beverly Juanita Dore (now Mrs. McIntyre married to Attorney Bernard McIntyre), the summer of 1976 when I was a junior at Clemson University and she was a graduate student at Atlanta University, a prestigious and historically black college. We were both working at the Beaufort-Jasper Manpower Office in our hometown which later became known as CETA (Comprehensive Employment and Training Act), and even later as JTPA (Job Training Partnership Act). This was a federal agency that provided summer employment to low-economic high school and college-aged youth.

Well, when I first laid eyes on Beverly, I made the unfortunate mistake of judging a book strictly by the cover. And followed the mindset I had internalized as a highly impressionable youth, "A light-skinned sister with long hair is stuck up and thinks she's cute." Gross error! For weeks I watched her interacting with others at work. I'm like, "Yeah she thinks she's cute. I ain't got time with that. I'm sticking with my buddies in the office that I know from 'The Island.'" (My hometown community of St. Helena Island.) But as I continued to check her out, I noticed that this was a genuinely sincere and warm-hearted person. And one day when she invited me to join the already filled-to-capacity group of young women in her sister's shiny black Cordoba headed to lunch at Western Sizzlin steakhouse, I happily squeezed in. And from that day forward, I embarked on the deepest and most special friendship of my life.

Beverly took me under her wing as her little sister. Her first major undertaking was plucking and arching my eyebrows. And you may say, "So what!" But if you had laid eyes on my big bushy uni-brow conquering my forehead, you would have begun to understand. This momentous event symbolized the first of an endless series of attempts of exposure to some refinement and remolding of me.

In fact years later in our friendship, Beverly was the one that persuaded me that I should acquire a more fashionable hairstyle during the late 80's and finally give up the one style I had desperately clung to since my "love, peace, and happiness" days of the 70's. My long straight hair hanging down past my waist, covering my backside. Or oftentimes, especially in the intensely hot and humid summers, pulled into a braided ponytail with large hoop earrings. That was my Sade look. My version of being in trend, for at least I was emulating one of the most exotically gorgeous contemporary singers of that day. But in the end, the asymmetric bob won out. Which wasn't bad at all.

Then there were the shopping trips. I had shopped at K-Mart and Roses discount department stores during the course of my childhood. For I mostly had worn hand-me-downs or sewn my own clothes during high school. In our family in those days, there just was no money to be had. The marginal money, which I earned during summer jobs, I had thrust quickly into my savings account to accumulate for college tuition. And Beverly also had limited assets, being a college student as well. Yet being the baby girl of eight, she always managed to finagle something out of one of her older siblings (of course that's how they were definitely raised—to help one another) for an occasional shopping adventure. Thus Beverly proceeded to introduce me to designer names and boutiques with specialty apparel. Here was a glance into a world I had never even given any thought to and certainly had no inkling of. I certainly had never heard of or even remotely knew who the heck Etienne Aigner was?

Don't hardly get me wrong, with my friendship with Beverly, everything wasn't just beauty tips and fashion. I'd spend the night over at her small and cozy, but ever such a lovely and immaculate home out in the neighboring area of Burton. We'd do this during our college days, but even on into my first years teaching, before we ambled down the roads of matrimony. Those were great days. I'd bring my school clothes for work the next day. We'd stay up playing backgammon. (In fact Beverly was the one who first taught me backgammon which was the craze at the time. They had elaborate boards set up in all the night-clubs and people carried them like attaché cases all about college campuses) or watching "Dallas," the infamous nighttime soap opera. Or just talking into the wee hours about the men in our lives that we anguished over. I even sojourned a couple weekend trips from Clemson University across the not-so-far state line to Atlanta University while Beverly was in grad school. And we'd spend the days exploring Atlanta in her fiery red convertible MG sports car. (Everything was fiery and full of life when it came to Beverly. From her personality, to her car, including the reddish-blond coloring she flaunted in her hair. She was certainly the opposite of miss homely and all-natural me. But Beverly's motto always had been "Allow people to be different," and she loved helping people, as well. So in my case, both fit.) Then at night we reverted to our equally favorite pastime of discussing and analyzing relationships, from family to girlfriends to boyfriends.

As I reflect on some of our conversations late at night, as we bundled up in her bed, I'll never forget the time Beverly debated about accepting a watch as a Christmas gift from her boyfriend. She said there was a saying that if you accept a watch as a gift from your boyfriend, "Your love would tick away." The same went for shoes but in that case of course, "Your love would walk away." Now in her circumstances she had the insight and wisdom to decline the offering. But as for me, I do recall receiving a beautiful and rather expensive silver Bullova watch from my college sweetheart. I was so taken aback and impressed with the gift, for neither of us had money. And he had had to work weekend after weekend raking one of the coach's humungous yards in order to save up the money. That's why that particular gift, that particular Christmas, had meant so much to me. I knew what it had taken for him to get it. But I should have heeded Beverly's prophetic advice. For that love did indeed soon tick on out of my life.

One of the most cherished possessions and experiences Beverly shared with me was—Her Family. Oh and what a family! I had no concept.

I had met them one by one and on very brief and fleetingly incidental moments. Of course I'll never forget my first visit to Beverly's home. You see her father passed on July 25th of 1976, the first summer I had met her on the job at the Manpower Office. We weren't really super close yet, but we were definitely office and lunch buddies. So I went to visit her along with the other girls from the

office. I genuinely wanted to show my support and not have her think I was
heartless and uncaring if I were the only one in the office not to come by. But
Lord knows that was a terrifying experience for me. I hadn't dealt with death in
the ten years since the passing of my own father. And I hadn't really learned to
cope with it at all. All I can ever think is what on earth can I possible say to make
the situation better. Nothing. And I end up sobbing harder than the family members. (Sometimes, well really always, I empathize too strongly with those in painful situations) But through the years, that's another thing Beverly truly taught
me. Though I still find it exceedingly painful and difficult, that I've got to offer
my presence during times of bereavement. And that the presence and showing of
one's self signifies such caring and in itself offers such a comfort to those grieving.
So through the years I've tried and I've actually improved in this regard. Thanks
Bev, again, for one of your many life learning lessons.

But the first time I truly felt the true presence and impact of the Dore Family
in its entirety and its unity, was probably the Christmas of 1976 at the home of
Charles and Geneva Cole on Meridian Road of Lady's Island. At the time if
memory serves me (That's what old people always say, and now that I'm getting
old too), I was a senior at Clemson and Beverly was a culminating graduate student at Atlanta University, both of us home visiting between semesters.

Well, when I entered that home, it exuded and overflowed with family love. It
probably was nothing genuinely too much out of the ordinary to them. But as for
me, there was just a spirit and a presence that wrapped me so warmly and so pro-
tectively. I felt shielded and guarded from any evils, perils, or calamities that the
world might fling my way.

And now internalizing that moment in time, I realize not only was I at a deficit when it came to my aunts, uncles, and cousins. (For I really believe as the
years had passed, I had succeeded in gaffing them off just as they had done me.)
But the realization now comes that I had just suffered the loss of Grammy (my
stepfather's mother) that spring. She had more than filled in for an extended family marked "insufficient funds." And now she was sorely and desperately missed.

But here was a home filled with all Beverly's brothers and sisters, cousins, and
none other than the mighty yet humble matriarch of the Dore Family, Mrs.
Emily Dore. First the brothers. (And let me interject right here. Not only were
they so very sweet, highly intelligent, but "finger lickin' fine, as well) There was
Hezekiah Jr., a successful businessman from Atlanta with his wife and children.
Freddie, an educator, from Columbus, Georgia home visiting with his family.
Louis, an established attorney, who resided in Beaufort with his lovely family.
Lorenzo, who was nicknamed "Bubba," was handicapped and lived with Mrs.

Dore. The youngest son, Vincent who was still in high school. Then the sisters. (Equally as "having it going on" in the domains of brains and beauty as the brothers. And they always were dressed so chic and stylish. Literally straight out of "Vogue" magazine.) Geneva was the oldest sister, a teacher, married with a family and was an additional mother figure for the entire Dore Family. And she was the one who was hosting the family gathering and Christmas dinner. Helen, who was another teacher, lived in Jacksonville, Florida with her family. LaVerne worked as a vocational counselor and had completed college at Hofstra University in New York. And then came Beverly, the youngest girl in the family. My tight friend. And soon to be like a sister.

Well we all assembled in the living room where the Christmas tree and a sea of gifts were overflowing from its reach. But ever more powerful and mighty was the overflowing of the host of family members squalled within the confine of those walls. Then grace was offered before dinner. And what a dinner that was! One of which I believe I had never seen the likes of. Turkey, ham, fried chicken, chittlins, collard greens, seasoned string beans, rice, macaroni and cheese, potato salad, chicken salad, candied yams, cornbread, sweet potato pies, sock-it-to-me cake, pound cake, and who knows what else. But it was all good. No, I'd say superbly delicious!

And Geneva had probably cooked the bulk of it. You see Geneva is the renowned cook of the Dore Family. Then and still to this day. She is a sensational cook and fortunately enjoys cooking and seeing others enjoy her labors of love. She's the family member that will cook on a day-to-day basis enough to serve 20, even now that her household is down to two people. But there's always someone stopping by to visit and she wouldn't dream of not having dinner to offer.

Now after we all had gotten our first helping of dinner, and no one had fallen asleep yet in a recliner or corner of the couch, we reassembled in the living room for the opening of gifts. Present after present was distributed to its rightful recipient and unwrapped to reveal the contents that would end in such joyous smiles and expressions of gratitude. But the gift that stole the show that day was undeniably the one Louis lovingly and surprisingly presented to his mother. So sweet, so clever, and so unique. I certainly had never seen or heard of the likes of it. It was a tree made of money. I believe I was just as excited as Mrs. Dore, even though I wasn't the proud owner. Who says money doesn't grow on trees?

But more incredible and memorable an impression than that gift was the final gift pulled from under the tree that Christmas Day. It was a tiny little parcel. And what do you think was inscribed upon it? "To Lynn. Love, Beverly." What an unexpected and total surprise. I certainly had no expectation on my part of receiving any gift that day, not in the least. At the time, Beverly and I, were very casual friends and the invitation to Christmas Dinner with her family was certainly a last minute thought. But the effect it has had upon my heart has been everlasting. (And I know you might be saying, "What was the gift? What was it?" Not that the actual gift was the significance, for here it was certainly so much the thought and love. But for those inquiring minds that just gotta know. My nosy ones, like me. It was a small bottle of cologne.)

You see this Christmas Day was such a unforgettable memory. So much of what I'm realizing is as I write this today. Not only had I not been with that much family since my father's passing. But also with his passing, our family ceased to celebrate Christmas as we had traditionally. (Don't think my mom is anti-Christmas, it's just that she felt that the concept of "give me, give me" for Christmas was not a true symbol and observance of Christ's birth. So since she had always participated in the traditional customs of Santa Claus, a Christmas tree, wish lists, Christmas cookies, and the whole shebang, particularly for my dad's sake, she opted to forego it all.)

And I know full well a lot of Christmas is too commercialized, money-oriented, and devoid of truly celebrating Christ's birth. But a lot if it does carry the true heart and purpose of Christmas. And what I particularly love is the love that is shared between family and friends as they offer gifts, break bread, and fellowship together. This display of love symbolizes the love that Christ has for us all. And there is none other greater commemoration of the Christ child's birth than that display of the power of love that we show sincerely and unconditionally for one another.

It had been such a long, long time since I had experienced the delight and wonderment of Christmas and the elated delight of the gathering of family. Beverly, thanks always for that special Christmas Day you shared with me. Sharing that day and especially your family with me, there is none other greater gift.

Consequently, I want to so badly share with you the foundations and depths of the Dore Family and what makes it such a special and strong family, but I'm realizing that would be an entire book in itself. So I'll attempt to share a few antidotes and glimpses that would allude to an overall general impression and concept.

One of the most incredible family stories is the saga of the roots of the Dore Family. When the Dore Family comes to mind, the two most overwhelming themes that arise are: Family and Education. For you see, the father of the family, Hezekiah Dore, Sr. was raised up with his brother James, in a small town north of Beaufort called Allendale, South Carolina. He was a racially mixed (or what some may refer to as a mulatto) child, born to a black woman and white man. His mother, the family endearingly has always referenced as DaddyMomma. I don't even know her rightful name. But DaddyMomma resided on a sharecropping plantation so to speak. And the owner of the property shared more than just the land with her. The results of their union were two sons. And from my understanding, this man acknowledged them as his children with gifts and the like, but they were never to live together as family. Also because of the economy, Hezekiah, Sr. had to stop his schooling at an early age to help provide for his momma and brother.

So the two greatest things that were lacking in Hezekiah's life as a child, family and education, he vowed he would ensure for his family to come. And sure enough, holding to his first promise, he raised his nine children with such an incredible bond of family unity and no other choice but to do for each other. Then holding to his second conviction and regard for education, he worked two jobs at a time to make it possible for each of his children to attend and graduate from college and even graduate school. An incredible feat with extremely meager assets in a period of time when grants and loans for socio-economically disadvantaged virtually were nonexistent.

I desperately want to share at least this one story that symbolizes the extent of this deep bond of family the Dores are fortunate to possess. When Louis and Freddie were students at Morehouse College, Louis was holding down a job while in school. But for whatever reason, Freddie was not employed. Yet what amazed me to no end. Louis recounted how on every payday, his daddy's requirement was that he bring his money home to the dorm and split it evenly with Freddie. Wow! Hold up. Hold everything. Did I hear this story right? Yes he insisted that he had to share his hard-earned money with his brother. Now I might have given him some, but he wasn't getting an even divide straight down the harvest he had no part in raising up. But not the case with the Dores. It was the literal sense of the saying "What's yours is mine and what's mine is yours." Talk about having each other's back. Their daddy didn't play when it came to that.

Another thing their daddy and Hezekiah, Jr. had the insight to do was to insert an "r" into their family name, going from Doe to Dore. They felt that since the name Doe was always used as a sample name on checks and legal documents, etc. that they'd rather insert the "r." So they therefore, had the "r" added to acquire the name Dore. Due to this undertaking and not understanding the extent of how close-knit the Dore family is, some community members accused them of thinking they were better than others. Accusingly they'd comment, "Why do you think they changed their name? All the rest are Does." But that is so far from the truth. All of them will readily tell you that their family name is indeed Doe.

The Dore Family is such a tremendously loving and caring family. And this is certainly not restricted to the family, but reaches to all those they come in contact with. And they are such a helping and kind family. I certainly have had the privilege to experience this first hand. For as closely knit as they are, they did not hesitate to take in and accept this little white girl into the inner circles of their family bond.

And lastly, I would be grossly in error if I did not make mention of, how intricately and carefully interwoven in the triumphs and accomplishments of the Dore Family, has always been foremost their staunch and unwavering Faith in the Almighty God and His power and strength. Reverend Hezekiah Dore, Sr. served as the pastor of several, four in fact, Disciples of Christ Churches in South Carolina. He served all four of them from the time he began preaching until he died. His home church was New Hope Christian where he served diligently until he went into the ministry and where all his children remain strong pillars of support then and now.

And in closing this chapter dedicated to Beverly and her family, I just want to say to her that she was the best friend I've ever experienced in my lifetime. I could share my heart and soul with her. She was always a true and genuine listening ear with heartfelt guidance, wisdom, and encouragement. Through the years, we've grown apart in our circles and loops of living. Going separate ways to raise children, pursue careers, different interests, and other circumstances. But that love within our hearts has always remained. I always kidded her that breaking up with a true friend is harder than breaking up with a man. And sure enough it has been for both of us as we've accepted life's ever-changing circles and paths. Though it continues to bring a pang and twinge to my soul, as my heart remembers the intimacy of a special friendship that we shared. It's so immensely difficult at times to accept that life changes and relationships change. "But Beverly, as you know and I know as well, even though we don't see each other and don't talk, we'll always love each other. That's uncontrollable. Love you always, girl, as my sister and my friend."

"Hey Beverly, remember the incident when we were shopping in Charleston at the Citadel Mall. We both had our hair pulled back. My dark, bronze tan was pretty evenly matched to your skin tone that summer. And an elderly white gentleman approached us in an excited rush and emphatically queried us in his loud and boisterous Geechie accent, "Tell me ya'll ain't sisters!"

Thanks always, sis!

14

Friends Come in All Sizes, Ages, and Colors of Packages

My very first friend in life is easy to recall. At the time, she was the only girl on my street. Her name was Nancy Miiller. And she lived on West Jefferson Street in Petoskey, Michigan. We probably became friends as soon as I became old enough to play with her coveted Barbie and Midge dolls and their vast and assorted wardrobes. (Always purchased with the earnings she'd made babysitting or helping to clean a vacationer's summer home across from her house. Which we enjoyed immensely for occasional slumber parties with just the two of us.) Nancy and I were the only girls on our street until our younger sisters were born. So even though I was four years younger than Nancy, I was a more desirable pick for a friend than one of her sisters, and vice versa.

And through our childhood years, we truly enjoyed each other's company, and she definitely taught me the ropes and filled in the gaps in some of my under-standings while growing up. I always looked up, to her in such high regard. As a pre-teen and teen she babysat and made good money with which she measured the worth of every little penny. I never really thought of it, of course as a child, but her household couldn't quite afford to be spoiled with an overage and wealth of possessions. Thus every article of clothing Nancy purchased was held in esteem and with high regard. I still remember her pulling out the storage boxes under-neath her bed to share with me her wealth of fine apparel. In particular, I recall drooling over the abundant array of pastel cashmere sweaters the box held: baby blue, pale pink, soft yellow, and the many other range of hues. Or certainly I'll never forget the actual one-hundred-dollar bill she showed me one day that belonged to her thanks to her hard work and hard saving. That was incredible! That would be the equivalent of a child today whipping out a thousand-dollar bill. I definitely looked up to her and admired her strong work ethic and respon-sibility.

Needless to say when I permanently moved from Michigan at age 12 and she was 16, we both would miss that special friendship we shared. And for my 13th birthday she sent me the most gorgeous chiffon dress, down to my new home in South Carolina. It was a little snug, and I only got to wear it probably one time. But it was definitely the thought that counts for I knew full well that wasn't a dress purchased at the dime store. She had paid a pretty penny for it from her hard earned and hard saved money.

We kept in touch through cards and letters. And of course through the years, they waned some, but never came to a complete stop. Even when I got married, she sent me a set of hand-crafted ceramic bowls designed by, the then recently-deceased and famed artist, Mr. Kellogg, from his Petoskey Studio. We continued our sporadic correspondence through all the natural progressions and stages of life: husbands, babies, children growing into adults, and our endless pursuit of careers and mere happiness.

Here I want to interject a crucial point for clarity in this chapter as well as the remainder of this saga. Not that it matters to me, but just so that you understand the racial implications of my social interactions. I can't assume you know that this or that acquaintance is black or this one white, etc. So for clarity sake, anyone in my Michigan years, were white, unless otherwise stated, such as the Martin Family. Michigan years were my White Years or White World so to speak. Anyone in my South Carolina Years, were black, unless stated. My Black Years or Black World. You see as you may recall, South Carolina did require you to choose which it was going to be, black or white. And by my mother's choice in a husband as well as my choice in schools, it was definitely going to be black. Anything other was the exception to the rule and worth noting. But of course with the Bahá'í Faith, it was always such a diversified and beautiful assortment of people. But I only interject this for clarity-sake so as not to confuse anyone. For the general public most times, does find the concept of my family rather hard to grasp. It's just too far removed from their frame of reference. And as a pop quiz, I want you to be ready to categorize for our race poll, what color each of my friends in this chapter were. Hint: Remember Nancy was in my Michigan Years. (Just kidding here.)

Yet at the end of my time with Nancy, what did I take from this friendship? I can see so clearly now that it was growth maturity-wise to be have the ability to interact and establish friendships with those persons who happen to be older than me. And from that point on a lot of friends were older, in fact much older.

That may account for one of the reasons I never dated guys my age. They always were significantly older. I mean I never did date any high school boys. I remember in ninth grade beginning to date a college student and continuing on and off until I was in twelfth grade and he was a first year teacher at Beaufort High. Then through high school were the occasional Marines that I'd date. And my senior year I also started dating the infamous Fuzzy in my life.

Earnell "Fuzzy" Johnson was eight years older than me and already had a son. We met while my sister-in-law would go on the military base at Parris Island to work in the ceramics shop. Fuzzy worked there with Lance, another friend of ours. Fuzzy was the sweetest and most sincere guy. He'd give you the shirt off his back. But unfortunately wasn't sweet enough to himself. He had become enslaved to drugs and alcohol. I guess sometimes the world is a bit too much to take in a sober state of mind, especially for a person with such a tender heart. And people deal with pain in different ways. Unfortunately staying high or drunk was how he dealt with his. No one could ever see what on earth an academically gifted young girl with a promising future ahead (Surprise, that's actually myself I'm speaking of), would see in this already deteriorating shell of a guy like Fuzzy. All they could see was his addiction. They never saw past this to the true virtues of his personality. And I had the dream that we loved each other enough that I could correct what I saw as a few minor flaws. Fortunately for my sake and the community's hope, we did eventually go our separate ways. I was young and certainly did not know at the time, that it's next to impossible to change anyone but one's self.

There were so many tell tale signs of a severe problem. One episode was while he was visiting my parents' home. He was on the floor of the living room, seated in front of me while I was greasing his scalp. Well, he fell into a deep, un-awaken-able state. It was so embarrassing, my family members had to step over him to pass by.

One time when he took me out dancing at the club on the Air Station, he fell asleep drunk in the car parking lot, before we even got to enter to the club. I spent hours unsuccessfully attempting to awaken him. Until it was now well past two o'clock in the morning and I knew I'd be in hot water if I didn't high tail it home soon. So I woke him up by throwing a cup of ice water on him.

Or there was the time when I begged for my mother to allow me to take my then-in-high-school, sister Sally out dancing at one of the clubs with Fuzzy and me. We went down to Ike's in Fuzzy's home community of Capers. Big mistake. He disappeared from the club for some time, as he usually would. But this time after dancing and "bus stopping" hours and hours away and the club was about to close, I'm like, "Where the heck is Fuzzy?" Tore up from the floor up, he was standing stiff against my little Toyota outside the club. I just knew he was dead. I couldn't get him to budge. Some guys helped me get him into the car, still out cold so I could get him home, but particularly my sister before I really caught it and she couldn't go again.

But the two final straws arrived when he ultimately and unsurprisingly lost his job and then later ended serving 30 days in jail for probably driving drunk with a suspended license. Love can go but so far. Then too much becomes just too much.

Now with all this dating, especially with these older guys, I'm sure you've assumed that I was rather promiscuous and hot in my pants. Well, this was quite the contrary. I simply enjoyed dating so that I could go out dancing, go to the movies, and go out to dinner at no cost to me and yet enjoy some male companionship. I certainly was from a family of rather meager means. So older men were simply one source in widening my exposure and experiences. And I definitely was still a member in good standing of the Virgin Club at Beaufort High, even though some of the membership was beginning to dwindle. You see one of the main problems with boys my age, they were hardly interested in me for basically, I was a nerdy four-eyed bookworm. Another major reason we didn't see eye to eye. They had one thing and only one thing in their minds, to get in a girl's drawers (panties if you're unfamiliar with that term), and I flat wasn't having that. Older guys respected a girl's "no" and still held an interest in other qualities of a young lady so the relationship still continued. Evidently they truly held the belief, "Good things come to those who wait."

Yet one of my bestest (I know a lot of these words aren't real words, except they always seem to express a feeling just how I want it. I guess you got to be in that "place" to really feel it.) But yes, one of my "bestest" friends in my childhood and entire life, was my dear friend, Mrs. Virginia "Comesee" Green. She is probably only about 45 years my senior. And when we first met I was probably nine, and by the time we became true friends, I was probably 15 and she was right around 60. She was already a widow with grown children she had adopted and raised, but was now raising her niece's baby who was named Tonya.

Virginia was a member of the Bahá'í community of St. Helena Island. She lived in Lands End on St. Helena. And before my mother got married to Elting, she was one of the landlords my mother rented from. We rented a small flimsily-constructed cottage that was situated on her property, directly behind her main residence, a typical three-bedroom, red-brick home.

Why a shack, you ask. When we had grown up in a three-story, four-bedroom, double-garaged home directly overlooking a bay of Lake Michigan? And half of our street was summer resort homes. It was a downright gorgeous view.

Well the answer is, Mom "always" had "too big of a heart." And well, she basically gave a half-decent home away to Bahá'í friends, Dr. Jenson and his family, who were in desperate need of a chiropractic office/residence. That was Momma.

Well, the ceilings of the shack, our new home, were so low that when Elting came to call on my mother. (That's the right term for courting. Right?) Well, he'd have to lower his head as he came through a door or even as he attempted to stand up in the room. Remember that he was a tall dude, six foot six. I don't know the height of the ceilings, but they were hardly adequate for him. It was like watching a giant entering a matchbox. I was always intrigued with amazement of this vision.

And once my mother married Elting and we moved to Tom Fripp which was on the other end of the island, I really missed Miss Virginia. So from time to time I would spend the night with her on a Friday or Saturday. And we'd have a ball! We'd stay up late in her little sunroom that had been converted into a den—snacking on Lay's green onion potato chips, sipping sodas, and watching wrestling. Which Miss Virginia Green would swear to me was genuine and real wrestling with which I would so adamantly counter her with the charge that it was all hype and mere acting. She offered the counter attack that she'd watched it live at a ring in Savannah. Which I informed her that certainly it could be contrived just as a live play is done. We never did come eye-to-eye on that issue. But nonetheless we remained confirmed pals and best buds.

The greatest legend of Virginia and Lynn were the tales of our endless travels for we were undoubtedly, strongly confirmed road dogs. Oh how, we loved to hit the road. Being a widow that was well provided for insurance-wise, Virginia was hardly hurting for money. And as she constantly reminded me, she had no intentions of any man eyeballing or capturing the inheritance her husband had left her. Not after she had put up with all his womanizing through the years of their marriage. Including the time she took a baseball bat to his windshield and put sugar in the gas tank of his GTO, after hunting his car down parked at some other woman's home in the middle of the night. Virginia did not play! Not even a little bit.

But anyway whenever an eye-catching Bahá'í event captured our attention, we set our plans in motion. Virginia hated to drive, but she didn't mind providing the transportation and gas. And I didn't have transportation, but at age 16 with my newly coveted possession in hand, a driver's license, and enough spending change, just say the word "go," and I'd drive as far as Virginia's heart desired. There our two little heads could be spotted, headed down the highway in her royal blue 1970 Volkswagen station wagon. In the driver's seat a little white teenager clad as a genuine hippie, long straight waist-length hair parted straight down the middle of my head, complete with hip hugger bell bottoms. And Virginia in the passenger seat, a middle-aged black woman with initial signs of graying, many times sporting some polyester pants and even a trendy-at-the-time dashiki.

I mean you name the Bahá'í conference or event during the 1970's and we were there. Blue Field, West Virginia; Oklahoma City of course in where else but Oklahoma; Orlando, Florida; and Key West, Florida were my greatest adventures with Virginia. Even dozens of short trips within the state, like to Hemingway, South Carolina where we'd visit the Louis Gregory Bahá'í Institute. Later she journeyed on by herself once I had gone on to college and in cases where mere spending change alone was just not going to cut it in footing my bill. Like her trip to the dedication of the temple in Panama and pilgrimage to the holy lands and shrines on Mount Carmel in Haifa, Israel. Virginia really had experienced the Bahá'í Faith in a lot of varied venues. She had truly been blessed, as well as me, for the opportunity to accompany her. I was from a home of very low means and wouldn't ever had been afforded these experiences otherwise. And it was a culmination of these experiences coupled with others that ensured my unwavering consecration in the Bahá'í Faith.

And occasionally as we made these trips, we reluctantly allowed a passenger or two to invade. For we truly enjoyed our friendship with each other. But never were they allowed to drive. Once was enough, for me to learn that I didn't take well to other drivers behind the wheel if I was too deliriously drowsy. It seemed the competency of their driving ability was not well measured or appreciated during these times of sleep deprivation. So I ended up regaining power of the wheel anyway. Like the time we embarked on our adventure to the 1973 National Youth Conference in Oklahoma City. Oh what a journey. This time we had Lamont Taylor, another youth from the neighboring area of Dale, and Charles Glasser, a young adult residing in our area, with us. And why did I ever ask Charles to take the wheel, but needless to say it wasn't for long. Charles being a somewhat uptight dude most of the time, commenced to steering the car in a manner that commenced the steering wheel to begin a vehement shaking that would not cease. His defense, "It doesn't drive the same as my car." No joke. But after a mile or two, he should have adapted. Therefore the syndrome I just spoke of took over so I completed the 24-hour trip virtually single-handedly. What alternative did a girl have?

Another rather memorable trip, was our drive to Florida in 1972 to the opening year of the newly unveiled, Disney World in Orlando. Our passenger this time, none other than, a passenger of often preference, Mr. Luther Willis, an older Bahá'í gentleman friend also from Dale who probably was about Virginia's age. He kind of fancied Virginia and she enjoyed his friendship, but that was it. She always reminded me as I guess she was reminding herself that no man was getting their paws on her in order to get them on her money.

So for the trip, it was agreed upon. Virginia would provide the vehicle, Lynn the driving, and Mr. Willis all the expenses, including meals, lodging, and tickets. Yes, I'll agree it was a little one-sided, but hey he was the one that wanted to wine and dine us. I just figured he really wanted to go to Disney World, but didn't have a way to get there. Of course, I was a bit naïve at the prime old age of 16. So here we were headed to Disney, what appeared as a middle-aged black couple and a young white teenage girl. Don't know how people would figure me into the picture. But all went well and we had a grand time. Or at least I thought all was well.

But after we got back and some time had passed, Virginia teasingly informed me that as far as Mr. Willis, I had "thrown my candy in the sand." Now just what in tarnation did that mean? I had yet to acquaint myself with all the old-timey sayings of the Low Country. So Virginia proceeded to fill me in with the facts that Mr. Willis had liked me, had shown a huge interest in me by footing the entire bill to Disney World, and I hadn't given him the time of day since that. Really? No way! That man was old enough to be my granddaddy! So from then on, the rest of our travels were solo, just Virginia and me. And guess that's how I liked it best anyways. No strings attached. No foolishness.

Being a parent of two teenagers now, it is so stupendously incredible how my mother allowed me this utterly huge independence as a young teenager. Just imagine driving halfway cross-country and back. Granted I was with a responsible adult. But just to believe in me enough that I could accomplish it and to let go of the over-protectiveness innate in all mothers. It's simply incredible. But boy do I thank my mom for that for I've never had a fear traveling anywhere. Just hand me a map, some gas in the tank, and I'm on my way.

Another quite older friendship I acquired and highly valued was that of Mrs. Eulie Horne of Oceanside, California. This time my friend was a mere 60 years my senior. I was 25 and she was 84. But we became the best of friends. I met her when I was a newlywed residing in that small town in Southern California. To show how small the world can be, I came to find out that her daughter and my mother had been teenage friends in the early 1940's while attending youth sessions at the Bahá'í School in Davidson, Michigan now called Lou Helen School. Truly, truly a small world. But the two of us for some reason hit it off and we became fast and firm friends. We'd go to lunch or dinner, and an occasional movie. So for her birthday we went out to the movies to see, "On Golden Pond" with Henry Fonda, Katherine Hepburn, and Jane Fonda. She was placed in a total state of shock and horror, as she commented on the senseless use of foul language to ruin perfectly beautiful film-footage and an equally beautiful story. As she then went on to inform me, she had never been to a motion picture show since she was a young girl. So by what was then 1981, the movie industry had changed just a tad from fifty years prior.

Later in our friendship, she did share with me a trick in handling such situations, as inappropriate language or even coping with viewpoints she did not want to hear, in a Bahá'í meeting, for example. She would simply turn her hearing aids off. Miss Eulie was definitely a trip. And that's what I've always loved about older people and children, they pull no punches. What you see is what you get. Not all this politically correct and what-you-want-to-hear mumbo jumbo. They're just straight up with it. The truth.

I'll always treasure Eulie's friendship and hold it in such high regard. She said I wasn't just one of her Bahá'í meeting friends that she'd see from meeting to meeting. But I was a true friend that would come and sit for cookies, tea, and conversation. Let me tell you, if you don't have at least one tight friend that is 20, or preferably even 30 or 40 years older than you, depending on your age, or when you do the math, their years actually add up to "dead," then you need to seek one out. Believe me they're not hard to find for they're so often overlooked for the simple reason that they move too slow for most of us preoccupied with our so "very important" fast moving, rat-on-a-wheel lives. But if you ever take the time, oh the gift of wisdom, knowledge, unconditional friendship, and just outright joy you'll receive.

Which brings me to bear in mind such another priceless jewel, I can't stand to continue with my story and without mentioning her. Miss Laura Shell, also known as, the Jazz Lady who for one of her final missions in life was as a DJ on WLGI Radio Bahá'í in Hemingway, South Carolina. This lady was the epitome of cool! When she entered a room or walked passed, the breezes alone of her ultimate coolness could even chill you on out. I always admired her from somewhat afar, with a courteous hello and small conversation, as we gathered at various functions at the Louis G. Gregory Bahá'í Institute in Hemingway. You couldn't miss her. She was a dark-complexioned woman with beautifully permed, shoulder-length white hair. (Later in life as sickness attempted to rob her of her flamboyance by stealing her hair, she never yielded. Instead she sported an even more improved crown of glory, a resplendent, shortly groomed, white Afro.) And she always set off the beauty and glow of her facial countenance with the hippest clothing, full of gorgeously blended colors and patterns of fabric contained in her attire. Whatever she wore, it was always, simply put, just downright cool! And I was continuously fascinated and held in a state of complete awe by her audacity and self-confidence and never allowing a moment or second thought that anyone would not be in total favor of her acceptance.

I recall meeting a young black man in his early twenties, one hot July afternoon on the side porch of Louis Gregory Institute. I was chilling out after having taught a hectic class in the morning of raging nine and ten-year-olds. I noticed I had sat down next to this rather handsome young man, and thought for a change I'd step out of my normal box and actually initiate a conversation, especially since he had an unfamiliar face. I knew most of the young men by either their parents or grandparents, but this guy was new to me. So I proceeded to ask him his name and where he was from. And whether he was a Bahá'í. Then what had brought him to the Institute that day? He then responded with his story of being invited by Miss Laura.

"Well, how do you know, Miss Laura?" For I knew she had no kinfolk in the area. She was from the New Jersey area.

"I met her last night in the club. And she invited me out." Wow! That blew me away. What was Laura doing in a club anyway? And I'm secretly and enviously reflecting, when I'm eighty-something, I hope I'll still be grooving to the body-swaying tunes in a club myself. That's pretty deep, but reassuring to know that I wouldn't have to give up my love of music and the club scene in my older years. I knew then that she was definitely my role model and inspiration to living life to one's fullest.

So it was about a year before her passing that I one day struck up a lengthy conversation about my home and the upcoming Penn Heritage Days Festival, followed with an invitation for her to visit which I was confident she would decline. At the time, we weren't really all that tight. But as that weekend approached in November, I got a call from her road dog and partner in crime, Mr. Obe, an old-hippie of a bead-making and jewelry-making man. They made it on in on a Friday evening and stayed the whole weekend.

And as Obe held down his jewelry booth at the festival as one of the multitude of vendors, Laura and I had the time of our life. Fish fry and blues on Friday night. Saturday, digging the many performances of Gullah storytelling, gospel choirs, and even a champion double-Dutch exhibition.

Then on Saturday night, we left Obe to rest and go to bed. But not Laura. She was ready to go to the club. So here we are heading out to the Elk's Club at our regular time, about quarter 'til twelve. Laura totally ready, not a moment's hesitation. Laura was well at home in the club like it was nothing, as it surely was for this 80-year-old woman. And we hung 'til the lights came on at two. If it was a club that stayed open later, I knew full well she would have been able to hang 'til whenever. She even apologized for not dancing, as she usually would have, but that she was just getting her strength back after fighting a rather rough bout with a serious illness. I was scared to see her with her full energy. I'm sure I wouldn't have been able to keep up with her.

And on down times back at the house, we'd nestle into my number one conversation place in the house, the kitchen. So as I stood at the counter and stove throwing down on some of my all-time specialties for Laura, like my practically-too-hot-for-even-Cajuns shrimp gumbo and srumdillicious, beggin-for-mo' carrot cake; she sat propped in the corner and pitched in by serving story after story of episodes of her excursions, as a feisty and fiery fine young thang. What a delightful time we had. Unforgettable. So when she did pass from this world, I had no regrets. We had had such a great sendoff together. What a special and precious memory I hold onto forever.

Now don't get me totally wrong, I have had one or two friends my age, but literally that's about it. One or two. Okay maybe three or four. But really not much more. During your childhood, you base your best friends off spending the night over to their house. Not that that's really an accurate indication for some kids aren't allowed overnight company. But during my elementary and junior high years at St. Helena School, Melissa Jenkins, Earnestine Warren and Debra Kinlaw, actually had me spend the night over. Later on in Junior High I was pretty tight too with Lenora Green, even though we didn't get to spend the night over with each other.

Spending the night with Debra was a rather educating and live-enhancing experience for me, which taught me such a valuable lesson to not assume that everyone lives in quite the same lifestyle. Believe me, having only come in contact with middle-class, Midwest households, I was still pretty wet behind the years when it came to a lot of things. So when Debra invited me down to spend the night in Scott Plantation on the Island, of course I was so excited and ecstatic to spend the night over with my friend. So friend-wise I was set, but mind-wise I was totally ill-equipped.

No one had prepared me for this moment and the harsh reality of being in a home with no running water and no indoor bathroom. Yes, I had learned to pump water from the hand pump on the electric pump when a severe thunderstorm had our electricity out on the island for a couple days. (Back then there weren't enough influential and wealthy whites to make it a top priority to restore it any more promptly.) But no ability to later turn the running water on, did not compute. And to Debra, I know it was no big deal. She had dealt with it throughout her childhood, and evidently quite a few of the islanders back during the late 60's were still dealing with no indoor plumbing. But this was totally a new concept to me.

Yet since I was getting rather used to and even enjoying new adventures, I thought, "Hey this is way cool." So watching Debra's mom add water to the boiling pots on the gas range with a fresh bucket of water and wash dishes in a porcelain dishpan were quite amazing. Later Debra showed me the outhouse at the far rear of the backyard. And that night she gave further instructions on the use of the infamous "slop jar" kept in the bedroom, for the outhouse was not lit, and you didn't want to encounter any critters in a night trek out to the toilet. Everything was clipping along pretty well. We had taken our sponge baths, were all "jammied" up for the night in our pj's, and I was even psyched up for the "slop jar." Even though not super delighted. But what should appear in the middle of the night? None other than a thirteen-year-old girl's most dreaded occurrence even in the midst of a regular bathroom—my menstrual period! Holy moly, all I could do was plea sudden illness, as I made a mad dash to the phone for my mother to come bail me out. I just couldn't deal with the whole sanitary napkin scene without a proper mental preparation.

Fortunately Debra felt bad for me that I had taken so violently sick so unexpectedly. But you know young kids and even adults for that matter, when you're ill equipped, you're just ill equipped. So I mention that little episode just to say, don't be afraid to be friends with people of different backgrounds, be it racial, age, gender, religious, or even socio-economic. Your life will be greatly richer for it. For these meaningless differences we attribute as valid differences are nothing. You know full well that friendship supersedes all barriers. We make barriers through our minds. But the heart knows no such things.

And several years later, you'll be proud to know that I did fully overcome my spoiling by modern conveniences such as the running water thing, when I spent a week with another Bahá'í teenager at a Bahá'í family's home in the middle of the doonies without water again. This time I was in a burg or probably even too small to be called a burg, but at any rate the official location name on the highway sign read "Turkey Hill." Yup, that was the for-real name of that place. Turkey Hill. But I stayed there a week in a home with no running water. Which I wouldn't say I didn't give it a second thought. That wouldn't be quite the whole truth, but this time I didn't go whining home with my tail between my legs. I actually toughed it out and found it to be really no huge deal.

In closing this chapter out that initially wasn't even in my original outline of chapters, but looks like it may be actually the longest chapter, I close with one of my very bestest, bestest friends in the whole wide world. And that could be none other than my sister Sally. Yes, I know you're saying, I have a lot of sisters. But this one I had the longest. Only since I was about four years old. And even though when she first arrived on the scene, hi-jacking my prized position of "the baby of the family," with my venomous outburst to my momma, "I hate her! And I want you to take her back," we later became the closest and best of friends.

Of course this really didn't occur until fourteen years later after I headed off to college and realized how much I loved and missed that child. Out of all our siblings, we were indeed the closest in age and by then had a quite a lot in common. Especially when Sally visited me on my college campus, Clemson University, and when she began college at the University of South Carolina. I looked out for her, but we also enjoyed so many great times of partying before our years of motherhood began. That slowed us down a tad. Sally was off to travel the world with her husband, an officer in the Air Force. And always in the most remote locations: Kansas, North Dakota, Holland, Germany, Italy, and finally Georgia.

(But always remember the reference to "partying" is never to get confused with other people's definition, which means getting stupid-face drunk. No we never drank. It always just meant to us dancing, dancing, and more dancing. That has always been in the blood of my entire family. From Momma on down.)

And later when Sally married four days prior to my wedding, and we both went on to have two children, with my oldest only two years behind hers, things like that further-tightened the connection.

But also society-wise, Sally and I always fit in the same box or category. So to say. We had rode the same fence rails in life. Had had many of the same experiences, coming from the same family, same upbringing, same schools, and sharing the same pigmentation. Yup, that was my one and only sister with a white complexion. Not that all people even get it to this day that we're indeed white. A lot of people still want to say we're "mixed" or "biracial", and that we just came out very light. Sometimes I feel it's easier for our black community to accept us. As if accepting us as actually being white could be construed as selling out to the enemy.

Of course, her experiences were hardly the carbon copy of mine or her reactions to them. Sally was and is the assertive, stand-up-for-yourself type. I've always been the easy-going, lie down and suffer doormat. So you see our personality types in themselves have shaped our lives much differently. But in the end that's my tight. So we, and as for the rest of my family, went through a lot of mess that life in general hands you with the added pressures that racism throws down on you, and still we still emerged victorious and triumphant. Thus I've found this to be so true for my entire family, "When the going gets rough, the tough get going."

15

"Work is Worship"

Another huge gift I received from my mother and family as a whole, other than my knowledge and love of God, was my fiercely strong work ethic. Of course, the two are elaborately interwoven. Being raised in the Bahá'í Faith, I'm not quite as knowledgeable in Biblical referencing as I am in the Bahá'í Writings. But I do know that through all God's great Teachers and His Teachings, the same divine truth radiates. So when the Bahá'í Writings teach that "Work is worship," I know full well that this is a divine principle held highly in regard by all truly God-fearing men and women. And it was taught to me not only through word, but more importantly by example. "Let deeds, not words be your adorning."

My mother taught us as most mothers did and hopefully still do that "Anything worth doing is worth doing right." Oh mothers love sayings and that was one of her all time hits, as she sent us back to the kitchen to rewash the sink loads of dishes because one or two glasses were spotted with a "smirge" of grease. (Sorry again for the made-up word, but I love playing with words. Goes back to my childhood and such word crafting as "edumacation" or even sister Sally's all-favorite, "scoobating." Just easy and simple fun.) You see Momma had an explicit system and process of dish washing for the millions of soiled dishware a huge family such as ours would create. So for her it was to always, always, always start with the glasses, the plates and bowls, then the silverware, and only lastly the pots and pans. That was to ensure that glasses following greasy pots being washed, were forever banned. But that was a simple example of mom's take on all jobs. "Don't forget, work done in the right spirit is worship," Momma would forever remind us.

Momma taught us well the importance of work through her spoken word. But as for dad, he taught us through example, working all kinds of hours and in all kinds of weather conditions, including snowstorms and blizzards, as cable manager for our small town of Petoskey, Michigan back in the 50's and 60's. I doubt if viewers' channels ever went out for the duration we experience today. And when dad wasn't working on his salaried job, he was working on his bigger job that paid zilch. Yup, none other than his full-time job as dad. But how he performed that so well himself.

Dad was *always* there for us. A morning kiss goodbye, a midday meal, a little league game, a PTA meeting, a Sunday afternoon ride in the country, tobogganing down a hill full force, reading a bedtime story, or simply watching TV with us at night. Dad was always on the case. Not that Mom wasn't, don't get me wrong. But I have to always give it to him for so many dads think it's just mom's job, and hey we so desperately need you dads, too. Moms instinctually know, but dads for some reason don't quite get it and either need a little shove or a lot of encouragement. So whatever it takes, I don't mind doing or saying it.

And as far as we the children, oh we had our share of time to worship through work. Particularly after my father passed, my mom remarried, and we moved onto my stepfather's farm in South Carolina. Back at our home in Michigan, you had the basic kid jobs of an average residence: dish washing, putting out the trash, raking and mowing the yard, shoveling snow, cleaning your room, and making your bed. But on a farm. It's true. You could virtually work from sunrise to sunset and then some.

When it came to work, it was now on. I don't even know quite where to begin. You had the huge household of what seemed liked hundreds of children and what their upkeep and the house itself required. Then there was the expanse of sufficient farm acreage to ensure that we didn't have any idle time for the "Devil's workshop," let alone to catch our breaths. We always joked that Elting married Mom to get some free hired hands or indentured servants to tend his fields and animals. Of course, that was pretty much a big joke for being little white middle-classed young-uns raised in a small town, we certainly knew nothing about real work and certainly no knowledge of downright manual labor in a field. But all that was soon to change.

Elting loved to grow vegetables. What some people may refer to as a garden, was certainly a misnomenclature. For when you have several acres of crops planted with rows upon rows that never end in either direction, I refer to that simply as "fields." So most afternoons and on weekends, we were out working in the fields. Either planting, weeding, or picking the huge array of vegetables and fruit. I mean we had it all. Of course the big cash crops of the area which Elting would load upon on his big flatbed truck to sell at the packinghouses: tomatoes and cucumbers, or "maters" and "cukes." Then there were some of his other favorites grown for family, friends, and neighbors: corn, okra, peanuts, sweet potatoes, watermelon, and cantaloupe.

And man, would that heat and humidity jump down on you and devour you like a raging incinerator. Not to mention a plant called "nettles" I came to discover. So very innocently disguised with soft, delicate white flowers, but at its base it had leaves with tiny spurs on them that as your ankle brushed past them, they quickly adhered to your skin with a fierce burning and itching sensation that about made you lose your mind. I don't care what I did to cover my legs and ankles, those nettles were out to get me, through the fabric of my clothes and all. Yes, granted upon my first encounter, they really did a job on me for I unknowingly was geared up in shorts versus long pants and socks. No one thought to hip me. I guess they thought, let "Hard Head" learn for herself.

But my main thing, those rows and rows in the fields never came to an end. Even with five or more of us out there at a time, they truly never ceased fire. And to this day when someone mentions yard work, gardening, even planting a few flowers, all my mind interprets that into is "Fieldwork—run!!!" Those things may be great for those who never got a chance to spend much time out in nature's elements and feel the earth between their fingers. But believe me, I've had my share. That's merely glorified fieldwork. I'll hire someone any day or merely be the ridicule of the neighborhood for not keeping my grass cut quite to their standard specifications.

Yet after my observing the total situation of working out in the fields for awhile and taking all the negative factors into consideration and coupled with another important observation. My stepsister Maxine always coincidentally seemed to suffer from menstrual cramps every time it was a field day and remained in our grandmother's house those days, I decided hey I'm out for the count too. So I itemized the entire list of indoor duties I would take on rather than join my brothers and sisters in Saturday fieldwork and submitted my finalized proposed contract to Momma with a down-on-my-knees, hard-down begging for mercy.

Not that that the agreement was a fair exchange of manual labor for the household tasks were longer than the rows, but at least they weren't in the blazing sun amidst unmerciful, human-attacking plants. Oh and don't dare think for a minute we were at least in the good favors and fortune of air conditioning. No, not even the schools had that modern convenience during the 60's. It was either pedestal-standing or window fans to attempt a meager alleviation of the rising temperatures. Otherwise some ice water in our finest glassware, compliments of a Welch's grape jelly jar or sporting the latest Hardee's cartoon character along with an equally vital necessity, an old worn and ragged towel around your shoulders for wiping excess sweat as the beads rolled down the nape of your neck.

So nevertheless my proposal was accepted and my fieldwork began to diminish. But oh how the housework mounted and mounted. We always had a good minimum of eight persons residing in the household at any given time, sometimes add an additional one or two, depending on whether anyone was home from college or the military. And Momma was still in the baby manufacturing business so I always had at least two younger brothers or sisters in diapers. Oh and you can guess by now, there were no Pampers or Huggies in our home. Cloth diapers were the chosen apparel. That with no dryer. Fortunately we did have a washer.

For a long time it was an old-timey washer with an open-topped drum and rollers above to wring the clothes out one by one. Well, I'll never forget the time when I got the brightest of bright ideas to try those rollers out on a more personal level as well as quicker, not even awaiting the clothes to finish agitating or more less even pulling an item from the wet sudsy pool of clothing. You see, I may or may not have mentioned this, but as far as common sense, I wasn't richly blessed in this realm. My mother always confirmed this fact, but attempted to make me feel better by reminding me of my great aptitude in academics and "book-sense." So much for that. It worked out fine in school. But when it came to life, it many times caused me quite a few problems. Such was this case in point.

One Saturday morning before I had actually taken on laundry duties, still in my pajamas, I thought I'd check out how the rollers on that washing machine actually worked. The washer we had had in Michigan was more modern and all the movable mechanisms were out of view once you closed the top down for the wash cycle to begin. I thought (well actually I didn't use that process much in this incident) I'd just insert the end of my pajama top into the rollers and see just how that worked. Oh, and by the way, I just happened to still have my pajamas on my body. Well, I didn't have a clue how to stop or reverse the process. That thought hadn't entered my mind until the washing machine had pulled me in almost to my neck. At this point I'm hollering bloody murder and my older stepsister comes running to my rescue, pulling the cord from the ceiling outlet in the light bulb socket, in the nick of time before the rollers had eaten me whole. Thank goodness we later upgraded to a more modern washing machine before I actually took on the household laundry job.

Therefore the never-ending rows of fields, were now replaced with the never-ending clothes lines that were of such a length we had to prop them up with large wooden sticks at each midpoint to ensure that the clothes wouldn't drag the ground and that the occasional breeze could capture their tenants. So along with line upon line of trousers, slacks, blouses, shirts, undershirts, socks, and underwear were the countless baby clothes, baby blankets, bibs, and a sea of diapers, diapers, diapers everywhere. Oh, hanging them up wasn't the biggest job. How 'bout taking them down, folding them, and finding their rightful place amongst the multitude of dressers within each of the bedrooms. And I don't care what anyone says about clothes hung out and they smell so fresh. What about the roughness of those clothes taken on during that line-drying process? Almost rough enough to break your skin when drying off with one of those towels.

Then there were the floors to mop and wax. As you may be catching on by now, no we didn't have carpet either. The entire house was wood flooring. So every Saturday morning, in between hanging loads of clothes on the line, I mopped and waxed the floors while everyone else was out and about doing either fieldwork, yard work, or dealing with the animals. Then I'd replace the diversified assortment of throw rugs that my younger brothers and sisters thrilled themselves in sliding on like an ice rink to end in the delight of our mother screaming for it to halt immediately. What else are parents for, but to ruin your fun?

Oh and did I mention kitchen work yet? We had plenty of hungry mouths to feed. That meant a lot of cooking and later our all time favorite, cleaning up the kitchen and washing dishes. And that's right, no dishwasher. So many times I'd either cook myself or help Momma cook. But then the dishes were either on me or my sister Sally. And Sally being four years younger than me definitely heard the call of playing much more strongly than her duty to pull her fair share. So many an evening before the dish washing began, we held a near to most knock-down-drag-down fight as to whose rightful turn it was to bust the suds. Then would begin the drudgery of washing dish upon dish, glass upon glass, and oh you know those pots never end. We'd have every counter in the kitchen full of dishes and pots drying until Momma yelled out, "Get those dishes dried and put up!"

Now as far as the work went outside, I did clue you to the fieldwork, but then there was the other work outside. One thing about living out in the country, there's no bi-weekly or weekly trash collection day. Nor were there any county dumps to frequent. Needless to say, your backyard was your own dump and landfill all rolled into one. For the most part, you had the fieldwork that all hands on deck were obligated to. But then you had the rest of the chores that fell into two pretty hard and fast realms. Housework for the girls. Outdoor work for the boys. So when it came to digging those colossal big-enough-to-bury-a-mammoth-dinosaur trash holes, my brothers were the ones called to duty. Thank goodness. They had to dig those holes using only two feeble shovels, probably 10' by 10' with a six-foot depth.

Then there were the animals. Don't ask me their purpose. Good question, but I truly don't have the answer. I know that we raised those huge hogs to sell to the slaughterhouse. And occasionally my stepfather would knock one out himself, hang it from the large oak outside our back porch, as the blood drained out and my younger brothers and sisters watched in both horror and intrigue. Then the grand finale would be when he would butcher it into small enough parcels to be housed in our deep freeze and dispersed to some of our neighbors and friends. The grossest part would be forgetting about the new occupant of the deep freeze, opening it to locate a freeze pop and seeing that hog's head sitting up oh so politely, looking like, "And why pray tell are you disturbing my privacy?" Down went the lid of the deep freeze, as I'd light on out of there, vowing never to return to the scene of that crime.

Now my grandmother did raise chickens for eggs and occasionally to stew a hen for dinner. But all the other animals remain an unsolved mystery. We had the cows that we never milked or slaughtered. I guess they were for mere atmosphere of a small farm. There were always one or two horses. Well, yes my stepfather used the horse to plow those rows upon rows of fields that I so dearly adored. Oh, and the horse would even provide free lawn mowing if you'd occasionally tie him up in the front yard. From time to time we'd have ducks squawking and quacking about. We even had a goat one time that I imagine served as a garbage disposal, especially seeing that we didn't recycle aluminum cans back then. He had a grand time with the few he found. For believe me, we were mostly a grape or red KoolAid kind of family. (Yes, it was always called red KoolAid as kids, no matter if it were strawberry, cherry, or punch. It was simply "red KoolAid.") And if we were fortunate enough to get our hands on some soda, it was normally in those return-for-deposit glass pop bottles.

With all of these animals, they naturally gave me a run for my money. Or in other words, we just didn't hit it off. Luckily I rarely had to deal with them unless we were short on male assistance that particular day. The rooster I utterly feared. He was known to not allow you to come next to his turf or his women. Then the largest of the hogs, terrified me completely. I remember trying to get feed for him out of the shed. I didn't realize he had broken out of his pen and so here came the attack hog after me, thinking I was trying to stand in his way of getting his meal. No more. I believe he was at the door of that shed and had me hostage well over what seemed an hour or more.

Oh, and my first and last time upon a horse. And I preference this with the reminder that when common sense was being issued in the family, they ran out on me that day. As is quite evident with this account. But one of my brothers helped me up on the horse's back for a short jaunt around the house. Nothing earth shattering. But then he decided he wanted to visit his trough for a midday snack. And as he's going under a low-lying tree limb, I'm trying to push it out of the way. Bright, real bright. Sure enough the branch of the oak tree didn't move, but I was the one that came plummeting down to the ground on my tailbone. Yup, I ensure you that was enough horse encounters for me in my lifetime. Just best to leave well enough alone.

Now outside of the animals on the farm, Elting loved the creatures of the ocean. But at least by the time we came in contact with these, they would usually be dearly departed. The shrimp, the flounder, the mullet (which I hated the taste), the crabs, and oysters. I loved and still love shrimp. Could eat it for breakfast, lunch, and dinner "24/7." But you never know how much work those rascals are to prepare until you meet the pleasure. So every Saturday or so my stepfather would arrive at the house with a huge aluminum tub of probably 100 to 200 pounds of shrimp. And oh what a joy. We'd have them on a large makeshift table made from a huge piece of plywood, under that infamous oak tree by the back porch, all hands available, popping off shrimp heads from early that morning for several hours until we'd popped the last head. More stockpile for the freezer and neighbors. Not that anything lasted in that deep freeze for long. All those toiling hands were attached to tired and hungry bodies. So at least we did get the opportunity to partake of the fruits of our labors.

As far as hard work, it hardly contained itself to our farm. That of course was out of the necessity of growing up in a large family back in the day that didn't know or want to know what food stamps or welfare was. But also with being poor, we didn't have money for clothes, let alone extras. So that's when it came down to seeking work that yielded monetary compensation. In other words a paycheck! Gots to get paid. So we all had jobs as soon as we were old enough to look like we were old enough. And fortunately most of my brothers and sisters were rather tall for their age so it did work. We'd mostly work in the tomato packing houses during the summers until in the early 70's they came along with the Manpower Program that provided subsidized employment in public, nonprofit businesses and offices for disadvantaged youth. Then we were good to go.

But before that came to pass, I remember my older stepsisters always making a hustle finding whatever jobs they could find, from the simplest to the more serious. I remember my stepsister Maxine even selling candy bars for the traveling country store housed on an old repainted school bus. Or the serious sacrifice my stepsister Omega made when she had sat out of college a year to go to Jersey to work full-time at the Maidenform factory in order to come up with enough tuition to continue her education and graduate from Benedict College. (That was before grants and government subsidized student loans.) But oh how we giggled with glee when we received a package from the residence of our Uncle Willie Smith in Newark, New Jersey where Omega was staying at the time. Those packages always contained the silkiest and most decoratively designed panties and brassieres. A far cry from our worn out and somewhat dingy used-to-be-white, cotton drawers. And at Christmas time, Omega was our favorite and most cherished Santa Claus. She would send a huge box loaded with what you'd think was the latest toys off TV. But no we didn't want toys. We couldn't wear those to school to fend off taunts of our old and worn out hand-me-downs. We delighted in new clothes, actually purchased for our specific name and size on the shopping list.

And to this day I have to fight off the urge to be a clothes-shopping glutton. I have the clothes halfway under control, but the shoes. That's totally out of control. I even have a large collection of miniature shoes. Thought that hobby would help me cut down on buying real shoes. Didn't work. I guess when you grow up with one pair of shoes that had to do it all: school, play, and even worship service, then you just develop a starving hunger that never quite goes away, no matter how much you feed it. So that's me. Luckily I'm not alone. I see there's a lot of women addicted to shoes out there. "Hey, did you all only have one pair of shoes growing up, too? Or are you all just naturally greedy? In other words, what's you all's excuse?"

And I always highly commend my parents, including my stepfather, and entire family for that matter, for I had a lot of older stepsisters that served as excellent role models when it came to teaching me the importance of hard work. As large as our family was and as poor as we were, we were never once on welfare, food stamps, ADFC, or any other assistance, other than the assistance of the Lord and the belief that "God helps those who help themselves." All of us always worked and worked hard. Not just one, but usually two or three jobs at a time. That's always been our family. And whatever job we've taken on, we give it our all. That's one thing I am so very proud to say about my family. We're all known as highly competent and extremely hard workers, whatever our chosen "field" of work. (Just can't get away from those fields, can I?) And thankfully it's had the domino effect even down to our children.

And in concluding this discussion on work and work ethics, I remind you that many of you may or may not have been raised with such work values or work ethics, but I venture to say that most of the older generation such as I was. And all I can say to you now is that our children learn by example and experience. If we don't provide both, our example and their own experience of good old-fashioned hard work, who's responsible for the end results? If our children today don't have a strong work ethic, who's at fault? It's no one's but ours', the parents'. You may not want them to go through all that you went through or have it as hard as you had it, but always remember experience is the best teacher. Don't do your children too many favors. In the long run, they're not favors, but actually crippling and debilitating excuses. (Don't mean to preach. But for real.)

Therefore I'm so very grateful that I learned from my family by seeing and doing, the importance and necessity of hard work in one's life. Knowing what it is to work hard for and earn what you get in life. Knowing that life doesn't come easy. But that once you've worked hard for what you have, you can feel infinitely proud of your accomplishments because you did it. No one gave it to you. You didn't expect anyone to give it to you. You got your own on your own. And you can't beat the feeling and high that sensation yields. All you can tell yourself is "Job well done," and be in peace and joy with yourself. You have to feel your purpose in life and what contribution you're making to make this world go round. Otherwise, what's the whole point?

16

Raising the "Younger Set"

Our family always had "sets" of children, like series of waves converging on the seashore. The first set were the eldest of the family, my stepfather's six children from his first marriage. And for "coloring" purposes, yes they were black. The second set of four, I fell into, my mother's children from her first marriage. And we were the white ones. Then came the final set, to which we normally referred to as "the younger set," the four youngest from the union of my mother and stepfather. These were my biracial or what our family and community always called "mixed" children.

Between this range of fourteen children in my family, we had quite a gap in ages, at least a span of 30 years between the baby and the eldest child. Most of the eldest set were off in the world embarking on life by time the last set evolved. That left me and the rest of my middle set. But my brothers from that set were now in mid-teen crisis, and basically not in the picture, as well as very irresponsible. Anyway the remaining sister from this set was initially the baby and still played that role. Responsibility certainly wasn't one of her virtues at this time. And since I was the only accountable, remaining member of the middle set, the heat fell on me. I was deemed one of the major caregivers as the "younger set" was born, along with my stepsister Rosalyn until she graduated and eventually left the nest too. I never really thought a thing of it. Back then, children certainly weren't given choices of whether we wanted to do something. So I thought nothing of taking care of my younger brothers and sisters. That's just the way it was. Really, no big deal. So as each one came along, I just continued to help Momma as much as possible, and became like a second Momma to them. Though, after Daniel and Felicia were born and therefore after learning the joy of laundering cloth diapers for two infants in a household at once, I did rather brazenly inquire of Momma, "One boy, one girl. Now Momma don't you think that's enough?" Evidently not, next came Victoria and last on the block Darrel.

115

Since as Elting and Momma were very active and well-known members of the Bahá'í Faith, they oftentimes were elected or appointed to serve on this committee, that task force, the local assembly, a state group, as a national delegate, or even as a travel teacher out of the country. As much as possible, we traveled together as an entire family to meetings, conferences, and Bahá'í school sessions, squashed and squished into our worn, but trusty, olive green Chevrolet station wagon, singing Bahá'í songs to the top of our lungs 'til the driver couldn't take it a moment more. But the other times, when my parents had to go solo, it was more times than not, me holding down the fort at home.

The rattling of pans, washing of dirty drawers, the mitigater of disputes. When it came to the "younger set"—that was me from about the age of thirteen on. And that still remains my official capacity in the family. Fortunately at my current station in life, the cooking has diminished to an occasional cookout, a family dinner, or the traditional Lynn's birthday cakes. I'm still called in as the mediator for resolution of conflicts that erupt amongst the family, probably because I'm a great listener, attempt to see all sides, be fair, and heck I've been doing it all these years. I guess the only thing I don't do at all any longer is wash their dirty drawers. Thank goodness for that alleviation.

The one thing though I never quite learned to do when it came to my younger brothers and sisters, particularly my younger sisters was to fix their soft, but thick nappy hair. But I never really learned to do hair of any type, even my own texture of hair. As my coif certainly still affirms to today. And thank goodness the Lord saw fit that I didn't need to inflict the same non-hair styles on any mixed children of my own. So thank you Lord for my two boys. A low cut works all the time. And as far as my eldest son's 'fro, he's now a young man and can handle his own business. Which I must admit he keeps shaped and maintained almost as nice as the heads of Afros back in the day of the 70's. And as for my stepdaughter Dee, there was always a hairdresser to be found, and fortunately she was soon managing her own hair.

But as for my youngest sisters, Felicia and Vicki, it was purely pitiful how I tried to pull their hair into one ponytail, with no grease or oil on their scalp, and hair flying every which way within seconds of its completion. Or don't mention attempting to pick their hair out into what was the somewhat distant resemblance of a natural or Afro. Oh, and of course we never had a pick anywhere to be found so it was always sitting on the front steps of the house with a kitchen fork filling in for the job. Wow! Did we actually used to do that?

I was always the adventurous type and liked to expose the "Younger Set" to new experiences. No I wasn't ever much for "playing, even as a child. It seemed I was always attempting to be a teacher already, from my youngest of years. So there'd we be, me jumping in the driver's seat of our family's station wagon with Daniel, Felicia, Vicki, and Darrel always in tow. Part of it was I wanted them to always go and see things, and the other part of it was that they were usually in my charge. Now Sally, my sister from "my set," was sometimes in the mix, but not usually. She would be gone doing her own thing with her buddies. And then later it would be just the two of us when we were getting ready to do some serious hangin' out.

The only down side of continuously having my younger brothers and sisters at my heels was that people always misconstrued that vision. Their take on things was that I must naturally be a young unwed teenage mother. Of course if they had actually attempted to do the math, having my first child at ten is a tad bit unrealistic. But some people always want to come up with the worst scenario, especially when they see racially mixed children in the picture. Just never enters their limited minds that it could be remotely possible to be a healthy and legit situation. But that's cool because from an early age, that along with everything else, forced me to become resilient to the judgments and accusations of anyone other than my Creator. So in others words, "I kept on keepin' on," always with Daniel, Felicia, Victoria, and Darrel trailing and traveling along into various ventures and venues.

Our all-time favorite escape was the beach. Oh how we'd love to head out to the beach at Hunting Island State Park. We'd all pile into the station wagon (or later my beat-down, pale-yellow Toyota Corona), clad in whatever beat up and beat down hand-me-down swimwear or made-into swimwear we could muster up. Beg for a dollar or two to put enough gas in the tank from the pump at A.J. Brown's corner store and get us down the nine or ten miles to the beach.

Of course, we'd always pack some peanut butter and jelly sandwiches, or bologna if we were really living high on the hog that day, and a jug of good ole grape KoolAid with ice already melting and watering down its contents. Lord knows there wasn't funding to frequent the snack bar. We didn't even ask. You know our kids today, really got it good. They can just say the word, and usually a soda or a snack readily appears in a moment's notice. It's just a given. But back in the day, we didn't even imagine in our wildest dreams that occurring. In fact if it did ever happen, we would have suffered complete hysteria.

We always had a ball on the beach. Riding the surf, jumping the waves, building gigantic sand castles and elaborate forts, burying one of my brothers up to his neck in the sand, diving for sand dollars, collecting shells as we walked the surf's edge, or sometimes actually swimming just beyond the emergence of the large crashing, incoming waves. Such great fun that no one ever had time to even notice the gawking eyes about to fall out of their sockets or mouths hanging open about to drag along the sandy shore. Sorry if our beautiful blend of colors in our family was a problem to some people. But that was simply "their problem." It certainly was never a problem for us.

Now back then I wasn't quite so obsessed with turning my skin a glowing tanned tone in the summer through that highly unhealthy practice of sun bathing. But for my black readers, let me tell you, white people, me included, really catch it trying to acquire a tanned complexion of skin. And hasn't it always been so completely ironic that some of the most racist of racist whites, truly tear themselves up in the hot summer sun trying and some actually succeeding to be black, at least in skin color? That's definitely one of those Arsenio Hall "things that make you go hmm." Though I'm sure there's some astute and astounding psychologically expert explanation and opinion on this phenomenon.

But I always did envy what I called the perfect complexion, that caramel-colored light brown, even skin tone my younger brothers and sisters were so blessed with. I mean they never had to wish they were darker or wish they were lighter. To me, they were always just right. Somewhat like a little story our mother used to tell us about the explanation of the creating of God's diverse and different races. The story refers to God baking cookies. The white race, a batch coming out not quite done. The black race being left in the oven a bit too long. And the biracial batch coming out just right. Don't ask me where my mother came up with that. She probably made it up for the "Younger Set" to ensure the squelching of any potential self-esteem issues society might throw their way. At any rate, I guess I must have always concurred with her. 'Cause I've got to give it to my younger brothers and sisters. They always did have such a pretty skin color.

But talk shows today battle about the trauma of raising racially mixed children in today's society. And really I just don't get it. Maybe they haven't interviewed the right families. But I'm sure my brothers and sisters wouldn't want it any way else. To be blessed with the best of two worlds. Why not? Why do we want to make it a problem when it's not? Just because they happen to be biracial.

We even want to trip on the identification and classification of racially mixed people. This is ludicrous. Complaints are made about mixed celebrities, such as Tiger Woods for example. "Why doesn't he want to admit he's black?" "If a police officer stops him, he's going to be black then." Hey let all people be proud of who they are. We should be. And if society wants to classify, at least allow people the freedom to classify as they best see fit. Why must Tiger Woods discount his entire Asian bloodline in order to say he's "Black" and black alone? Why must he comply with society's antiquated and racist classifications? Why must we buy into that decrepit system? He's not ashamed of being black, but neither is he ashamed of his other heritages. Let him celebrate all the many strengths that went into his composition.

Yes a racist society affects us all whether we're white, black, Hispanic, Asian, Native American, or any other race, or any mixture thereof. But there's certainly nothing wrong with God's children and His creation. If there's a problem here, it's not His problem He's created, but rather one we, mankind has manufactured ourselves.

As the Bahá'í Writings affirm, "O humankind! Verily, ye are all the leaves and fruits of one tree; ye are all one. Therefore associate in friendship; love one another; abandon prejudices of race; dispel forever this gloomy darkness of human ignorance."

17

Uncovering the Myth: White Schools Superior to Black Schools

In making comparisons of the black schools to the white schools during segregated and "Freedom Choice" policies, the question always reoccurs, "Were the white schools actually better?" Well, according to whom you ask you'll undoubtedly get a sundry of quite varied and opposing responses. From my personal experiences of having attended both black and white public schools during elementary, junior, and high school periods; my response would rightfully so be quite different from someone only exposed to one side.

To accommodate federal legislation for integration during 1965–1970, Beaufort County utilized their policy called "Freedom of Choice," which allowed students to attend any school, regardless of the school's racial composition. This affected one percent of the black enrollment. You see the educational system had brainwashed the general public to believe that the traditionally "white" schools offered a superior education to that of the "black" schools. This was so much so that some black parents chose to enroll their children in these "white" schools during Freedom of Choice, even when they would be forced to endure daily the riddling with the bullets of racially derogatory slurs, psychological abuse, and oftentimes even physical violence. And what was the purchase of merchandise made in exchange for this price they paid? What they believed to be a more superior education.

But this was not the case. Yes, the quality of the facilities and the materials in the black schools were indeed lacking, but hardly as far as a school's most indispensable element of success. The teachers! They held such an acclaim and charge in self-worth ensuring success in black students. And the results of this phenomenon have never quite been replicated.

As I compare the black schools during the times of segregation to the schools that resulted during initial integration, there's no comparison of equity. Just comparing my education to that of my husband who is eight years older than me and completed the majority of his education at George Washington Carver High in Edna, Texas. Yes a black school. (Did the name give it away?) His knowledge of academics used to blow me away. Here I was a college graduate with a bachelors and two masters degrees. And he used to run circles around me with just a high school education. (He couldn't comprehend why something as basic as a "gerund," I had never heard of. And I was equally amazed how well versed he was in so many things that somewhere in my high school and college years had not been afforded me.

Yet the critical difference here was that he had attended a black school throughout his secondary education, graduating in 1967. (Just prior to the "Dark Ages." When I attended high school, 1971–1974 that was the early years of forced integration, I called those years the "Dark Ages" of Education. I had received what I'd called a mediocre to adequate education versus his of an above average to superior education.

To illustrate this more clearly, he as a First Sergeant, a noncommissioned officer in the Marine Corps (meaning no college degree), always had to write the reports that his commissioned officer (college-degreed) in charge could not do competently. Just what is that saying? And the only reason I was able to compete successfully in college was that I was competing with other graduates of the "Dark Ages."

Even the sixth grade education Grammy completed at one of the small one-room schoolhouses in the black community about matched up to what I had acquired. Maybe not in the area of math and sciences. I did have the privilege of having some strong, traditional (what I call truly "old school") teachers in those disciplines. But as for English, literature, and social sciences, I was batting zero in the area of good instruction. What can I attach the blame to? It's hard to say. Can I attribute it to the attitudes of those involved in the integration process? We had the same students, parents, and staff. Just together now in one system. Or is it an overall laxity and apathy that was already developing in society at large that I was unaware of? Good question. Be it as it may. I and many others suffered and some continue to suffer through an educational system that is not a successful educational experience to all segments of our population.

In reflecting on my education, I want to share my personal experience. For I've seen both sides. I attended St. Helena School, a black school, for elementary and junior high until mandated integration of all schools in 1970. St. Helena

School was for students in first through twelfth grades. Its doors had first opened in 1954 as one the "Separate but Equal Schools." Students were taught by family, community, and teachers that education was the vehicle of success. The school was well disciplined because we knew what our purpose was, and we respected our teachers without even a thought of any other alternative. The saying, "A hard head makes for a soft behind," was well understood by all students for it had been instilled in the youngest of children as mere babes in the households of the St. Helena community. Mrs. Keith's fan belt made a lasting impression on me as I incredulously watched her use it only once on a "hard-head" boy during my year of fifth grade. And "going to the office" was almost unheard of. Those would have been extremely isolated incidents, which I truly didn't want to have any knowledge of because when we reached home, it wouldn't have been a pleasant tale to tell.

Our teachers at St. Helena were strict like most of our parents. They loved or cared for us just as our parents did. And we loved our teachers dearly in return. Their intentions were obvious. Their major concern was for us to be successful academically, as well as in our future careers and endeavors. And their philosophy was clearly "By Any Means Necessary." If it meant giving you an allotted amount of licks with a belt or chops with a wooden ruler or paddle, endearingly named "The Board of Education," when you failed yourself. Be it failing to do class work, failing to do homework, or failing to behave that was your poor choice in judgment and the teacher's job to insist that you made less of those decisions resulting in failure and more of those resulting in success. This was one key factor in ensuring that all students worked and achieved to their highest potential in their acquisition of academic knowledge.

Another vital ingredient to the success of St. Helena School was remembrance and praise of God and supplication of His blessings in all our endeavors. We began each day of instruction with the Pledge of Allegiance and devotional service, which would consist of prayer, Bible scriptures, and a singing of a popular spiritual. One of my fondest pictures in my memory is my ninth grade teacher, little petite and soft-spoken, Miss Rogers, reading her daily Bible verse for the day. Now that certainly would be a wonderful tactic in beginning to combat today's ninth graders. (My husband that currently teaches at the high school level assures me that they are his roughest customers.) Why did we ever annihilate prayer and the requesting of divine guidance in the schools?

One of the characteristic activities of the black schools was the Friday assembly. And St. Helena School was no exception. Every Friday afternoon was set aside for Assembly programs. The entire school congregated in the gymnasium for the Assembly program that would be presented by the scheduled homeroom or club for that week. We'd begin with prayer, the pledge, many times the Black National Anthem, "Lift Every Voice and Sing," but always the closing with our school's Alma Mater.

And every student was afforded the opportunity, in fact required, to participate in the presentation, usually in the form of a play, skit, poetry, recitations, musical, or dance selections. It provided opportunities for talents to be discovered and cultivated. Even the typical "troublemaker" could find his niche within the scheme of the school, and a "turn-around" might become evident. It's what we educators call, "positive reinforcement," as opposed to always giving attention and credence to reinforcement of negative behavior. The students also felt they "belonged" because they were actively involved and engaged members of the school.

I remember to this day, standing on the stage in front of the entire school, elementary through high school, being allowed to offer the opening prayer for that particular assembly. (That original gymnasium still stands on the campus of the newly built St. Helena Elementary. Boy do I have warm and comfy flashbacks while I'm sitting in that gym today.) We were all taught we were "Somebody" and that we could achieve the dream and the gleam of what our eyes envisioned. Such a vital and crucial building block to guarantee a successful life to come.

In eighth grade I experienced one of my first, what I call "higher order" teachers. Mrs. Mary Drake began to provide the navigation routes that provoked such levels of thought in such content areas I had previously been totally oblivious to and ignorant of. What a year of true awakening for me. First I began a rather safe tiptoeing through a small rippling stream. The project was to create a scrapbook reporting on eight different famous black Americas excelling in varied areas of expertise. For example: education, politics, sports, entertainment, science, literature, etc. With the aid and assistance of my older stepsisters and several old issues of *Ebony* and *Jet* magazines (vital staples, then and now, in most black households), I was able to execute this task fairly well.

Our next excursion, was literally an actual "excursion." This time stepping up the intensity a bit more. Traversing the Charleston Bay. Mrs. Drake arranged a field trip for the class to tour Fort Sumter in Charleston, which is our neighboring coastal city to the north of us. We were to reinforce through a first-hand environment, but fortunately not first-hand in its entirety, a sequence of highly significant, century-influencing events. South Carolina's succession from the States, the first shot that echoed out of Fort Sumter to begin the Civil War, and the infamous seizure of the Confederate ship, "The Planter," by a slave and later

Congressman, Robert Smalls (who happened to be a homey from Beaufort). The study of the Civil War was certainly virgin soil for me in my treasury of learning. And I certainly found it rather puzzling and absurd how our nation had engaged in civil warfare in order to resolve what the War for Independence should have already guaranteed to all Americans: "Life, liberty, and pursuit of happiness."

My greatest plunge in the ocean of black history was two required readings that year assigned by Mrs. Drake. *Uncle Tom's Cabin*, a largely-based historical fiction by Harriet Beecher Stowe and *Black Like Me*, an autobiography of a segment of John Howard Griffin's life. What the path of knowledge these two books began to embark me on somewhat compared to what the viewing of the series *Roots* accomplished for the entire nation. Following the day-to-day battles of the characters in these novels so intimately and emotionally attached me to their blood, sweat, and tears. And *Black Like Me* afforded me an education past the era of slavery to that of racism and discrimination as it continues to exist in our society today. (And just as what Griffin's book did for me, I hope that my book can somehow attempt to provide, a glimpse at understanding how racism having affected one insignificant person as myself, can be damaging to such a vast population of our society. For it not only harms the discriminated, but the discriminator as well. And this disease is so crippling and debilitating to the true potential of America.)

As I type yet another word in the text of this book, I thank Mrs. Drake for another invaluable education she provided. I almost forgot her other position at St. Helena. Not only did she teach eighth grade social studies, but she also was the typing teacher. So in eighth grade she also taught me typing. And this skill I have found to be a priceless tool that I've carried my entire life. Through the summer jobs in high school of typing in the offices on the military base. To typing research paper upon research paper in undergrad and graduate schools. To being able to secure a job in California as a clerk typist (more proficient than those with secretarial degrees) when no teaching jobs were available. To being able to teach word processing and keyboarding to Adult Education students. To being able to type my own teacher evaluations on my laptop as I observed classroom instruction as an assistant principal. To teach composition writing, word processing, and keyboarding to fourth and fifth graders. And now to compose this book sitting by the oceanside under a nestle of trees, as I rattle-tat-tat on my laptop the chapters of my life. Wow! Mrs. Drake. One year of typing in eighth grade and have all that that I owe to you? Oooh, when you truly examine the power and impact of a teacher throughout your life.

Mrs. Mary Drake has since passed on, but I will always say in her memory, "Truly Thanks" from the bottom of my heart and soul. Thanks for being a dedicated, committed, and serious teacher. Thanks for such a valuable and real education, enlightened by such highly-choice assignments and experiences.

As I continue to recount the impact of St. Helena School, I must say that education was a major focus of not only the students and teachers, but of the entire community. Not only was the community engaged in school activities, but this was reciprocated by the faculty's involvement in the community. School and community were one entity. "The community was the school." Teachers ensured that they met parents of all homeroom students through home visits. Teachers were required to attend the monthly Community Sing held at Penn Center, which was a major social event. And though this was a requirement, teachers looked forward to attending and continued to become even more accepted and involved in community life. This is essential to a successful education program. It can't be "just a job." That's not what it is to be a teacher.

The school also served as a showcase of the community. The majority of social activities abounded from the school involving concerts, competitions, performances, and special events. One of the highlights of the school year was the May Day celebration. This event included the traditional wrapping of the May Pole, which had continued to be observed in some elementary schools until recent years. Generally a beauty and talent pageant would be held in conjunction with the crowning of Miss May Day, and performances were held to honor the queen and her court.

The Eagles' football and basketball games were always full to capacity, and school spirit and pride were evident. Students especially enjoyed pep rallies for the teams. Also everyone knew the school song, and still do to this day. The St. Helena High School Band had an unwavering reputation for its showmanship and perfection under the direction of Mr. Wesley Felix.

Mr. Felix gave us all so much in so many ways. He impressed upon us and reinforced many of the same values that we learned in our homes. One in particular, "Anything worth doing, is worth doing right." Mr. Felix believed in what educators so frequently refer to as "High Expectations." That was not merely a belief or terminology. That was a reality in action. The St. Helena High School Band was the epitome of excellence, never less than the best. We practiced daily until dark and murky shadows had drunk up every drop of light. And parents began to stew and rumble as they sat in their parked cars on the sidelines of the practice field and under the shady and voluminous oak trees. As we practiced and practiced, over and over and over and over, the same routine until it was right. Always nothing less.

Not only performance, but appearance was the best or you didn't perform. No exceptions. Band uniforms and hats immaculately clean. Band shoes and major-ette boots freshly polished white. During practice and performance, marching with knees up 90 degrees parallel to the ground, no not just the majorettes, but the entire band. No sheet music was allowed outside the confines of practice.

All Mr. Felix's efforts, they were always for us. Not for his glory, but for his students. I don't recall Mr. Felix being honored as Band Director of the Year. If he was, he never alluded to it. For me, he would have to have been Band Director of the Year, every year. None surpassed or even begun to touch him. He was nothing less than total excellence. Even when we were transferred to Beaufort High School during integration, and Mr. Felix was selected as the Junior High School Band Director. It was never about himself. It was still about the students. He kept being himself, excellence in action. And his band, the St. Helena Junior High Band, ran circles around the Beaufort High School Band. Still the Show Stoppers.

To this day St. Helena School remembers and dearly cherishes Mr. Wesley Felix. He wrote our Alma Mater Song, which the children of St. Helena Elementary continue to sing.

I thank Mr. Felix, as one of my tremendously outstanding and superlative teachers, for teaching and touching the thousands and thousands of us students during his career. And for teaching us about pride and excellence, a lesson that has gone with all of us throughout our lifetimes.

It was such a privilege and honor for me to join the St. Helena Band as a jun-ior majorette when I was in fifth grade, and I continued until St. Helena High School Band ceased to exist. Special school activities and special teachers ensured that students would continue to look forward to attending school. Dropping out of school was unthought of and unheard of.

Consolidated schools such as St. Helena School were utilized and the policy of Freedom of Choice was adhered to until 1970 when integration was mandated by Health Education and Welfare's (HEW) findings of noncompliance with sub-stantial school desegregation, which would have resulted in several million dollars of federal funding. Immediate and complete compliance followed. In other words, "Money talks."

So my freshman year of 1970–71 I attended an "integrated" St. Helena Junior High. And my sophomore year of high school it was mandatory that I attend the also integrated Beaufort High School, which was the former white high school. I experienced a great deal of negativity in relation to this transfer from St. Helena High to Beaufort High. First of all my high school principal was demoted to that of a junior high position. As well, my high school band director was also demoted to a junior high position. This was ludicrous and enraging to my classmates and me. Doc was a highly respected and competent principal. And Mr. Felix was the most renown and gifted band director in South Carolina.

You see all the black high schools and faculty members in leadership roles such as principals, guidance counselors, head coaches, and musical directors had been downgraded to merely elementary and junior high schools. These individuals were retained mostly at the junior high level. (And I found this to be the general policy in most school systems across the nation in compliance with the integration status.)

Needless to say, I and many schoolmates elected to drop out of the band due to our to disappointment and disapproval of the situation. I basically "dropped out" of the holistic school experience and all its social amenities. I held to the one item I needed from that institution, a high school diploma with a high GPA that would afford me a college scholarship and get me the heck out of there. I never did attend even one football or basketball game. I didn't desire a Beaufort High School ring. I didn't even purchase invitations to my graduation. My only happiness was that I was soon to be leaving. To this day, I avoid any situation that would cause me to come in contact with that campus. I never did feel that I "belonged" at Beaufort High.

But thanks to one very special young lady whom I'll never forget, she made Beaufort High somewhat palatable, Patricia Bee. She was incredibly something else. Talk about a Black Pearl. That was her. She was every bit of six-foot, but walked with such a grace and regality that would make Princess Di envious. Patricia sported the most perfectly-shaped natural. And she was really all about being black and proud. She was secure and confident within her own skin, but didn't mind befriending me, the displaced one. I was basically for the most part, alone now. You see many of my classmates from St. Helena Junior High had bought into the misconception that they would have difficulty competing with white students. They shunned the college-bound and honors level classes like the plague. Only a few brave souls didn't give into this false phobia. And for Patricia, she was as equally confident in her height appearance-wise as was her confidence in her academic altitudes, as well. That girl was what you definitely called just plain and simply, "Smart!"

It was in one of the higher-level classes where I first met Patricia. And we were fast, firm friends throughout our high school years. You never saw one of us without the other. Inseparable and just plain "tight." Even through being snided by their Majesty the Popular Ones for daring to be students that actually studied, conquering the rigors of our course overload, and overlooking the antics of the silly high school boys who we despised. I could have never endured Beaufort High without the support of such a true friend as Patricia Bee. God bless you for that friendship, Patricia.

Also by my senior year I was beginning to get pretty tight with my good friends, Annette Mitchell and Cynthia Williams. Though we mostly became closer after graduation from Beaufort High and college. Those were my hanging out buddies. We loved to go clubbing at least 'til the church hijacked Cynthia completely.

And there even were a few white students who humored me, actually a few boys in my chemistry class, such as George Madlinger, Mike Boyne, and Jerry Webster. George was truly a sweet soul. But the others, I don't know, they could have been just trying to copy off my chemistry test.

Beaufort High School was almost completely devoid of excellent teachers. Several I must admit come to mind, but most of them were remnants of the old schools. There was Mr. Cletus Ferguson who made Algebra II & Trigonometry as clear as crystal. Mr. James Johnson who had me waking up at two am to complete a 27-step proof in Geometry. And even the such sophisticated and stylishly chic teacher I so dearly loved, Madame Begley who tore me up in French II. ("Who happened to be white. But I didn't hold that against her." Just kidding. Really.) You see it was the hardest and most challenging teachers that really set it off in me. I had so much I was determined to prove. And what better a place than in a classroom with the most academically vigorous teachers?

But my all time very best teacher was Mr. Joseph Sherman. He was my Chemistry teacher, my senior year at Beaufort High. What made him the very best is that he expected us to do our very best and would not accept any less? He was a very, very challenging teacher because he had to be. Chemistry is a very, very arduous science. It demands time and attention to acquire its knowledge. That year when I was in his class, he taught everything we needed to know about Chemistry and then some. We had heaps of homework every night, but it gave us the vital and necessary practice. And when there were times we were confused, we could remain after school with Mr. Sherman for additional assistance. He also would meet with students every Saturday morning at Penn Center to give us free tutoring on his own personal time.

Later when I attended Clemson University the following year, Chemistry was one of the basic courses required our freshman year. This Chemistry class was an extremely large class, which was held in an auditorium. I had never seen so many students in one class. About 300! (That's as many students as were in my entire high school graduating class.) Well, fear tried to grab my hand and talk me into doubting myself and believing perhaps I wasn't as smart as all those other students. But I had a duty to myself and to Mr. Sherman to prove that he certainly was "The Very Best Teacher." Turned out I aced all my tests that year in Chem 101, and it didn't even require that I study. You may say how is this possible? She must be extremely gifted academically. Not really. But having had The Very Best Chemistry Teacher, I had already been superbly prepared and taught more than I even needed to know for high school Chemistry and Chem 101. I'll always remember Mr. Joseph Sherman as "The Very Best Teacher" and hope that many other teachers will continue to follow in his footsteps, by preparing students more than adequately for successful futures.

Yet while still attending Beaufort High, I was quick to learn of the general public opinion, that St. Helena students were inferior to Beaufort High students and that we would encounter an extremely adverse transition in academics. This was such a common opinion that I was even brainwashed to the point of belief, as contrary as this was to what my teachers at St. Helena had confirmed in me, to always believe in myself. I came home from my first day at Beaufort High School with my first migraine headache and was convinced that I was going to "flunk" every subject. I had to pull myself together. I had a lot on the line. Not only my future, but this unfounded stigma that a black school and its students were inferior. That just did not set right with me. I was enraged and furious. So I came out armed with the words and wisdom of James Brown again, "I don't want nobody to give me nothin'. Open up the door. I'll get it myself." And I did! Three years later, I graduated with a 4.0 grade point average from Beaufort High School, ranked #2 in a graduating class of 300, with a full scholarship to Clemson University. (And you know I packed that same "attitude" for that trip to Clemson since my entire life I've always felt I've had to prove myself.) Fortunately, what do I attribute my accomplishments to? The lessons I learned from my caring and loving teachers at St. Helena that I was "somebody" and that I could achieve whatever I dreamed of.

You see one of my greatest desires was to become a teacher. The influence of my parents and my religious beliefs as a member of the Bahá'í Faith were the sources of my high regard for the teaching profession. Our writings declare, "The education and training of children is among the most meritorious acts of humankind." My parents instilled in me the extreme importance of an education and an educator's high station of service. Teaching is one of the noblest and most praise-worthy of all professions.

Through my experiences as a student, I was privileged to benefit from many outstanding teachers that have served as role models for my career as an educator. Embedded in my heart and mind are the spirit and dedication of these teachers. The qualities these teachers possessed made a lasting impression on me. High expectations, high standards, and genuine concern for students.

At present, I find the educational system and attitude of students in a state of emergency. I'm alarmed, appalled, and shocked with horror when I hear black students inform me, "Yeah, getting good grades and being smart are 'acting white.'" What's up with that? What are we as a society teaching our youth? It's certainly not the message that black children learned when I a child.

I feel that today it continues, that many black students are unsuccessful in our schools because they are not hearing crucial messages from their teachers. "I love you." "I care about you." "You belong." "You are somebody." "You can accomplish whatever you dream of." These were the basics of instruction in the black schools. Let's get back to these basics! Then educators can begin to make a true impact on students.

18

"Momma, I Hate White People!"

What brings a young white girl to one particular day, when she blurts out just as matter-a-factly to her mother, "I hate White People?" What brings a person to a point in their life where they truly despise their own race? I passionately and truly felt this way during my years as an adolescent. As if just going through the stage of adolescence weren't enough. I had taken my mother slightly aback as I emphatically bleated out this proclamation to her. Being a mother to such a multitude of children, this was hardly her first or last problematic situation to resolve. And even knowing what had spurred this venom out, she ever so warmly and calmly responded as only she could, "Well, Lynn don't you love the Bahá'ís? There are white Bahá'ís." She also knew how to grab a hold of my heart and my intellect within the same breath and moment in time. If she ever mentioned God or the Bahá'í Faith, she knew full well where my deepest grounding and foundation lie. And it would pull me back to reality.

"But! Mom they're different." (Referring to the Bahá'ís that happened to be white.) Since I had had to learn to deal and operate within a system based on race, I had developed my own personal strategy of categorizing and classifying people. (This was definitely a survival skill in the South during these times.) There were black people, white people, and Bahá'ís. And as far as the Bahá'ís went, I never had to break them down into boxes. That wasn't necessary. From all my past experiences and dealings with members of the Bahá'í Faith, they truly existed as one people. And if they weren't forming distinctions amongst themselves, why would I have? Of course, the Bahá'í Faith had always taught and practiced their fundamental belief, the Oneness of Mankind. (The Bahá'í Faith had been integrated since its founding in 1863 in Iran. And what I found so uncanny is that the year of the Emancipation Proclamation in America, which abolished slavery, was none other than the same year—1863. Sometimes God's work and His plan is such a mystery to us. Other times it just slaps us silly in the face.)

Yet truly what brought me to this point of expressing such hatred and contempt when I had been raised to love all God's children? I believe it was having now the undeniable exposure of living within the daily realms of and bouts with racism. Here I had come from complete naïveté as a child living in northern Michigan now catapulted and submerged within a black southern environment and lifestyle. I think it would be natural for me to be processing and internalizing quite a bit of racially discriminatory data in my memory bank. You see that saying, "You don't understand a man until you walk in another man's shoes," we have all learned in some aspect is oh so true. Basically that's what I did, "walked almost my entire life in another man's shoes." And it wasn't quite a smooth stroll or pretty depiction of life. I really saw firsthand and felt the discrimination and degradation thrust upon black people in their daily living. As if life in itself doesn't have enough turmoil. And one thing I could never begin to fathom was the "why" of it all. Just "why?" Simply because of a color of our skin. My totally analytic mind could never begin to comprehend. So it really infuriates me when mainstream society makes implications that racism and discrimination do not exist. How could they possibly know? When have they ever walked in those shoes?

Oh how I've gotten more than a good glimpse, actually a good dowsing and drowning. All the way back to Miss Beatty's fourth grade class at Beaufort Elementary. When my little unknowingly, already-brainwashed classmates informed me that I couldn't play with black children. And I mean, just what was that? Who were they to tell me what I could or could not do and with or without whom? I liked their nerve. But they were simply miniature representatives of the bigger versions at home, the lines of authority that wove and interlocked into one huge monster of a longtime, ingrained and entrenched system. And this was the exact time and place in my life where I felt the thorny bush of hatred begin to germinate and flourish within my being. I'm not happy or proud to say this, but I saw this as a natural cause and effect of its progression.

Later I realized, but for the complete grace of God that I was raised within a home that taught love and unity of all people. For I could have just as easily been born into any other home. We don't control from whence we come, but we certainly do control our destination.

Yet as a young girl and adolescent, there were many a night I prayed to God that He would grant me my highest wish and aspiration that He would turn me black. With the smoothest milk chocolate skin and the most beautifully-crafted Afro with a good grade of nap that would hold a carefully-picked natural. That was my prayer. (And at one point in my life, I just couldn't resist temptations any longer. Since I couldn't grow an Afro, I endured the seven hours it took for my sister Felicia to braid my very too-long hair into a multitude of waist-length corn-rows, complete with beads.) But really I just wanted to have a "place." I have loved the place of "blackness" and the St. Helena community accepted me, but I wanted to really be a true part.

Besides, all I had seen thus far in "whiteness" represented racist views of hatred and negativity in regard to blacks. Thereon in, I purposely dressed differently and presented myself in a unique style and manner for fear least there be any interpretation or affiliation with a group of people such as that. Besides they certainly didn't want me. And hey I didn't care for them too tough at this point either. I figured I'd just let them be in their white world and just let me be in my black world. But if the Lord would only make me black it might work out a little simpler. (Not to mention later in life when it was time to get a husband. Now that was complicated.)

And so many things from that moment on stabbed into me from the depths of a racist society. Why when I watched television at night with my older stepsisters or Grammy, there barely ever appeared a black person's face on the screen? Of course growing up in Petoskey, Michigan in my little middle-class white family, it never even crossed my mind. But once I began walking in these new shoes across new paths, I'm like something's not right here. I'm asking my stepsisters, how can you stand to watch TV with sometimes not a single black actor or actress to be seen the entire night, sometimes the entire week? This was messed up!

Or when we walked into a bank, why was there *never* a black bank teller to greet us and handle our money and our bank transactions? Or yet on the other hand, heaven forbid the picture when I got to Clemson University and I promise I'm not exaggerating, out of a janitorial staff of several hundred they were entirely black. Not a white face in the entire place, not when it came to cleaning up. That was conveniently reserved for blacks. Yet almost every class you entered on campus, had a white American or foreigner's face at the front podium. I could count the black professors practically on one hand.

And don't mention the looks of wretched disgust and contempt for my family as we walked down the street, entered a store, stopped for gas, or walked into a restaurant. Really any time we made a move outside the black community of St. Helena Island or the Bahá'í community. Any move we made in public, all eyes were on us. And as I said, they were usually quite menacing looks and looks of disdain. Or the simple never-ending stares of total disbelief.

I'll never forget an old white woman at a McDonald's in Columbia, South Carolina. On this venture, my boyfriend OJ and I had gone to get some lunch while I was there for the weekend visiting him. We were parked in the car in the McDonald's lot eating, when I felt these eyes glued upon me. Sure enough when I looked up, an elderly lady sitting under an umbrella at one of the outside tables was staring me down. I gave her the once over. Then I came back a second time. Home girl was still in a permanent and unyielding trance focused on me. I had to do something to pull her out of that comatose state. So I began staring back at her for what seemed an eternity. Usually this little tactic would work and break the spell. This time it failed. Wow! What next? I was grabbing for straws. So without much thought, I stuck my tongue out at her. Yes, I did. I don't know. It was complete desperation. But all I know it did work and she finally snapped out of it, remembered her home training and proper etiquette, and got her eyes the heck on off me.

But we never had too many casualties worst than that. And if there were times when my family and I were in danger, I certainly wasn't cognizant of it. This is probably the time in my life when I learned so well how to walk into a room and be fully unaware of who is there and whether or not they were looking at me. And I certainly couldn't be concerned as to what they thought of me and whether they liked me or not. This I learned at an early age. So to this day, watch me as I enter a room, particularly a large room where I don't know everyone. I automatically replay this coping mechanism of unawareness and aloofness. It's not done by design. It's simply a survival tactic I developed back during these days of constant stares of disdain and disapproval.

Racism continued to knock at my door and slap me in the face. Always. It just refused to go away. And the far greatest infliction was the economic and employment thing. Here a black person, would have the necessary education and all the qualifications and certifications, but there would always be an excuse for not hiring. As James Brown so simply but emphatically declared to America, "I don't want nobody to give me nothin'. Open up the door, I'll get it myself." How much simpler can a message come?

And unfortunately the bulk of my absorption of rounds with racism was encountered in the South. (Yet I'm hardly so naïve to believe that the Northern or Western segments of our fair country are racist-free realms. My memory will always take a hyperlink to my aunts and uncles' tantrums thrown when my mom remarried. And of course I was kind of too young when I lived in the North to have digested racism yet.) So what remains is that my most vivid racist encounters were of a Southern flavor.

And the remnants of all the stereotypes I still house in my closets stem from these experiences. Some of the symbols I equate with racism are pretty weird and far-fetched, but they still make me cringe, a slight chill runs down my back, and a radar of suspicion and skepticism emerges. And I realize full well these are unsubstantiated, biased, and downright prejudiced stereotypes. Evidently something or some experiences along my life developed these little mental faux pases inside my head. So when I look at things from the other side and put myself in the other man's shoes, I readily see how someone else can come up with some of their same type of stupid little misconceptions just as well. And I'm telling you, subconsciously something jabs me in the ribs each time I encounter one of them. And I'll give you just a glimmer of some of these "things" that get to me. The twangs and belts of country western music, even including Charlie Pride. The high-pitched and draggin' Dixie drawl of some southern accents. High-on-the-hog, up-in-the-sky, monster-wheeled trucks. Plaid shirts of any color or concept. Even a house with columns or pillars on the front porch. (Way too much like the master's old plantation house I've seen in movies during the days of slavery.) And I realize that these encounters and visions do not represent a racist person, but unfortunately they send my mind reeling and wondering. It's like an antenna goes up and I have to catch myself in order to return to a normalcy in my evaluative and rationale thinking patterns.

But one symbol I can't control in my thought process is that doggone Confederate flag! And I know that's a whole story unto itself. But it sends me into an immediate and involuntary convulsion. I am hardly ever successful in battling with myself in the persuasion that the person in the vehicle or in the house with this Southern badge of the Confederacy could possibly not be sending out a clear message of love for the Confederate States. Not when their way of life in these states was a thriving economy based solely on the barbaric rites of slavery. I know there's exceptions to every rule. But why would someone even want to be remotely confused with being a racist or proponent of this dreadful system? I don't get it. And one day I'm going to have to be crazy enough to walk a little nearer to those paths, I don't think I can do the shoe thing. But I would like to have somewhat of an understanding with the true proponents of "It's not hatred. It's heritage." If these people truly do exist. I mean I have some German heritage, but I don't get the urge to fly the Nazi flag on my front porch or sport a Nazi car tag. So one day that will be my challenge to attempt to understand.

I've had to face myself head-on and truthfully, regarding my own racist and prejudice views. I realize my prejudices are a little uncanny and different for you don't find too many people that are prejudiced against their own people. And if you've grown up in American society, believe me, you are not prejudice free either. It's probably just a different turn on things. We have definitely all encountered misjudgments and misconceptions based on the cover of a book after opening and reading the contents. But I challenge you to call yourself on it each time you find yourself guilty of a narrow-minded and unfounded bias, to stop yourself dead in your tracks and make a rational and fact-based conclusion rather than one based on what society has misfed us. And for myself after many maturing experiences, I finally came to a point in my life where I didn't hate any longer.

Now I always thought growing up in two cultures was a great advantage. And I still believe that, but there are some down sides that accompany that bounty.

The price you many times pay is not fitting in or not belonging. Which I have found, as emotionally independent as I am, I oftentimes suffer from loneliness. I "think" I'm an "island," but that basic need of belonging often attacks me unexpectedly and relentlessly during my deepest moments of solitude. Not that I've ever sensed a shame of who I've now evolved into. But only the need and desire remains to so desperately belong.

You see I always thought that I just happened to have the personality to be a loner. And today it hit me hard like a hammer. I've been a loner not by choice. But frankly I just don't belong anywhere. There's no niche or category where I truly belong. Famed jazz musician, Doc Holladay, entitled his autobiography in reference to this phenomenon, "Life on the Fence" in which he tells of his life as a white jazz musician amid a jazz world in which many of his colleagues and surroundings would be predominantly black.

This Fence is a firm reality. Just watch children in general, as they follow their progression of schooling. Oh now in elementary they may all play together. Most of them don't even know or care what color their little friend is. Then before elementary school is completed, they now refer to this one and that one as black or white. And yes they may still have their little outings and sleepovers together, but they are beginning this fitting in with the Fence System. By middle school you begin to see the separation. And by high school the System has succeeded. All the white kids now hang exclusively together. All the black kids now hang together. With only a few minor exceptions of those who can think for themselves and refuse to buy into the System. This is not a hunch of mine, but unfortunately a stark reality. If you say I'm wrong, don't kid yourself. Just look into any school cafeteria in the country. Just look at the kids your kid is friends with. And most times they have been totally transformed before they realize they've been bamboozled. The sad thing is that sometimes the System is so successful that they never do notice they've been had.

Or don't even mention the people that don't mesh with either side of our society's two-sided system with the fence or railroad thing. Such as Hispanics, Asians, Native Americans, Jews, Arabs, or even multi-ethnic peoples.

And recently my niece who is also interracial like my son, queried him after his first fall semester at Clemson University. "What! So you're not black enough, Jack?" So when Jack returned home for his spring break, and proudly makes statements such as "People think I'm black" (rather than mixed). And "A lot of people on campus know me. Black campus that is." Or also "I'll be living in the dorm called 'Chocolate City' this fall."—I now know the real reason why I'm happy and I smile through and through for my child.

He is able to belong! (Something that definitely never happened at Clemson when I was a student there and still hasn't happened.) I don't think I recall that feeling since those blissful and carefree days of being a student and member of the band at St. Helena School.

There is fortunately one other group where I do belong and that is universally people embracing. It's amongst the Bahá'í World Community for being a refuge amongst a world of hatred and discrimination. Thank God for them. Truly! The Bahá'í Faith and its members have been such a blessing for so many of us now and in the future that are caught "on the fence" without a side to take. Thank you Lord for Your new revelation for today. That we must truly love one another unconditionally regardless of race, religion, or background. Just judge me on my personality, my attributes, and my virtues, please. Or as Dr. King so eloquently phrased his proposed plea, "I have a dream that my four children will one day live in a nation where they will not be judged by the color of their skin but by the content of their character."

To ensure that this "one day" soon arrives, the Bahá'í writings admonishes the blacks and whites of America. "Let neither think that the solution of so vast a problem is a matter that exclusively concerns the other. Let neither think that a problem can either easily or immediately be resolved. Let neither think that they can wait confidently for the solution of this problem until the initiative has been taken, and the favorable circumstances created, by agencies outside the orbit of their Faith. Let neither think that anything short of genuine love, extreme patience, true humility, consummate tact, sound initiative, mature wisdom, and deliberate, persistent, and prayerful effort, can succeed in blotting out the stain which this patent evil has left on the fair name of their common country."

And in closing this chapter, I must close on this note. Yes, I do accept that the Lord created me just the way He meant for me to be. There was a reason for me to be a white person living in a black world. And part of that reason is for me to have the experiences and abilities to make the statements and challenges to Americans about racism that I'm making in this book. Yes, I do still have a small fantasy in the back of my mind that it certainly would be so cool to really be totally black through and through from the outside in. But no I don't hate myself for actually being white on the outside. And on the lighter side of things, there are many white people I think are rather attractive. Just ask my husband my feelings on Jean Claude Van Dam or George Clooney, the gray-headed knock out from Batman.

But back on a serious note and another even more paramount statement. In taking account of myself and my actions for that's one of our moral obligations, and particularly since you can't truly control anyone else, I've come to terms with the racism within me. Thank God that I've matured and grown in intellect and spirit to know within myself that no I don't any longer "hate white people," not even racist persons whom I once would have referred to simply as "redneck bigots." I must love all people. That's God's request and requirement. Don't get me wrong, many things prejudiced people do, I do I hate, but I can't hate them as a person. For all people are part of God's creation. And love is truly the strongest power on earth if we'd only use it. So I thank God for my journey in life thus far and for giving me the enlightenment and wisdom to love.

19

A Test of Faith: "Why Richard?"

One of the most life-altering experiences of my life was the day my brother Richard became a quadriplegic for the remainder of his life. And this is a day I even dared to think about questioning God. That summer I was soon to be a rising senior at Beaufort High. Working hard, saving hard for graduation day, and soon to breakaway to college. Frolicking in all the fun these fanciful thoughts of soon-to-be independence brought me. But all those thoughts and idle imaginings soon came to a screeching halt, the moment my brain comprehended the words this news brought to me, "Richard has broken his neck and is paralyzed." Such a simply put statement. Oh but where my mind and soul were off and running to.

I'd heard of other families in newspapers, in magazines, on the television news reports, or in movies, suffering such an unfair blow in life. And even after going through the experience of my father's drowning, nothing hit me as hard as this thunderously collapsing skyscraper. Why had God allowed this to happen to Richard? Why was our family going through this insurmountable grief and pain? What had he done wrong? What had we done wrong? How could this have happened? To us? These things only happened to strangers. Never within your actual real family. Why? Why? Why?

Richard was only 21 years old. Just out of the Navy. Just beginning his life. So I couldn't begin to stop asking why?

On the day of the accident, July of 1973, Richard was swimming and diving with friends at a swimming hole on Lady's Island. Trying to get a rope down from a tree, he decided to dive into the water. Hitting a shallow area, his neck was broken, and he was immediately paralyzed—a quadriplegic. The doctors didn't know if he would survive this injury. Initially he was in the Intensive Care Unit of the Medical University Hospital, and then the Veterans Hospital in Charleston, and later the Veterans Spinal Cord Injury Unit of Rehabilitation in Richmond, Virginia for months upon months, rehabilitating. But how do you ever truly ever rehabilitate from a total loss of your power to be ambulatory and independent?

The early years of Richard's life he had grown up in a beautiful ski resort area in northern Michigan, an excellent setting for a young man who loved outdoor activities. Richard had played little league baseball, enjoyed swimming, snow skied, went snowmobiling, tobogganed, ice skated, and played hockey. During his junior high and high school years, he continued to enjoy outdoor activities; he wrestled and pole-vaulted. Also he enjoyed some of the benefits that his new home in South Carolina provided, swimming and body surfing in the ocean.

Being such an outdoor-loving young man, Richard had chosen to serve in the Navy, just as his father had. Being an exceptional swimmer, he was an Underwater Demolition Team diver. He was assigned to the U.S.S. Farragut and went on a Goodwill Tour to South America. One of the unique and memorable occasions of Richard's Navy career was when he crossed the equator on August 13, 1972. He went through quite a grueling initiation into the "Solemn Mysteries of the Ancient Order of the Deep." He spoke in depth recounting the details of this event; his framed certification of this induction always displayed proudly in his room.

Even after leaving the Navy, Richard's theme of enjoying the outdoors continued with obtaining employment as a roofer with Pinckney Roofing Company of Beaufort. All this is to say, Richard loved the outdoors and loved to be on the move. Where else was he when it all went down. Outdoors in the fresh summer air, enjoying swimming and diving into the water with his buddies from work. That was Richard; always enjoying the outdoors.

First day I laid eyes on Richard after the accident left me powerless. I've always been the faint one at the sight of blood, when indulging needles, feeling the pain even in others, the smell when entering a hospital, visiting the doctor, or just talking about any of the above. In other words I'm a complete ninny when it comes to illness and suffering. So you can imagine when I walked into that intensive care unit. There's my big, strong, athletic brother—helpless. They'd shaved his head completely bald and he was uncomfortably situated on a small-stretcher-looking thing, barely even wide enough to hold his body, which I quickly learned, was called a gurney. Of course there were tubes and machines making continuous readings that were running in every direction possible. And lastly, though my mother did forewarn me, but I still wasn't prepared, my eyes and mind synchronized to comprehend just what it was to have two steel rods going into either side of his head directly into his skull. This was to ensure that there was zero movement, which could have the possibility of fatal damage before they did surgery. That was once he was stable enough to endure that next procedure.

Well, I kept a prayer going in my heart and mind to give me the strength to last the five minutes allowed for me to stay and for him to be aware of my presence and support. As soon as I receded to the hospital corridor, every bit of the strength I had mustered up fled my body. And I immediately passed out cold on the deck. Momma was concerned but not surprised. That was my normal reaction to far, far less. She was simply astonished that I had endured at all. She had gravely warned me of the danger of me passing out and jarring his delicate and fragile position in the least. But I had vowed to her that I would rise to the occasion. And I did it with His helping Hands.

But life doesn't give you long to ask why, why, why. It's immediately time to pray, pray, pray as you do, do, do. So I proceeded to pray and do as I responded to the immediate and desperate needs of the family. Momma needless to say, rode in the ambulance directly from the scene of where the accident occurred, a small, man-made lagoon now posted "Off-limits." She accompanied Richard by his side through the 70-mile ambulance ride and the initial two months of his hospitalization in intensive care at the Medical University Hospital in Charleston. From the initial news of his accident, she was gone. Never did she come home once until she was assured that his condition had stabilized and he had been moved to a regular room. Even with which she still remained weary. Who would check behind the nurses to ensure that the doctors' orders had been executed in rotating that gurney on time and without fail? Finally she felt he was on a capable and reliable schedule. So now she would come home for a night or two to sleep in a bed rather than halfway napping in the hospital chair by his gurney's side. Nothing like a momma to be there for you.

That was a rough year for us all, including me. I was a senior in high school taking a full load that year, so long before I ever became a career-working mom; time management had already come into play in a large way at this time. I was the oldest at home so the weight fell on me. I drove the 90-minute drive up to Charleston and back each day to take Momma fresh clothes, toiletries, food, money as it was available, and complete any other necessary transactions. Then when I got home, it was my younger brothers and sisters to care for. My baby brother probably being about a year and a half at the time, the rest of the crew preschool age, and Sally in Junior High. So the two of us ran the household. Meals, household duties, bedtime routines, bathing, fixing hair, and getting the younger ones off to school. I think now, how did I ever do it and manage to maintain straight A's? A lot of prayer saw me through. I needed all the power and strength available to me.

Some other feeble attempts at assistance were en route. Richard's wife, Sharon, who had mysteriously and rapidly appeared as she had disappeared from his life during his three-year stint in the Navy, including a "Dear John" letter while at sea. They had jumped in and out of marriage as quick as the latest fads that accompanied their teenage years, being only 17 and 18 with an infant on the way. Crazy. Plumb crazy. They were mere babies themselves. Certainly they were not equipped for the strain of marriage, a child, and a long distance relationship as newlyweds. Things weren't working out during the "good times," and now things had hit rock bottom during the "bad times" with a husband being totally paralyzed from the chest down. So I give her credit. She gave it a try for almost a year. But it was really almost too much even to handle for mature partners in a lengthy and stable marriage.

Next arrived my brother Tom who was the closest in age and relationships to Richard. He flew in from Germany, being there stationed in the Army. Since he didn't have much of his three-year obligation to Uncle Sam remaining on the books, the Army graced him with an early discharge, taking the gravity of the emergency into account. Of course that was wonderful moral support for Richard, having his closest brother by his side. They had been through a lot in life already together. And this was yet a higher hurdle to scale.

You see when we lost our father during our childhood, Tom and Richard were in their early adolescence. As if traversing the rough and jagged path of puberty and adolescence weren't enough in themselves. Thereupon came our father's death, my mother's remarriage, relocating to a totally divergent locale, losing old friends, making new ones, a new father, a new family, dealing with a complete change in cultures, and coping with the South's racism. That was a total overload for Tom and Richard, resulting in a foundation of rather turbulent teenage years.

And my brothers never handled it well to put it mildly. Oh how they did rebel. They ran away on numerous occasions, including the "permanent borrowing" of our stepfather's car. They smoked, they drank, and did drugs. They cut school and eventually dropped out. They hung out with all the wrong people in all the wrong places. And as a direct result headed straight to jail. Fortunately at that time, many judges allowed juveniles a second chance by going into the armed forces as early as 17. So Tom ended up in the Army for his three years and Richard in the Navy for his three. The military was a good remedy for it afforded my brothers the necessary structure and discipline in their lives that they had fallen between the cracks, with a deceased father and an unaccepted replacement.

They completed their GED's for they undeniably were very intelligent, just lacked someone to keep them on the straight and narrow. They finally learned enough responsibility to hold down a job. And shortly thereafter, even dropped the poor-choices in leisure time that they had acquired.

Of course later I did begin to see the "why" for this unimaginable and unbelievable event in our lives. This close vision of the life hereafter, first hand for Richard and close enough to be first hand for Tom, had an immediate change of their view of life. Richard later confessed that this accident that almost took his life, actually had in truth saved his life.

Richard had always been extremely strong physically and mentally. But now began his spiritual growth and development to an equal level of strength. And unquestioning evidence in God was how he exceptionally survived this ordeal. I don't know how many of us could have endured such a test, for the next 22 years Richard was for the most part confined to his bed. But he was not bitter and angry at the world. In fact, Richard had a very humorous personality and fun-loving spirit.

On any occasion you visited Richard, his room would always be cold and "windy," for he always insisted on having a fan circulating—(no actually blowing air directly on him). He said this was one of his ways of escaping mentally to outdoors (which he loved so much).

Richard had always been very strong mentally. Though he had only completed his formal schooling with a G.E.D., everyone that knew him, knew his knowledge and education far surpassed the high school level, and perhaps even that of college. As a youth he had been an unbeatable chess player. After his accident, he also became extremely proficient and capable with his many computers and computer components. He was fascinated with and appreciated languages, and was self-taught in the Japanese language. (I never asked him why. But knowing Richard, perhaps he wanted to read computer manuals directly in Japanese, rather than the English translation.)

Richard also enjoyed reading several genres of literature: fantasy, legends, science fiction, mythology, and particularly philosophy. Richard, I would say, was a philosopher in his own right. For anyone that has ever attempted to converse with him in one his "deep" conversations, would concur fully with this.

Richard's most significant strength was acquired thanks to his accident, his spiritual strength. Instead of taking his condition of paralysis as a handicap, he used it as an asset. He focused on spiritual development. He began an in-depth study of the Bahá'í writings and encouraged the Bahá'í community in their studies of the Writings. He initiated and facilitated for the Baha'i Community, a study class of our most holy book, the Kitáb-i-Aqdas (The Book of Laws). This was a study class that had been firmly established and a constant for the community.

In closing this chapter dedicated to the memory of my brother Richard who passed February 28th of 1995, I now must explain to you the special strength, guidance, and relationship he provided to young people. The children held a very special place in their hearts for Richard and he treated them as his own and truly believed it is the total community's obligation to raise and develop children. True to the words, "It takes a village to raise a child."   .

Richard provided strong fatherly guidance and direction to myself and my brothers and sisters who were the youngest in the family, particularly after my mother became a single parent and head of household for a second go round in her life. He counseled, advised, scolded, and chastised as needed; yet was always patient with us, understanding, and had a listening ear. Even after the younger siblings grew up, he continued this role with our children, his nieces and nephews. He taught them how to play chess (which his nephews tribute their Uncle Richard to this day for teaching them and engage in ongoing matches), worked and played on the computer with them, watched science-fiction and action movies on the television with them, even cartoons to their delight, and fussed with them when they got out of hand. Richard always had patience and kindness coupled with sternness.

I dearly miss Richard's physical presence in our lives, but rejoice in the knowledge that he is no longer constrained physically and is now able to soar to unlimited heights in the spiritual world. Spiritually he is still within all of us and his guiding presence will always be.

20

At Clemson, Trying to Find the Beat

As the family station wagon pulls off from the entrance of Manning Hall, with a large majority of my life within it (my mother, my stepfather, my three younger sisters, and my two youngest brothers), I'm thinking what have I gotten myself into. Here I was in a totally new world soon to be immersed in something I had never really encountered much of, a white Southern environment. I was entirely unprepared, both socially and psychologically, and otherwise. A little note here: "Never choose a college on academic merits alone." Unfortunately this did not occur to me until it was too late. In my case, as usual, I was out to prove myself. Based on my lack of finances, I had opted to choose a state-supported college within the state of South Carolina. Then based upon my SAT test results, I researched as to which of these institutions would offer the most difficult challenge academically.

It was Clemson. Little did I know the limitless challenges it would provide far beyond the scope of academics. For as far as the majority of my coursework, it was rather lacking in vigor. Again in comparing black and white schools, even on the post secondary level, there undeniably was a fallacy in the stringency of Clemson University's educational challenge.

One of the most beneficial reasons for a black student to attend a predominantly white university is the image this represents to mainstream society as well as the networking developed in their chosen field. Later giving them an edge in securing employment in a predominantly white-run job market. Yet the downside is missing out on the wealth of socialization and support available at a black institution. As I so very soon found out.

One of my first tasks in settling into room 9B-1 on the ninth floor of Manning Hall, was to get some grasp of the old and familiar. So after unpacking, I painstakingly arranged a collage of all my family members on the bulletin board beside my study desk. Of course, it was quite a few pictures because I wanted to be able to glance up at any moment I began to feel a twinge of "missing them" and they'd all be right there in front of me to comfort me. I never really thought about it because that was simply my family, but it was rather a diverse spectrum of complexions, from the rather deep dark chocolate, to the rich caramel color, and last but not least, me—French vanilla. Now that I had that "security blanket" in tact, I ventured out about campus.

Later on, I finally met up with my roommate, Lisa. Lisa was an upperclassman, a junior. I had corresponded with her once during the summer to introduce myself, but that was about the extent of it thus far. The suite mates had already informed Lisa that she had a black roommate, based on the faces of my family that had helped me move in. Then confirmation to her was the photo collage of multi-colored hues and tones of my family members so triumphantly displayed on my board. Needless to say, she didn't seem overwhelmed so that proved to be a good sign. For let me tell you I would need a friend or two, to pull me through some of the bumpy hills that lay ahead.

Lisa Kaminer grew up in the capital city of Columbia, South Carolina and her extended family was from Chapin, South Carolina. Therefore she was definitely a white South Carolinian girl, but not in my formerly stereotypical understanding. (As we all realize by time we've gained any sense of wisdom in this world, many things happen in life for a reason. Well, I wasn't at Clemson University by mere chance.) If you may have recalled, I wasn't to fond of "white people," particularly from the south, and that's putting it nicely. I for the most part truly felt that I despised them. A large part of my education to be gained at Clemson was in the realm of understanding whites and of course I reciprocated this with exposing my new white friends with acquainting themselves with my black friends and family. Now this was unfamiliar ground for both parties involved, Lisa as well as myself.

Lisa being a junior, already had a boyfriend in the vicinity. Jimmy lived off campus so she split her time between hanging out with him and hanging out with me and some of her other friends in the suite. When we did hang out, we might play cards, listen to music, go to campus activities, go eat, go to the movies, or shop some. But not shop that much. Lisa wasn't big on clothes and I didn't have the money. But we did have a commonality which most people share, but from different perspectives. She loved music and so did I, but of course they were quite different worlds. Lisa enjoyed rock and my love was rhythm and blues or as we called it then, "Soul Music." So we'd take turns listening to albums on her turntable. She'd play the Doobie Brothers, and then I'd play the O-Jays. Prior to my Clemson days, I hadn't even heard of the Doobie Brothers. So we were both broadening our exposures. And one of the greatest gifts in music exposure I received from Lisa was being introduced to Carole King and her "Tapestry" album. What a musical delight that I soon would treasure. Carole King produced such raspy, soul-stirring melodies I grew to idolize and adore.

Now even though many times, I didn't have a hanging buddy, I didn't let that stop me from adventuring. So during our first week of college, the university sponsored a street dance to welcome the freshmen. What a welcome! A Rock and Roll band. And my sole diet of music during junior high and high school had been "soul music." Being deathly allergic to hard rock, I told myself it would be all right, that I did indeed need to be open to new experiences and I would grow to appreciate them. Wasn't this all part of college? So I reluctantly trudged from Manning Hall over to the parking lot of the Sikes Hall administration building where the dance was underway. Being a huge dance lover and suffering withdrawals from no dancing for the last week or so, I made my way into the crowd to immerse myself in my #1 pastime—Dancing! (This was to be one of my first and greatest educational lessons at Clemson.)

Since I had never really listened to rock music, I got out there and as any dancer unconsciously does, listened for the beat. Well, was I in for a rude awakening. I couldn't determine a beat so unaccustomed and out of touch was my sense of hearing in this new and foreign environment. All through high school, I had prided myself in being a great dancer. I could go into any black nightclub and hang with the best dancers there. The simple task of dancing on the beat was never a worry or concern. But suddenly now it was. I refused to give in. I kept moving about, trying to adapt all my best moves, groves, and gyrations to this music. After an hour or so of complete failure, I came to the conclusion that there was no apparent, discernible beat that I had the ability to hear. And I also concluded that maybe this could be the reason that a large majority of white people experience difficulty "dancing to the beat." If white people are accustomed to dancing to rock music, then when they try to dance to rhythm and blues, they are still accustomed to hearing the rock music and therefore can't dance to the beat. A major revelation in "things that make you go hmmm!"

An abundance of learning experiences continued to manifest themselves during my collegiate days. Sun tanning was another one of the top priorities amongst coeds. Since Manning Hall was a ten-story, high-rise dorm, many of the residents were avid participants of the sun worship ritual that was held on the roof of the building. In fact, after taking the elevator to the tenth floor and exiting a door to the rooftop, there was an actual deck built here for the distinct purpose of sunbathing. I was nonetheless amazed by the extremely calculated offering of an area specifically constructed for students to suntan. No other purpose, but to suntan. Very intriguing.

Me always yearning to be black, or at least mixed, with a more appealing skin tone, I was definitely down with the concept of darkening my skin. So on my first available sunny free afternoon, I sojourned on pilgrimage to the sun temple atop Manning Hall, joining all the other adherents and disciples that were scantily clad and laid out in sacrifice upon the planks of the wooden deck. The smell of coconut ascended from these glistening bodies drenched in Hawaiian Tropics suntan oil. And sunscreen was definitely not a vitally sought after ingredient in tanning products at this time since the public, certainly knew nothing of a hole forming in the Ozone. And there I lay greased down in Coppertone, soaking up the rays. Happy as a clam, knowing that each moment that I bask in the sun's radiance, the darker and more beautiful my skin would become. Oh happy day. I religiously made the proper amount of flips in lying position, from back to stomach and top to back, to ensure an even coloring of my pigment. But one thing I either didn't realize or had forgotten was that heat makes you sleepy as all get out.

So after having fallen asleep for what must have been a few hours after making the final flip to my back, I awoke realizing that I had overstayed my visit with the sun. My skin was definitely a reddish hot pink. And boy was I in excruciating pain. I had endured a mild sunburn or two before, but this felt somewhat worse for my eyes were swollen and puffy to such a point that I could barely open them.

Well I was soon to encounter Miss Louise as my wounded body staggered back to my dorm room. Miss Louise was the maid assigned to ninth floor. She was my daily connection and warm touch with a dose of blackness. She had become a friend and like a mother away from home. So when Miss Betty laid eyes upon me, she sure blest me out. "What you doing up on that deck with those white girls? You don't know nothin' about that. They're up there frying their bodies to a crisp! Look at you. Can't even open your eyes. You've got sun poisoning. Go get some cold compresses for your eyes. And don't you ever let me catch you up there again!" I learned my first important lesson at Clemson, follow all sun tanning rules faithfully, including a foundation law that one must fully respect and honor the strength and power of the sun.

Now don't think that I had never had any experience at all with tanning, but yes it was extremely limited. My family, particularly my mother, loved to go on family outings to the beach to swim. But tanning was definitely not the purpose of our family expeditions and I was rather ignorant about this activity called sun tanning. I don't even recall owning suntan lotion or oil prior to college. And believe me, my black siblings and friends had no intentions of further deepening their skin tone. In fact, the ideal time of day for blacks to frequent the beach was the late afternoons and evenings as the sun began its early trek of descent for the day. And from avid sun tanners, I learned that mid-day when the sun was at its highest epoch, was the greatest intensity of sun absorbing time. (In fact, I thought if you stayed at the beach long enough, it was fun to watch the beach turn from totally "white" in the early part of the day to eventually all "black" as the day progressed.) But nonetheless, such was my first serious endeavor with sun tanning.

Much of my first year at Clemson was spent engulfed in my studies, trying to ensure that I aced every course and beat out as many classmates as possible. My goal was to continue to prove my worthiness as a student educated in black public schools with just as much if not more knowledge as those white students from the vast array of private schools throughout the south. Of course, once I uncovered the true worth of most privately founded southern schools and academies, I found them to be virtually worthless in exceeding public schools.

For the foremost reason of the rapid outgrowth of these institutions in the late 60's and early 70's was in direct and immediate response to court-mandated integration of public schools. And this was one of the South's answers to ensuring the continued propagation of segregation. It definitely wasn't to provide improved educational instruction, as I soon learned firsthand, as I ran circles around the products of these institutions, their students. Now in encountering them in classes at Clemson, they certainly had proven to yield no competition.

Yet in my free time that I did find at Clemson, I soon found that the campus didn't offer me much in terms of enjoyment and socialization. The drinking age at this time was 18 so much of the entertainment focused on drinking, "beer busts," and concerts that made beer heavily available. Needless to say, a non-drinker and dancer who loved soul music, amidst these thousands of drunks at a blue grass or rock music beer bust, was like finding an oyster in thirst of water in the middle of the Sahara desert. I certainly did not fit into the scene, nor did I want to. After a few meager attempts, I did not want to endure these agonizing and torturous engagements. I therefore, gladly found refuge in the home with a circle of friends and activities of my dear childhood friend, Ingrid.

Ingrid lived five miles away from Clemson University in the small town of Pendleton, and she also worked as a secretary for the engineering department on campus. We had known each other through the Bahá'í Faith and enjoyed each other's friendship at many conferences we had attended through the years. So we rekindled our friendship, and thankfully "the girl" (that's me) was saved. And don't let the name Ingrid fool you, Ingrid was black. At last a refuge and environment that I was familiar and at home with. So we would meet each day in Schilletter Dining Hall for lunch. And seeing she worked in the engineering department, which was comprised of a large enrollment of foreign students, particularly in the graduate department, our table at lunch often appeared to be perhaps a committee of the United Nations. And just like the small amount of blacks stuck together on campus so did the foreign students. So I soon met a large array of students from across the globe. There was our soon to be close friend, Abdul from India. Then another friend that I remained friends with throughout my entire bachelors and masters degrees was Tems from Nigeria. During my years at Clemson, I must have had friends from at least every continent.

Ingrid and I were fortunately not limited to a superficial "lunch-only" friendship. Ingrid welcomed me totally into her family, home, and life. I was a new member of the Jackson Family at 2-20 Crenshaw Street. The large part of my weekends, I would spend at Ingrid's apartment in the small housing project of Pendleton, hanging out with her and her two young daughters, Yolanda and Denise. Ingrid would cook. And my favorite of hers which I had never had prior was Rice-a-roni. (Don't laugh, but I had never eaten much "boxed" foods. Most of the food I'd eaten being raised on a farm was "made from scratch.") Our favorite board game at the time, was Boggle. Ingrid loved this word game and we would always play it. And many times we would just hang out watching TV. Not to mention the fact, that I actually was able to become recharged and updated with some good old soul music. Because any black home worth anything has to have a radio or some form of music. But most of the time we spent discussing all the drama surrounding Ingrid's many male admirers. That I would say was probably the most fun. Out of all of this inclusion within a black family, I felt at home again.

And through it all, Ingrid was my very, very best friend, in addition to my faithful and loyal roommates, Lisa and later Brenda. For Ingrid was always there for me! And oh how you will see how she was there for me in some of my darkest and most frustrating times at Clemson.

One other fortunate support system that I did have the luxury of was my brother, Tom also choosing to attend Clemson University. So by my sophomore/junior year, Tom had transferred from the Beaufort campus of the University of South Carolina. Though he was still somewhat a newlywed, his wife did not join him until the following year. I certainly enjoyed having a small piece of my family to share many comforting times with, such as simply watching TV together, as we had done as children. And later when his wife and stepdaughter moved up, I even spent my summer in between my bachelors and masters degrees, residing with them in their small apartment in Clemson.

My sophomore year at Clemson I decided to move my residence from 9-B Manning Hall to 5 Finley Street. Lisa wanted to move off-campus and had come in contact with a friend who already had an apartment. And since I knew that I could definitely get along with Lisa, I didn't want to chance what roommate the Housing Office might send me in the fall. So in August, Lisa and I moved in with Brenda. And we all hit it off fine. They were definitely easy to get along with and I reckon they were nice enough to put up with me. I learned to tolerate Brenda's playing her new Jimmy Buffet album 3,878,019 times in a row and she obliged the endless times I played my Earth, Wind, and Fire "Reasons" album.

I also learned that Hearts must have been the white-version of Spades and that I definitely wasn't missing anything when it came to playing Bridge because I wasn't about to play a hand if I would be the dummy. We enjoyed each other a lot, even though I continued to be too uptight and serious about my studies. Therefore, I soon earned the nickname "Stoneface" when I wanted to study and my roomies wanted to party. Or other times when I felt the apartment should immediately be condemned as a disaster area, but they felt all we merely needed to do was purchase more paper plates rather than wash dishes. But all in all we were fine. And still are. We visit each other, call, and send cards. I'll always love Lisa and Brenda.

One very important lesson I learned from Lisa and Brenda was that I didn't genuinely hate white people. I grew to understand that you can't hold people totally accountable for how they were raised, their environmental effects, or the experiences they've encountered in life. Brenda Wannamaker's family was from a small town called Swansea, South Carolina. Though Lisa and Brenda were from quite different economic backgrounds. Lisa having been from an upper middle class and Brenda from a lower middle class or in other words, Lisa's daddy paid her way to Clemson and Brenda had to work and take out a loan. Don't even mention me, I'm sure I was in the lowest of the lower class. Luckily I was there on a four-year academic scholarship. That was one definite plus of Clemson in my eyes. But at any rate, though Brenda and Lisa were from somewhat different backgrounds, they both shared this specific commonality that most southern whites shared at this time and still do, they had never socialized with blacks. And both of them admitted to me that they had always known blacks, but never on a social level. Though they'd known blacks personally, it was always someone that cooked for them, cleaned for them, sewed for them, or was like a nanny to them. Though always on a close level, it was in a service capacity, not one of exclusively socializing. Extremely big difference. And after living together with me, meeting and hanging out with my black friends and family, they concluded that "Hey black people are just like white people." They had never had this opportunity before. It was a breakthrough for them and it was definitely a most valued lesson of life for me. For the feeling was mutual. "Hey white people are just like black people." And that there are some white people that are nice and that I rather quite like. Undeniably, I had come a long way from my childhood feelings that "I hate white people!"

21

"Why Do You Date Only Black Guys?"

This is probably the question throughout my lifetime that has gotten under my skin and kind of bothered me the most, "Why do you date only black guys?" Like I had a choice. It's almost like asking a black girl, the same question. And really after the first couple times out of hundreds of times it's been posed, it's made me wonder about it myself.

To my younger people, let me remind you that I'm definitely "old school." So we didn't ask guys out; we waited for them to ask us out. I know that's a strange concept, but those were the times. So at Beaufort High School, I knew exactly why white guys didn't ask me out. I was that strange white girl from a black family, from a black school, who always hung out with black kids. Or whatever fragment or version of that they knew. Who knows, they may have even believed I was black. Sometimes I wished it so much that I certainly at times believed it myself.

But now even at Clemson, not a single white guy ever approached me to ask me out, for my telephone number, a subtle flirt, or even a simple hello. Out of 20,000 students, the 10,000 male students had no way of knowing my "Black Connection." So why wouldn't a single one of them talk to me? Was I so totally ugly and grotesque to the human eye? I mean with contact lenses, I had even ditched the "four eyes" stigma of my glasses. Yet I was truly developing a complex. Not that I really cared if a white guy asked me out for I grew up in an environment where I had become more accustomed to and comfortable in the company of black people. But for curiosity's sake, just what was it, the reason white guys hadn't ever been attracted to me? This is the question I've always and yet still do ask myself. So when someone asks me as they always have, "Why haven't you ever dated white guys?" I actually become irritated. "I've never done anything to them." In fact throughout my years of high school and even college, white boys for the most part avoided me like the plague.

Yet only twice in my entire life, have I gone out with "a white guy." Both of these guys were during my final year at Clemson. I had already completed undergraduate school and was now in grad school completing a masters degree.

Nick was a grad assistant in the education department, just like me. We both took classes together and had duties around the department. Nick was a nice guy, but never in my wildest imagination could I ever fathom a white guy asking me out. It just did not compute. Nick and I were buddies, which was strange enough because for the most part, white people just weren't naturally attracted to hang with me. And don't ask me why for I certainly don't know. But Nick was a mid-size average-looking guy, probably of Italian decent, with a fun-loving, sweet personality. Now that I look back, yes he was from the North, in other words a Yankee. And maybe that's why I was even considered. For I guess those Southern boys have a high-powered radar to pick up on the lightest range of a "Blackness" reading.

But Nick asked me if I'd like to go see the mountains. Here I'd been at Clemson for four years, in the foothills of the Blue Ridge Mountains, and it hadn't even crossed my mind to go see them. My roommates and other students were always talking about going to the Blue Ridge Mountains, and going white-water rafting at Table Rock or another spot on one of the rapid rivers, or even hiking or camping. But none of these ever appealed to me. I just don't know. Could they have just been a little too "white" or just too outdoorsy for me? At any rate, I was never tempted in the least to adventure into these realms. So I guess it was a combination of things, the fact that Nick was nice, I'd never actually thought to go see the mountains, and the fact that I had for the first time in my entire life been asked on a "date" with a white guy. And I'm sure the last caught my curiosity more than any of the other factors.

So I bravely offered an affirmative response. There's no way he could have even remotely been aware of the significance of this date. But this was definitely making history in my life. So he drove me up to the Blue Ridge Parkway to see the mountains. It was incredible. We even hiked up the side of a slope near the shoulder of the road and picked wildflowers on the hill. Very lovely time. We laughed, we played, we enjoyed the beauty, and enjoyed just hanging out together. It was a splendid day.

And what continued to be incredible is that evidently he still liked me after the date because he asked me out again, this time to dinner. For those of you that can identify with the college days of a poor, struggling student, you'll recall the limited funding. So I realized that this guy really did indeed like me for he took me to a really nice seafood restaurant and had to pay out a nice little bill for dinner. And another time he took me to an Italian restaurant. But all this was soon to cease, the day he saw a passion mark on my neck, the telltale signs of my lingering addiction to the OJ relationship, even though we were officially broken up. Being a normal red-blooded American boy, of course Nick had tried to kiss me, but I told him I wasn't ready for that. But now he could see for himself that though I said I wasn't seeing anyone, that yes I definitely was. There was no need for words. My telltale signs did all the speaking. I felt so badly. I hated the fact that I had hurt him. I really enjoyed Nick, but unfortunately my heart was still with OJ, and it wouldn't allow me to move on. So Nick really never had a chance at this time in my life to be nothing more than a friend.

That year was my banner year for white boys, for a second one stumbled my way. These were the first two white guys and the last the last two white guys in my life that ever entered from the dating aspect.

I met Jack Fitzler during spring break of that same year. (And let me certainly set the record straight before I go on. My son, Jack, is definitely *not* his namesake. My son is named after both of his grandfathers, my father, Robert and my husband's father, Jack. Just wanted to be crystal clear on that. Don't want to hear it later, "You know she named her first born after an old boyfriend.") But I was visiting my Bahá'í friends, the Cerquas, at the military housing complex on Laurel Bay, on my way out of town, returning back to Clemson when I began experiencing some minor mechanical problems from my Toyota Corona, otherwise grudgingly known as the "Lemon." Certainly not uncommon, it could have been easily disguised as a F.O.R.D. at the time, "Fix Or Repair Daily." But here I had met this tall, extremely tall, handsome Marine. I'd usually made the reference as tall, dark, and handsome. But in this case, I stand corrected—tall, white, and handsome. And definitely a knight in shining armor for he rescued me from the perils of an inoperable automobile. Whatever the problem may have been, Lance Corporal Jack Fritzler, had me back on the road again.

Jack was undoubtedly a fine specimen in hunkliness. He was only six foot eight, built rather nicely, and finished off rather handsomely. He was a nice-looking fellow I must admit. In fact later he shared the fact that he had even done some work for a catalog, modeling underwear while in college. And somehow we must have exchanged telephone numbers for we actually began dating after I graduated in May and returned home to begin teaching.

Our first date was quite memorable, not the date itself, but rather the conclusion of the date. I can't even remember now where we had gone; all that remains embedded in my mind is the grand finale. I was staying with my parents at this time so when he drives up to the house and parks in the yard, we begin into a huge and lengthy conversation, really a debate, about my family, and more specifically my parents. He told me that he had really enjoyed my company but had a definite problem with my family. Then he proceeded to inform me of how the Bible strongly forbade marriages mixing races. Whereas, I politely asked him the precise location of this Scripture within the confines of the Holy Word. And after much rambling, he admitted that the reference was from a religious magazine, which I reminded him, was definitely not to be confused with Holy Scripture.

After that, he went on to share his sentiments regarding the entire black race from his extremely limited source of understanding. He told me how all black people were unclean and smelled. Of course, this was based on rooming with one black guy thus far in the Marine Corps. Interesting how these enormous stereotypes are actually based. And I shared with him my feelings of the oddity and absurdity of his statements. Because from the thousands and thousands of incidents and interactions within the black community, for the most part, black folk are very particular about cleanliness of food, the house, clothing, just everything, and particularly their body. So I don't know where this guy was coming from. Definitely off the wall.

But we all come into each other's lives for a reason. And it was evident why I had crossed this man's path. For he definitely needed a lesson in the realities of black people versus the falsehoods and myths fabricated and passed down through the ages by misinformed and uninformed individuals.

Jack proposed that he was willing to overlook his objections to my diversified family because he genuinely liked me. And evidently I was willing to overlook all that to experience this completely foreign and new concept for me—a white man! And not just any white man. Jack had the appearance and presence of a Greek or Roman god. I assume I was in a comatose and stunned state to fathom that I had actually been chosen by this man against all odds. Why else had I agreed to date a man that didn't properly acknowledge my family.

We were definitely from different worlds and of different mindsets. But for some apparent reason we continued the see each other. I think we both saw each other perhaps as a challenge of conquering and converting the other to the correct viewpoint. So we continued to date for several months. We'd go to the movies, out to eat, or for walks at the Waterfront or through historic Beaufort. Being an elementary school teacher, I had a habit of bringing quite an abundant amount of my students' papers home to be graded. So another activity that Jack and I would be engaged in was grading papers late into the night. While I think

Jack eventually grew tired of this recreational pastime with me, especially since we weren't quite romantically involved, and we soon continued on our separate paths.

It's funny, but neither of these white fellows had I ever kissed. We were not intimate, strictly platonic relationships. I don't know if it was subconsciously because they were white and this was unfamiliar territory or that these guys just weren't for me. But I didn't necessarily kiss every guy I went out with, be they black, white, or whatever. The majority of my dates were simply as friends going out to dance, to dinner, or to see a movie.

For as I now take inventory, I've dated within quite a few cultural and racial zones in addition to Black and White American: East Indian, Nigerian, Guyana, Taiwanese, and Puerto Rican. But I must say I always had a special weakness for Puerto Rican men, at least for those I had met in the nightclubs for they were sensational dancers. Certainly a lot of black men are great dancers, but I got to give it to the Hispanic culture, as well. And seeing my passion in life is dancing, you can see the connection and appreciation.

But back to the question at hand, "Why do I date only black men?" As you can see this is quite an inaccurate question for those who really know me. Yet I must say that I've always felt that if I had become involved permanently with a white companion for life that this would have truly been an interracial relationship culture-wise. For I feel so remote and distant from whatever the "White World" entails. I know I would have had a lot to learn and a lot to contend with. For one thing the music thing which is such a *huge* thing with me. If a guy is not down with the rhythm and blues and funk songs that radiate from the Tom Joyner or Doug Banks radio show, I would have had major concerns.

I've been married over 20 years now to a black man, and yes people identify this as an interracial marriage. In fact if a black man were looking exclusively for a white girl based on that merit alone, "Surprise, surprise." For after dating this one guy he confided, "You're probably one of the blackest girls I've ever dated." And yes on the exterior, I'm white and Bryant's black. But on the interior, I can not and do not ever want to change my cultural makeup, being black. So believe me this marriage was never a challenge racially, as most people would identify an "interracial marriage." I felt quite at ease and comfortable in this relationship. It's definitely been a safe place. Being within a black environment is all I've ever known. Simple as that. Simple as that.

So in closing this chapter, again for the record, I want to state, "I do not dislike white men! They just have never taken much of a liking to me." I suppose they just don't know how to take me. And that's all right. Nothing personal. "I ain't mad with ya'."

22

Love Hang Over: Discrimination at Its Deepest Level

Final exams for the fall semester were assailing upon us and we soon would part our separate ways to return home to visit family for Christmas vacation. But we still had a little time for some final moments of fun and frolic. Frequenting, the local Clemson bars was not my idea of entertainment and relaxation. The black nightclubs I was accustomed to focused on music and dancing. The bars in Clemson highlighted drinking, fooseball, and more drinking. So when Lisa and Brenda learned that an old rhythm and blues band would be performing at one of the bars, they quickly extended an invitation to join them, knowing this more than likely would be an evening I might enjoy. Little did they or I know how enjoyable and memorable this night would prove to be.

So the Chairman of the Board (one of my favorite bands when I was in junior high) would be playing at the Grocery on Thursday night, the 4th of December. I hoped that this would fill the gap in my soul for a body starved out for some satisfying soul music and a night of "sweat 'til you're wet" dancing.

We found a table in the large throng of people gathered in the renovated grocery store to nightclub, and thus still the residue of the name "The Grocery." The crowd was in their normal hype for a night of intoxicating fun, drinking drink after drink to reach an ultimate state of gaiety. There I sat sipping a Tab diet soft drink, quite content in consuming the long, lost familiar environment of a rhythm and blues club scene. The only difference—"That dancing, off beat, had to go!" How could they disrespect such soul-soothing music with such jerky and sporadic movements? Of course the crowd was white as normal, what else would one expect at a gathering of Clemsonites during these times. But all of a sudden I glimpsed several figures, moving in and out amongst the swarm of dancers out on the floor. But these were noticeably different for they actually danced to the beat.

What a rare and treasured sight for my sore eyes from watching time after time rhythmless dancing. These were guys, and they were black, and some of them were even cute. I was excited at the vain imagining of perhaps dancing with one of these guys. Well, I woke out of my dream and decided that I would jump out on the floor with my roomies and enjoy the music on a much higher and more meaningful level for me—dancing. And I was getting my little groove on, really forgetting all about my previous sightings, when all of a sudden one of these guys I had been admiring had come up to me and actually asked me to dance. (Later found out was Archie Reese who would become a good friend.) Boy was I thrilled—I felt like I was definitely for the moment in time, in a comfortable situation that I so enjoyed, black music and dancing with a black person—"to the beat." So that was cool and lovely. Then that fellow switched off with another and another one of his friends which is huge fun and guys normally do when they're really having a good time out on the dance floor. So I definitely loved it too. And at one point during these tradeoffs, I danced with one guy for a longer duration than the rest. We exchanged names, some limited conversation as we danced, and he concluded in asking me for my phone number. Was I still dreaming? I couldn't believe a guy was interested in calling me. "I'll give it to you, but I know you won't remember it." So I gave him the digits, "6-5-4-6-4-8-8." And we would see. During my clubbing excursions at home, it hadn't taken me long to find out that guys requested a girl's phone number at a considerably higher frequency than the actual amount of call backs a girl would receive. And I left the Grocery that night on Cloud 9, hoping that this time the phone request would correlate to a real live call.

Well, much to my delight, OJ did call me. Turns out he was a junior at Clemson, and in addition to being a student, his other major job was being a defensive back for the Clemson Tigers' football team. But outside of this celebrity status, which for being a non-sports enthusiast didn't excite me, I learned that Oneal Tyler, Jr. was from Fernadina Beach, Florida. His interests included surfing, swimming, diving, basketball, tennis, reggae music, and playing bid whist. And he was Catholic. I had never met any black churchgoer that wasn't Baptist. Nor had I ever met a black guy that surfed. Right away I could see this was a special and unique kind of guy. I definitely saw him as interesting. He was always so enthralled in and full of life. And he had a fun, yet so sweet disposition. We hit it off as good friends from the very start and soon grew to be inseparably and uncontrollably in love.

Two key incidents unmercifully placed my heart and spirit in the palms of OJ's hands. The first was the fact that he never pressured me for a physical component in our relationship, even though our intimacy had developed deeply. Just so we could be in close proximity to one another as long as possible, he would spend the night over to my apartment, actually sleeping in the bed with me, both of us fully attired from head to toe, in our jeans and t-shirts. Crazy, right?

The second contributing clincher occurred one night, after receiving the most upsetting and unsettling phone call from my mother. Momma never, never called. It just was so costly. So I knew there was something up. And though she wouldn't come out and say, the pain traversed through and through the telephone. I could see the tears in her voice. And I knew what was up. I couldn't bear to know my Momma's in pain and that I'm helpless to do anything. As Momma cried softly, I sobbed in OJ's arms. And OJ comforted me with the reminder that yes something could be done to assist. And I'll never forget how he dropped to his knees at the edge of my bed in the dark of the night and ever so humbly offered a prayer for my mother's trials and tribulations. There's such a strength in witnessing a man submit to God. With these key elements, OJ had truly captured the heart and soul of me.

And not only for me, but OJ had had a personality that people could not resist and naturally my roommates also enjoyed his company. And luckily so because we spent every free moment we had together. Not only did I become close to him, but to all his buddies. There was his menacing-in-appearance, but big-hearted teddy bear roommate, "Sweet Thaddy Daddy." Then his tight friends, Peanut and Ogden. As well as who could ever forget Nelson. He was the comedian and entertainer of the gang. He always kept us laughing when he was in the mix. Nelson really became one of my own friends in his own right.

As for OJ and I, we continued to spend a lot of time together. We played cards together, we watched television together, listened to music together, ate together, laughed together, cried together, and even prayed together. But always within the confines of my apartment or from time to time at his dorm room in Mauldin Hall, the "Jock" dorm. Or on occasions at the drive-in theater in Seneca. But never Clemson's movie theater. At first I thought nothing of it; we were both students and had little to no money to be going out on dates. Especially OJ because athletes were not allowed to work and definitely couldn't receive money.

And at one point, I was confident that things were progressing for he invited me to Catholic Mass. It had such significance for me that I still even remember the pale peach, polyester dress with a scooped neckline that I wore that morning. We had actually attended worship service together, and in public mind you. But as the months waxed on and we continued to always remain at home, I really started wondering what was going on with him. Was he ashamed of being seen out in public with me? Maybe he had another girlfriend. No impossible, he spent all his time with me. So finally I had to interrogate him and get to the bottom of things. It was eating me alive.

OJ explained how he had dated a white girl his freshman year at Clemson, and the coaches had gotten wind of his choice in female companionship. Coach Red Parker had sent one of the senior players on the team to deliver a message that it was their firm polity that he was forbidden to date white girls. He evidently chose to continue to see the girl, and though they could not take his athletic scholarship away, they punished him by taking away his greatest love—playing football. He was benched for several years. In fact, when they finally allowed him to play his senior year, newspaper reporters commented, "Where had this OJ Tyler, suddenly appeared from?" And he wasn't about to let that go again. In other words, I wasn't something he wanted to purposely draw to their attention. Well this was to be my first and most devastating bout of many with racism at the almighty institution of Clemson University.

I wasn't particularly thrilled with this information, though I was relieved to know there wasn't another girl in the picture or that I was too ugly to be seen with. It did hurt, though I made light of it by slumping down in the passenger seat of his maroon Ford Cougar while driving on campus or past the vehicle of a football coach. And the greatest sting came to bear at OJ's final home football game of the season when they introduced all senior players that would come out escorted onto the field. Well, OJ explained to me fully how he had promised a dear friend, Diane McDonald, to escort him for this activity. And that he had made this commitment to her long before we were officially going together and she would be very disappointed if he didn't hold to his word. Not to mention how kind-hearted and sensitive OJ was. Though it seemed legit seeing it was the girlfriend of his best friend, Ogden. Well, love sure as heck does blind you. I took it hook, line, and sinker; though I wasn't at all pleased with the verdict. My roommates gave me much grief and told me it was absurd and crazy that I, as OJ's girlfriend, wasn't going to be at his side for such a significant occasion as Senior Day. In fact, I couldn't even bring myself to attend the game that day. I sat at the apartment alone crying my eyes out, while everyone else devoured another Saturday's worth of Clemson football with all its amenities. This was one of many sad celebratory days that would come for OJ, but not for me. Though he would always try to make things up to me running over to my apartment the moment he had finished his obligations with the team, it never quite erased all the pain.

Here I had fallen hopelessly and helplessly in love. I was out of control and the situation was totally in control of me. I loved OJ more than I had ever loved anyone else, including myself. It was such a beautiful feeling much of the time, and such a devastating feeling other times, especially when racism reared its ugly head in collaboration.

The off seasons were much happier times. OJ didn't have all the football obligations and public engagements. And so these times were far less complicated. Though during summers, we often times weren't in school together, we found times to visit each other. OJ visited my home in Frogmore (now named St. Helena Island) on numerous occasions. Which further increased my perception of what I hoped had signified an element of a serious relationship. On a couple of occasions I had met his brother who lived in Atlanta and even his father several times, when he visited Clemson to assure that OJ's car continued to be road-worthy. But was I ever invited to his home in Fernadina? This definitely should have been yet another strong indicator of a major obstacle. Still yet, I would make the five-hour drives to Clemson to visit him in summer school or even during his internship at the State Mental Hospital in Columbia. And we were in constant touch by phone. These were definitely happy times. Though all this was soon to come to a complete and unexpected dead end.

Upon graduating that May, I had decided to stay on at Clemson for graduate school. They had offered me an assistantship in the education department and this would pay for the majority of my masters degree. I would be crazy not to take it for the money's sake, not to mention that OJ was still completing his degree. But upon arriving on campus that August for school, it didn't take long to realize that OJ and I weren't quite the same.

A primary example, soon after settling into my dorm as a graduate resident, I suffered a somewhat superficial injury from a fall. One night as OJ escorted me across campus from Mauldin Hall to Geer Hall, my new resident dorm in the "Shoeboxes," I stumbled on a curb and came down with quite a force. Well, it turned out I had taken a bigger bang than I was aware of. By morning, my leg wasn't too bad, but I was continuously in a state of dizziness. Every time I sat up in bed, I about passed out. Well Melanie, my roommate who was the other grad resident of the dorm, demanded that I get on over to the campus infirmary. Which I gladly agreed to for I didn't know what on earth could be wrong with me.

Well, the doctors diagnosed me with extremely low blood pressure; I guess a reaction to the trauma I had incurred. But it didn't stop here. Oh no. They wrapped my bruised leg in a cotton cast, ran an IV in me, and actually hospitalized me for two nights. Now this is where the real trauma began. I had never spent a night, a day, or even an hour in a hospital-at least not as a patient. Then as if matters weren't bad enough, OJ calls me and informs me that he's headed down to Columbia to visit some of his friends he met during his internship who are now returning to their respective schools. And volunteers his TV to keep me company during my hospital "sentence." Thad would be dropping it off early that afternoon because he's got to get on the road. Keep me company! That's certainly not the company I had anticipated or needed. As the nurses overheard me sobbing upon conclusion of this conversation, I overheard them rapidly requesting an order for pain medicine. But no pain prescription could be written to eradicate the pain I was experiencing. Just one of the endless letdowns and heartbreaks.

After surviving the hospital ordeal, OJ ultimately confided in me that the root of the problem was his mother, that she was not pleased with him dating a white girl, and that to make her happy he was looking to find a nice young lady who was black and would be acceptable to her liking. He concluded that we needed to break up and go our separate ways.

But we never actually did break up for almost a year or more. For the record, we did not "officially" go together. But we were in constant contact with each other and continued a sporadic intimacy. The "friendship/intimacy" thing was tearing me apart, but I didn't know how I could let him go completely. And he evidently didn't want to totally let go of the relationship either. This had to have been one of the saddest times of my life. I cried that entire year. How could it be possible to be so in love and feel a mutual love, but not be able to be with that person?

And what made it even worse, here I had chosen to pursue my masters degree at Clemson University, largely because OJ was still here. Because Clemson definitely was not one of my favorite locations in this sphere of existence. Yet as soon as I embarked on my masters program, OJ informed me that we're history. Here I am stuck in Clemson, sad and lonely. And to add insult to injury, after completing my masters, I would drive up on an occasional invitation to still visit OJ on weekends. And he would do the same in visiting me in Beaufort. One thing I never could figure out though—I loved him and I truly believed he loved me, but why were we broken up?

Yet inevitably the exploits of racism won out, and this "endless love" did indeed come to an end, with OJ informing me that he had found an acceptable young, lady whom he had fallen in love with and was making plans to marry.

Well, naturally this thrilled me to no end. But I wished him well and finally attempted to go on with living.

And years and years later, for we periodically kept in touch as good friends, he finally gave me the truth of why we broke up and never really could be. After hearing about the passing of his mother, I commented about the fact that I had wished I had met her but I knew she did not approve of our inter-racial relationship. Well I guess he couldn't lie on his deceased mother, so he finally admitted the truth after almost 20 years.

He told me how he had endured racism throughout his years in college at Clemson and when he looked at living a lifetime in an inter-racial marriage, he knew he couldn't handle the pressure of that. I thanked him for his honesty after all these years. And it finally brought a much-needed resolution to that saga and drama in my life.

OJ had loved me. But evidently the love wasn't quite sufficient to take the stand that proclaimed, "It's you and me against the world!" Nor had he loved me enough to give me what I most wanted—him and a family. And apparently he didn't possess the strength and faculties to cope with the constant barrage and onslaught of racial assault at such a level of intensity he foresaw for an interracial marriage.

Things would have been so much simpler if I were "really black." But that's just it. Too simple. Life doesn't work like that. And it apparently wasn't part of God's plan for me. You know how He loves to strengthen us with His tests. (Sometimes I evaluate, "Do I keep failing them or does He just want me stronger?" Good question.)

But all of this is to illustrate the depths of how devastating and agonizing racism proves to be and continues to be in controlling the destiny and even the love in people's lives.

23

Rounds with Racist Roommates

My most totally wearing-down battle with racism (or should I just call it the Big "R"), would also become the roommate issue. You see through my years of undergrad, things were cool in the roommate department. Yes, they drank a little or no really far more than I was comfortable with and partook of illegal yet socially acceptable substances. Yet we were still "cool" with each other, and even grew to love each other. (They really would do anything for me to this day. Truly good and real people.) And they had stepped out of the ordinary box that I had come to know at Clemson, and had accepted me, my boyfriend, my friends, and family simply as individuals and with no other specifications. When it came to my roomies, nothing was based on skin pigmentation and the reading of your melanin level.

Therefore when Lisa and Brenda both graduated, in sequential years, I was left to embark on graduate school with a desperate search for a new roommate. Well, this should have been a fairly simple process. I had seen on many occasion the endless array of 3 x 5 inch index cards posted in every possible nook and cranny of the colossal windows of Lynch's Drugstore, posting the immediate and desperate need for roommates. I jotted down several numbers and so the search began. And before the end of the day I located a young lady in need of a roommate to share her apartment. She was a young, black girl struggling as a cashier at a nearby Bi-Lo grocery store, but she looked to be making ends meet. And so we shared the expenses of her apartment for several months. But then while home visiting my family for Christmas break, I received a call from Denise informing me of a soon-to-be eviction date for nonpayment of the rent. (Obviously she had been blowing my half of the rent I had been paying her.)

So my sister, Sally, who was also home from college, agreed to make the trek to Clemson to help me pack my things, very temporarily move in with my dear friend Ingrid, and very soon find another roommate. So it was back to the front windows of Lynch's Drugstore. This time it was an older white girl, employed as a teller at one of the local banks who had held down her apartment for several years, but wanted to take on a roommate to be able to work on her savings. So I'm thinking, yeah stability. No more eviction notices. A roommate who's older, more mature, more responsible, and all those good things.

Sally and I proceeded to load up all my meager earthly possessions into my old dilapidated Toyota Corona to haul to my new apartment that was rather upscale compared to my last dungeon of a dwelling. Upon numerous trips, my belongings were almost all set in place in my new spacious bedroom of this beautiful duplex apartment. I mean there's plenty of natural sunlight beaming in, I'm admiring my room, smiling and happy, going down for one final sweep of the car. And behold my dear friend, Nelson, standing in the parking lot. I met him through my boyfriend OJ, for they were both on the football team. He's like a brother to me, comes to visit me, we play cards together, and are just good pals. To know Nelson, you have no choice but to love him. He's so fun-hearted, comical, sweet, and good-natured all the time. In other words, just "good people." Haven't seen him for several weeks since we've been home on Christmas break, which feels like being sentenced to life in prison to a college student. So of course my immediate and natural reaction is to run up to him and get one of his tremendously huge panda bear hugs. I mean he just added further sunshine to my day, as I'm still beaming about my newfound apartment.

Well, the sun never could just shine long enough for me up there in ole Clemson town. The clouds came rolling on in like they had sworn a sacred oath and duty that they were obligated to *always* insist that my parade was rained on. And that's what precisely proceeded to go down. I'm joyously sharing my glad tidings of my new abode because believe me, Nelson had experienced my last residence, the cavern. But biding him good-bye because he's actually visiting someone else in the apartment complex and besides I've also got to get back to my sister as well. So here I am all jubilant and bubbling over. And bam, here comes the thunderstorm out of nowhere. I mean the clouds didn't even roll in to forewarn me. "Who is that?" nastily demanded my roommate with her voice reeking of disdain, contempt, and down right hate. And I'm thinking what on earth has occurred to transform this mature and pleasant young lady into a foaming-at-the-mouth demon alien straight from the underworld.

And she proceeds to interrogate and investigate into my dealings with this young man in the parking lot. I'm like, "He's a good friend." Really simple as that. What else is there to tell?

"Well, do you have other black friends?"

And now I know where the alien bigot cleverly disguised as a human being is coming from. It's my lucky day again, let's play Racism. Well I'm quite accustomed with this. And I felt the best thing to do was to just lay all my cards on the table and let her deal with that. "Yes, I do have other black friends. In fact I have a lot of black friends, my boyfriend happens to be black, and half of my family is black. Why? Is that a problem?"

"Well, they wouldn't be coming by here to visit would they?"

"Oh, yes most definitely. My boyfriend will probably be by almost everyday to see me. My friends visit on a pretty regular basis. Though my family probably won't be up until graduation in May."

"Well, I don't know if this is going to work," point blank. And I'm thinking, "Really what is going on in this demon's head?" And she continues to offer some attempt at concocting a mammoth tale that she feels will rectify her hatred for blacks, and particularly as she explains, she emphasizes "black men." She continues with the fact that she "has nothing against 'them,' *but*—" (and you know a three-letter word is truly on as equal a footing as a four-letter word). And on goes the fable of how *something* terrible happened to her when she was a little girl that involved a black man. And of course, she never felt compelled to tell me what this *something* was for she's unable to fabricate any more information for this story on such short notice. And I don't want to really hear another word of this falsehood and fabrication anyway. But I'm thinking of all the many loadings and unloadings I've already been through while she's telling me that she needs to think heavily about this.

Early the next morning, a knock comes to my bedroom door. Daylight has barely broken. The rays haven't even had an opportunity yet to stroke my head. And hey anyway, I'm used to sleeping in on the weekends at least until a decent twelve o'clock. So I'm already thinking, what time it must really be. Time to raise up on out of there. And sure enough. The enemy wants me to come downstairs so she can talk to me. Though she really could have saved her breath. "It's not going to work. I've been thinking about it all last night. I could hardly sleep. And I know it's not going to work."

I couldn't even get a word in edgewise if I had wanted to. "And I need you to be out by sunset." And I'm thinking, where am I? I'm thinking perhaps the "Twilight Zone" or Fosythe, Georgia. Though of course, Clemson is the next best thing.

I'm telling her as matter-a-factly as possible, "Alright." Nothing else to say. I'm certainly not going to waste my energy. I need that for packing up again, searching for a home again, and unpacking hopefully to remain there just for the next four months until graduation. Please, Lord if you see fit.

So here I am, "Ingrid, it's me again." How could I ever had made it through school at Clemson, especially graduate school, without her? I wouldn't have been able to. So it's back to Lynch's drugstore. Boy, is this getting old. Yet there's never a lack of potential roommates plastered across their display windows. But now I know the real question, can I make it with one of them? Though no, that's not truly the question either. The all-prevailing question is: "Are they a bigot or are they not?" So after several calls, I connect with a perky and receptive young and energetic coed. In fact, she's in a hurry making plans for a date with her boy-friend, but has time to meet with me.

Totally up-front with the whole nightmare of a saga with the racist roommate because I really don't have the strength and energy for any more of this drama. I'm telling her if you have any problem in the slightest just say the word. "Oh, no. I can't stand people like that! I really have a problem with people who are prejudice." So she's giving me a copy of her key as she's jaunting out the door with her little boyfriend. And I'm thinking whatever. I've finally got a roof over my head and no more of that nonsense.

I return to Ingrid's for the millionth time, to gather my belongings again or at this point they may have still remained in the car, but particularly to get my poor worn-out and enduring sister, Sally. As soon as we get all moved in and almost ready to chill out, the phone rings. It's my new roommate. I realize you will think this now has to be truly fiction and elaboration I've added here to either embel-lish a little or lengthen this chapter. Surely I would have never believed it unless I had had to unfortunately be the one to experience it.

And here she goes with, "You're not going to be able to stay. My parents pay for my apartment. And I don't have a problem, but they do. They're very old-fashioned and narrow-minded. And they'd have a fit if they came to visit and someone black was visiting the house." And I'm thinking no way do I want to return to Lynch's Drugstore or to haul my stuff to one more apartment complex.

So against all my basic principles and beliefs, I'm compromisingly pleading, "Well, where do they live and how often do they visit? Because I can just inform my friends that I can't have them over at that time." Boy am I desperate at this point. It doesn't even sound like me talking.

"They live in Florida. But they pop in at any time to check in on me. And they would stop paying for my apartment."

Okay I've heard this whole pathetic tale before, just a slightly different version, and I'm really not in the mood for any more games. I then emit a very weak and

surrendering "Alright." Click and we both hang up. Unbelieveable. Totally unbelieveable. Hadn't I purposefully been totally upfront with this girl? I just couldn't
comprehend. I was in a complete stupor and didn't know where to turn at this
point. And where else do you go when you don't know where to go, but home.
So the beaten-down warrior in this God-forsaken foreign land places a phone call
to who else, but Momma. And I'm crying and screaming through the line,
"Momma, I'm tired of these people. I can't take it anymore. They can keep their
damn masters degree! I've had it. I'm coming home."

"No Lynn, you've made it this far and you can't give up now. You can't let
them beat you." And she gives me one of those motherly talks that only mothers
can give: reassuring, convincing, supporting, calming, and loving me into what I
must do. I must complete my graduate studies, while simply using these stum-
bling stones as steppingstones in my life. And that was the course at hand, no
matter what obstacle they threw my way. Truly thanks be to God, for allowing us
to have a small piece of Him on earth through our mothers.

I politely repacked the few things I had unpacked, which wasn't much because
I wasn't even allowed the time or luxury of unpacking much of anything.
Reloaded my weary little Toyota and called Ingrid so she could add a scoop or
two of rice to the pot for dinner. My final task was loading my mattress and box
springs upon the roof of my car, which was rather difficult. And so my roommate's boyfriend who happened to be at the apartment as I was departing,
though the coward herself couldn't face me and wasn't even there, offered to
assist me by carrying it out and loading it on the car. Of course, I didn't turn him
down because it was really quite heavy and cumbersome for about a foot or so
hung down on both sides making my car appear as a giant mushroom rolling
down Hwy. 76 toward Pendleton. I guess the boyfriend had been sent to assure I
didn't trash her home and property in retaliation for this, as well as to collect the
key. And while tying down and securing my bed to the car, he apologized for her
actions. He shared his feelings that you just had to feel sorry for people who were
like that. (I didn't believe he was referring to the parents though I am sure they
are originators for teaching this hatred and distrust, but of the daughter.) And he
said it with a true feeling that emerged from his heart. So I truly appreciated the
kindness he had shared and extended to me.

Yes, and it's back to none other than good ole faithful Lynch's Drugstore, but
this time I can now tell you that it would be the final time. I located a rather
unorthodox hippie-type mountain woman of a roommate living in a small,
shoddy, two-bedroom, singlewide trailer. The appearance and personality of the
roommate and the dwelling were rather deficit and depleted. But I said, hey the

others appeared good on the surface, so hopefully the reverse will occur with this situation. And it did work, luckily things held out for those four remaining months until graduation.

Though a few days before graduation I incidentally overheard one of her drug deals going down in the living room, as she thought I was still asleep in my shoe box that doubled as a bedroom. After they had exited the trailer, I snooped out her little warehouse in the trunk that served as our elegant coffee table, there to uncover the numerous little plastic baggies that dispensed the students' favorite product of choice, marijuana. Here I had been living with a drug dealer for the final months to my procurement of my masters degree. I realize tuition is expensive and minimum wage doesn't quite pay the tab, but wow, we're lucky a paddy wagon never visited to cart her off, along with the "innocent bystander," namely me!

But let me tell you the truth, we certainly weren't best buds at all, strictly business partners in paying 50% of the rent, electricity, and phone bill those several months. Yet surprisingly on graduation day, she completely caught me off guard, and goes to show, don't ever judge a book by the cover. That girl, (and I feel bad now because I can only remember my private nickname that I never revealed to her, "Mountain Woman") totally caught me off guard when she gave me a graduation card with a check enclosed for fifty dollars. I know it may not seem like much to you, but under the whole roommate circumstances that I had encountered that final semester, it felt like a million dollars had been placed in my hand. It actually somehow began to make small amends for all those vilifications that had been assailed upon me.

In fact during the beginning of my final semester at Clemson, I had actually moved to five different residences in one week. Incredible! That's all I can say in regard to me completing a masters degree at Clemson University, in spite of the roommates, not hardly the coursework.

24

Trials and Tribulations Abound

Racism continued to abound in regularity like a reoccurring migraine headache to maintain my grounding and to guarantee a full awareness of my environment and circumstances. What was always so incredulously amazing to me was not only the blatant boldfacedness of the discrimination, but the public surroundings, personnel, and situations involved.

"Educated" (and I use the term loosely here) racists for the most part, keep their racist views private, only to be opened in the comfort amongst well-known people and comfortable surroundings. But sometimes, they evidently get a little too comfortable in certain settings, and forget the two items go hand in hand. So they may overlook the fact that they don't actually know whether all those present uphold their little racist beliefs and ideologies. And this was certainly the case one evening in one of my graduate classes at Clemson.

Ironically, now that I reflect again upon the details of the occurrence, I recall that it was actually in my Educational Supervision and Leadership class. During the course of those three-hour lectures, the professors would have a tendency and need to throw in a joke or two from time to time, to break up the monotony of the presentation. And so was the case on this night. The professor lapsed into one of his little stale epilogues of suppose-to-be humorous characters and events. Here he was recounting this rather lengthy and boring joke, and then came forth his grand finale of a punch line, "…and that would be like finding a nigger in a wood pile!" And he, a professor of educational administration graduate school, and the class, fledglings in the field of educational supervision and leadership, busted out into a din of laughter and sheer rapture at the "indubitably and incredulously humorous wit" of this pathetically shaming occurrence.

And here I am sitting in the mist of this throng of frolic, utterly frozen and stiff, with my mouth hanging so low it could have swept up the dust bunnies on the floor. Unbelievable! Flabbergasted! A nightmare, perhaps. No way that my professor, an employee hired by the state, paid with tax dollars, teaching at a state-supported institution of "higher" learning, molding our future leaders for our children's schools, could have said such a word in such a setting. But then seeing that he might have to soon call either 911 or EMS directly, quickly rushed to resuscitate me from my temporary cataleptic state with "Oh, Miss Markovich, I certainly didn't mean to offend anybody. I could have just as easily used any other term, like 'cracker' or anything else."

And I'm entirely incensed by this occurrence because it had broken one of "their" rules and had erupted with this in an area that I held to be a "no blatant racism zone." Yes, I do admit the instructor was white and the entire class was white. But still this did not adhere to the full intent of their rules and regulations for Racism 101. How could he have committed this gross and negligent act of racism right here, smack dab in the middle of my fine and lofty graduate education class? Then suddenly I regained consciousness and recollected my bearings. He obviously was secure in his position and aware of the nonexistent consequences that institution would have imposed. And truly where was I, anyway? Nowhere, other than Clemson University. So really, why was I even shocked?

Several months later during jubilant anticipation of graduation, the large majority of prospective teachers, sojourn to the Education Department's Placement Office with long awaited joy of procuring the "perfect" teaching position located in the "perfect" place. Well, I too certainly felt compelled that this would be the ideal avenue to pursue in finding a launch pad to all my dreams career-wise. Well—how *wrong* I was!

Appointments for interviews were all precisely scheduled. Candidates were outfitted in their "land-the-perfect-job" attire, sitting on the benches of Tillman Hall in suspense of their appointed time. Tillman Hall was a mammoth and dark looming dinosaur of a building. Hard, wooden, never-ending hallways and limitless ceilings that echoed as you walked. And waiting on a bench like an inmate anticipating interrogation before his ultimate execution.

The door finally opened with the summon for "Miss Lynn Markovich." I entered the small high-ceilinged cubby of an office, offering a confident and pleasant smile, though my innards were playing dodge ball. Behind the antiquated, wooden, desk reposed two middle-aged gentlemen. They comprised the teacher recruitment team for Beaufort County Schools. Immediately after I was seated in a chair in front of the desk, I was quite taken off guard. One lit up a cigarette and the other threw his feet upon the top of the desk as he leaned back in a semi-reclined position in this chair. I was shocked, as well as horrified! What kind of professional interview for recruitment of teachers was this? Well, as the so-called interview proceeded to unfold, my question was soon answered. One of the gentleman (and I use this term quite loosely) stated that he "*knew* my family." Being the naïve person that unfortunately my mother raised me as, I was slow to catch his point. I certainly was happy in the fact that this man knew my family because everyone that *truly* "knew" my family, always loved them. So this was what I thought was unmistakably good news for me.

But I didn't understand the full intent of this man's statement until several months had passed and I hadn't received any correspondence from Beaufort County Schools offering me employment. And soon his statement, "I *know* your family" took on a multiple meaning, and rather than being in the positive realm, I realized it was spoken in total disapproval, hatred, and spite. His acknowledgment wasn't to attest my family's reputation for integrity, faith, and hard work. Rather his proclamation didn't mean at all that he "*knew* my family," but rather that he "knew *of* my family." Two totally divergent equations! And his intent was now clear. In other words the unspoken and underlying equation was "I know that your mom is married to a black man. You're certainly from an unacceptable family and upbringing. And therefore, basically forget any hopes of obtaining employment in Beaufort."

So here it goes again, the constant badgering and harassment of the well wishers of racism. Got to do their job and keep it healthy, well, and prospering. Certainly don't ever want that it be diminished or eradicated!

No, graduating with high honors with a bachelor's and a perfect 4.0 for my masters, both from their prestigious and highly revered institution of Clemson University, certainly meant nothing to them. I had jumped through their hoops, put up with all their little initiations to racism—and still my degrees meant nothing and were virtually meaningless to any reputable and respectable "good ole boy" who had to perpetuate the thriving institution of racism. And as we all well know, it is truly *never* "what you know," but who you do or do not know, or in this case being known in a family of the wrong racial composition. And worse to them than a black family, one that's racially mixed. Remember their golden rule: "No mixing."

But fortunately I was able to play some of *their own game*. So I went to who I knew. The principal of my childhood elementary school, Mrs. Henrietta Wiley, was still principal of St. Helena Elementary. I informed her of my desire to return home to teach in the Beaufort area and of my encounters with the Beaufort "Recruitment Team." (What a poor joke and charade!) She was rather perturbed by the fact that my employment application was not even made available to her. If I had not come by personally to visit her, I would have assumed she had no openings. But she quickly righted their deliberate and blatant wrongs, and I soon found myself gainfully employed as a second grade teacher that year.

I never could quite escape the tentacles of racism. They followed me every step of the way, from Beaufort to Clemson and back to Beaufort. On one visit home on a weekend, my sister Sally and I went to visit a couple of Marines we had met in the club. They lived in Taylor's trailer park in Burton, just outside Beaufort. Well, we simply stopped by for a couple hours one night to just talk, laugh, and listen to some music. So memorable were the guys that I don't even recall their names. Yet the incident remains forever indelible in my mind. After a few minutes visiting, a neighbor from next door came knocking at the door, requesting to be invited to the party, thereupon listening to the music and eyeballing Sally and I from the door. Well, the fellows explained it wasn't a party and that they'd give him a rain check.

Evidently this proved unacceptable. For later when Sally and I walked out to my car to head for home, I heard a whizzing sound, soon discovering I had received the welcome basket to the neighborhood with four slashed tires. So let me paint a picture here. Two black guys with two white girls visiting. Enters a white guy. He requests an invite, but receives a rejection. Well, the whole episode doesn't sit right with him. The end result—slashed tires.

So we made it on home to the Island that night before all the air had escaped the tires. The next morning, I single-handedly put the car up on cinder blocks, removed all four tires, borrowed my parents' station wagon, drove to Beaufort to purchase a complete set of four times, took the car off blocks one by one, as I replaced the blocks with the new tires. Needless to say I was fit to be tied.

So I called the County Sheriff in the meantime. They have me accompany one of the Sheriff's detectives to this suspected guy's home. With a search warrant they search the contents of his car. In the trunk is a box cutter that they conclude most likely is the object that slashed my car tires. Of course I've watched enough police detective shows to know that that's not enough proof. But the clincher is that this misguided, attempted party crasher/successful tire slasher is a Marine classified as AWOL. (That's Absence Without Leave.) Not quite the same as not showing up to a civilian job. The military's penalty is prison. So the detective calls the Military Police. They come and handcuff him, carry him away to the brig, and all the while I'm watching. Because as Grammy always taught me, "Unjust does not prosper!"

And I think I'll end this segment with an additionally "whimsical" little encounter of the third kind (which I really try not to take much more than that. It's like you have to laugh to keep from crying if you know what I mean.) It all went down actually after I had graduated and was home and safe, teaching in a nest of a haven, St. Helena Elementary. And I was on one of my periodic return visits to Clemson. Of course, it was for love. Whatever foolishly idiotic reason would I purposefully expose myself to such a torturous environment. So here I am back at Clemson after a week of my ultimate joy, teaching in my little cocoon of a classroom. But it's the weekend and OJ wants me to visit. And of course, I'm headed out in my little lemon yellow Toyota (and yes it was true to the color of its name for I was stranded in midpoint of this route in the boonies on numerous occasions)on I-95 North and I-26 West to my favorite town in the world, Clemson, for just a little more torture and abuse.

Seeing school dismisses around three o'clock and I had to stop by my credit union on the way out of town to get cash for the trip, after a five-hour trip, I arrive in Clemson clearly after dark. I meet OJ at his dorm and he takes me to a small motel where he's already reserved a room for me, none other than the Thunderbird Motel. He goes in the Office to pick up the key, unlocks the room door, and then begins to assist me in taking in the few things I've packed for the weekend. Evidently he is in the room putting my bags down, while I'm still at the car, gathering a miscellaneous item or two. Out of nowhere forcefully and venomously erupts a middle-aged white man, I'm assuming to be the manager of the motel. And he's foaming at the mouth while barking out to the tops of his lungs, "No Mixing!"

And I'm staring at him in total confusion, perplexity, and downright dumbfoundedness. I don't know, to be through all these similar-type situations that I've experienced, you'd think I wouldn't be so completely naïve and slow to catch on. But evidently, my bewilderment is written all across my face and entire person for he reiterates at even a more deafening volume, "I said, 'No Mixing!!! Hurry up and git on out of here before I call the police!" At this point OJ has returned from the room and reached my side by the car. And the words are finally being computed, translated, and registered in my understandings of this immediate situation, as OJ is softly telling me that he's getting my things out of the room and we're leaving. And I concur for I don't want any trouble from this fool. And we both agree upon this move, without a word spoken in response to this man besides perhaps a simple and quite subdued and yielding, "Okay, we're leaving."

Where do we head? None other than my shelter and refuge in many a turbulent storm, Ingrid's home. Here, it is by this point, probably midnight but it makes no difference. Always, always, always was she there for me.

Of course, we were all totally enraged by this outrage of revitalization of Jim Crow days, but the problem was so many adherents either were unaware or refused to acknowledge that it was now almost 1980 and the Civil Rights Act had passed Congress for some time now. The next day OJ returned to the scene of the crime in full force with his total power to demand the return of his deposit on the room, probably with much of the defensive line of the Clemson football team. And that was luckily the end of that one particular advent. Though I still feel the owner of the Thunderbird should save himself and others a little less aggravation and re-post one of his old signs, "No Colored," and make an addendum, "And No Mixing of Colors." Save a little undue stress and time on him and others such as myself.

25

"Then Came Bryant!"

When I left Clemson and returned to my hometown of St. Helena Island to teach, I left behind quite a few sources of pain in my life. Don't get me wrong, it wasn't all bad. But it was just that the bad was so bad. My constant heartaches with OJ which were an indirect cause of my other major heartache, racism. And let me tell you the unrelenting beating down racism puts on you, is near fatal. As I'll always say, I'll never forget or regret my years at Clemson even through all the pain, for it taught me so much. How would I ever have understood the full strength, power, and depths of racism? How would I ever have known how sadly racism could have impacted my life or anyone else's in such a hurtful way, then and throughout my life?

You see racism doesn't just mess with you in a mere superficial way, but usually on such a deeper, more personal, and enduring level. It worked hard at attempting to conquer and devour me in two of the most important realms of happiness in one's life, my lifetime partner and my career. Most people have the opportunity to either marry their college sweetheart or at least break it off. Not me. Racism decided it would make my mind up for me and determine my fate. Even for the other most important love of my life, teaching which I had longed for since I was a child and had spent years and money training for. It attempted to rob me of that, as well. So I'd say racism and I have been acquainted in an intimate and personal way for sometime now.

Therefore last year, when my eldest son, Jack, informed me that his desire was to pursue his degree in Civil Engineering at Clemson University, I was weak. That's my baby! How could I allow him to throw himself to the wolves like that? Yes, 24 years had passed, but how much had really changed? Believe me this good ole boy system takes generations upon generations to elicit change and attempt to eradicate. At least according to their track record. So I cringed when Jack made his announcement. Yet I said to myself, let the boy struggle and strengthen in this world, just as we all must do. I can't shield him from life's afflictions. All of it is an integral part of his evolution to manhood. And he's got to learn and know racism to be able deal with it and face it head on. You see Jack had grown up in basically the same harbor and shelter of the Sea Islands, like his momma. So you can feel my concern.

Yet when I myself had completed my undergraduate and graduate degrees from Clemson, I happily re-spun myself into my cocoon back home on St. Helena Island. As a humble abode I located a little worn-in, but not too worn-out, single-wide trailer in Mr. Branton's quaint and well-kept trailer park on Sam's Point Road of Lady's Island. Just five miles from my first job, teaching at none other than my so dearly cherished St. Helena Elementary where I had begun my love of St. Helena Island's people so many, many years ago as a child. I was back home. Safe, sound, and secure from the torrential rains and forceful gales of racism. At peace in my surroundings.

Of course I still had my inner battles with continuing to let go of a relationship that racism never gave the opportunity to even begin to reach a stage of fruition or flowering. And yes, in that regard it still had almost demolished me from within. So I had to work harder to push remnants of that out my heart. I had the outside under control with regard to my career. Now I wanted the inside of me to be healed and in control, as well.

So I did what I knew best to heal the pain. I went out dancing. And hey the dancing always relieves the pain. And another side perk, usually I would meet a relatively decent young man to converse with which may or may not lead to eventually healing the total ailment.

Thus what I did do was commence to taking an overdose on dancing. I'd hit the club scene in Beaufort six days a week. Seriously. I had a regular club schedule, just as you have a regular work schedule. I mean dancing was serious business to me. So Friday and Saturday night it was disco-ing and hustling 'til almost the crack of dawn at the Image Club. (Here I first learned my preference in dance partners was definitely Puerto Rican guys. Boy could those guys hustle!) Then on Sundays the sound of Funk and R&B had us party like you just don't care and your blouse couldn't hold another ounce of sweat flooding off your body. That little workout would have been with those Marines at the Enlisted Club on Parris Island. (Which I vowed I'd never get involved with a Marine after growing up in a military town. So much for that.) Mondays we'd venture into the Bottoms Up Lounge in Port Royal and hang out with our home boys and amuse ourselves watching the lustful eyes of the old, decrepit "sugar daddies" attempting one last prowl. Wednesdays it was back to the Image for none other than, Ladies Night. And on Thursdays I'd begin my prelude to the weekend with the other troop of soldiers in town, the air wing at the E-Club on the Marine Corps Air Base. And then it would start all over again.

Yes, I know if you're paying attention here, you're saying, "What happened on Tuesdays?" Well, I guess I simply slept and rested up for the other six days of the week. Not by choice though. There just weren't any club happenings on a Tuesday night. Because believe me, I was trying my hardest to either find or at least feel happiness by any means necessary. Even if it meant an overdose on dancing. I had had my share of sorrow and pain.

And through all this dancing, naturally I met quite a few fellows. Hey, this was "back in the day." Quite unlike today, where you'll enter a club and see women dancing with women, men dancing with men, some people dancing with themselves, and one or two couples. Then it was strictly couples. (And specifically, I mean a couple as being comprised of a man and a woman.) So you see through all that dancing I did come in contact with quite a few guys. And I went to dinner or the movies with a few. But always remember girls, for it's surely true, "You've got to kiss a lot of frogs before you find your prince." And that's what proceeded to happen.

That very same year: my first year home, my first year teaching, and that year of all those marvelous days of dancing—along came Bryant. At the time I didn't have an actual boyfriend. But I did have a tight buddy and dance partner. That was Scott. And unfortunately he and everyone else got his relationship always confused with "boyfriend," rather than "dance partner." For let me tell my young girls, and women you know, I don't care how many male platonic friends you have and for how long, somewhere along the way (even if it's been years of friendship), they want to step up the pace to a higher level. Even if they never let on. It's there. Some finally 'fess up, and some never do.

In Scott's case, he didn't hesitate to tell me and the entire world how he felt. Even though I was quick to promise him that the feelings were not mutual. In fact, he even took the liberty of enhancing and embellishing the status of the relationship to the level of fiancee and betrothal. And what's bad, I didn't even have a clue. I'm just thinking, here's my pal Scott. And everyone else is looking to me as the future Mrs. Scott.

But these false rumors never came to light for me until quite some time after becoming acquainted with Bryant. In fact, I was with Scott the night I met Bryant. It was New Year's Eve leading into 1979. Quite unusually something we never did, we had gone to a house party. We were at someone's home in Laurel Bay, the military housing area of the Marine Corps Air Station. We were all pretty much coupled off for the evening. And Scott introduced me to all his friends at the party: Ikenberger, Sledge, etc. etc. and Bryant. And that was that. We were all engrossed in the main element of the evening, partying.

So as the house party began to lose its interest, we made pilgrimage by caravan to our closest Mecca of partying. Savannah, Georgia about 45 miles south of Beaufort. By the early hours of the morning, we had located a large club there still celebrating. So we literally danced the night away. And here I am driving back into town across the Beaufort River as the sunrise began to softly light the sky. With my accomplice of choice, none other than my sister Sally whom was home from college for the holidays. Somewhere along the night, Bryant and his date disappeared into the night just as unnoticeably as they had appeared. I really never gave him a second thought. He was just another friend of Scott's I had met, never to be seen or thought of again.

But hold up, how big do you think Beaufort is? It certainly is not. So Bryant's and my paths continued to cross and cross again. We'd definitely see each other in the nightclubs. Remember Disco Fever was the craze so we were always in the clubs dancing. Or he'd see Sally and me torturing tennis balls on the city court as he traveled home. Other times we'd bump into him on base. And it was really no big deal. For the truth to be told OJ still had my heart shattered. A real relationship was the furthest thing from my mind. Thank God that Scott was willing to be my dance partner and buddy with no mushy stuff. I wasn't up for that—"Dealings of the Heart;" I had had my share. Thank you, but no thanks. I couldn't stand the pain.

So life went on as such. Scott and I continued to hang out as he spun me round and around night after night on the dance floors. And all was well. Then soon it was time for Scott to transfer to a new duty station. And that was cool. I'd miss dancing with him and hanging out. But luckily no broken or aching hearts were involved. So Scott did indeed transfer. I remember seeing him off to catch the train at the Yemassee station. But that was that. We may have contacted each other once or twice after that, but it certainly wasn't very memorable contacts. For I certainly don't recall any dealings with him after that.

And I would continue to see Bryant in the clubs. We would make our cordial salutations in passing and go on. One funny thing though, I remember bumping into him at Parris Island one day. He was dressed in uniform of course. And from the first night I met him at the house party on New Year's Eve, I thought his first name was "Brian." It had never computed the fact that he was following the common military practice of being called solely by his last name. So I found it so absurd when I saw his name badge that read "Bryant." I'm like, "You're name is 'Brian Bryant?'"

And he's like, "No, my last name is Bryant. But I don't like my first name. So no one really calls me that."

"What is it?"

"Wilbert Joe."

"Oh." And I could see why he clearly wouldn't be too excited with it.

"So everyone calls me Bryant." And it was Bryant from that day on.

Some months continued to pass, and then one day toward the end of July as we chanced in meeting, he ever so nonchalantly asked me if I'd like to go to the movies with him. I certainly had nothing else to do so why not.

But you know I had to ask him, for I had met him seven months ago, "Why didn't you ever ask me out before?" And sure enough he had quite been taken in by Scott's rumor that I was not only his girl but his fiancée as well. He told me how he would never stab a friend in the back like that. But that as the months had passed and he'd seen me out in the clubs with other guys, he figured we had broken up. He was certainly just as shocked to learn we had never went together, just as I was to learn of this imaginary engagement Scott had with me.

But nevertheless, we ventured out that evening to the movies to see "Blazin' Saddles." I wasn't a big moviegoer at the time, but why not. What did I have to lose? Well, it was certainly an enjoyable evening. The company and conversation were good. And I found Bryant to be someone I would like to see again. In fact, after that night we did see each other again. Again and again. We were inseparable. We saw each other for every single day, without fail for several months. Complete with the big time date to the Marine Corps Ball, me in this grotesque and pathetic pale blue formal I had actually borrowed from a friend and Bryant in his dress blues uniform. I hadn't done anything like that since my Junior-Senior prom in high school.

I mean by now this thing with Bryant was getting some serious feelings involved. I was even beginning to stay in a night or two at his small and quaint efficiency cottage, stretched out in his living room, head to head, watching TV. Hey it's so funny but I had never even heard of or seen the television show, "Saturday Night Live" until I started dating Bryant. Of course, one would have to be home on a Saturday night to see that show. And Saturdays was one of my biggest club nights of the week. Needless to say I had never been home on a Saturday, and I certainly never was a big proponent of TV. When I was at home in my trailer, my stereo system was always pumping out the sounds of the Commodores, LTD, Peabo Bryson, or the likes. Music has always been my means of relaxation.

But of course Bryant couldn't lure me totally out of my love of club. Music and dance were and are too much attuned with my daily life support. So several nights a week, I still got my doses of dance. And he appeased me and compromised, by calling me at the Image toward the close of the night. One of the waitresses would call me off the dance floor and I would answer the phone. I guess I spent so many nights in the club, it was like my home. And Bryant knew where to track me down. "Hey baby, why don't you stop by on your way home." And that would be the icing on the cake of a great night of dancing.

Another highly attractive quality was the time and attention he afforded his six-year-old daughter, Dee, even though he had been separated from her mother since the child was two. But he'd driven down to visit Dee in Jacksonville, Florida on a regular basis and had brought her up to Beaufort to stay with him for the holidays and summers. For a single dad, also in the military, I was highly impressed. Most of the examples of estranged fathers I'd witnessed hadn't been a good situation. So Bryant was a breath of fresh air in the realm of fatherhood. Evidently these traits of fatherhood I saw manifested in him were images of those that I had lost when I lost my own father.

Then many a day, he'd call me on my job to see if I'd like to go to lunch. What girl in her right mind would refuse a lunch date, especially with a fine man like Bryant? It was summer and I was working with Beverly and the gang at Beaufort-Jasper Employment and Training. Bryant would drive up in his white Dodge Magnum. And he'd step out like a tall, handsome black knight in shining armor, but instead in his all white cool summer cotton slacks and shirt. I mean, the brother was lookin' fine. And calling on who? Me. He wanted me to join him for lunch. Fine with me. And I'd step out. There I'd be with my summer drenched golden tanned skin, with my waist long hair flowing down my back, in a sassy summer dress, complete with three-inch, to-die-for, sling-back pumps. I guess I thought I must have had it going on as well, as we drove down Ribaut Road with the t-tops off and the summer breeze tousling and toying with us.

Bryant even ensured he'd put his clincher on me, by hitting me where I can barely resist. He sent me a dozen long-stemmed red roses to my office. Now I'll tell you, flowers to me are like kryptonite to Superman, I was beginning to crumble and melt into a complete stupor. Everything had been cruising along fine, but unfortunately I was falling in love here.

Yet as quickly as this romance had erupted, it came to a screeching halt. And mind you with no advance warning. Now that's what always gets you. For a surprise attack always has you so totally unarmed and unprepared. I mean, and here's the nuclear bomb he put down on me out of the blue. "Lynn, we need to see other people. I can't just see one woman." What! Hold up! Hold everything. No, I wasn't even asking to be his wife or his girlfriend. I wasn't asking anything of him.

And I responded to Bryant two days prior to Valentine's Day, with my infamous Hypothesis Letter.

"*Hypothesis A:* Bryant finds great satisfaction and enjoyment in knowing that he has 'conquered' another woman. It gives him a feeling of accomplishment to know that he can manipulate a woman. In other words, 'He has made a fool of a woman.' Perhaps this is an attempt to avenge a past experience."

"*Hypothesis B:* Bryant truly cared a lot about Lynn in the beginning of the relationship, but the fire has dwindled down. And Bryant does not want to let go of the relationship entirely."

"*Hypothesis C:* Bryant still cares a lot for Lynn and perhaps to the extent of love. But he is scared of a committed relationship. Yet any true relationship entails some type of commitment between parties to establish and maintain a relationship. Perhaps Bryant is scared that such a relationship may hurt him and would prefer not to enter therein."

So much for my hypotheses. And besides what did I know about men? I certainly had been batting zero. And where were Oprah and Dr. Phil when I needed them?

So here we go again, heart. For I certainly had feelings for him by this point. Well, what can a girl say or do. So after my shedding of tears and my well-thought-out response letter to his Dear Jane announcement, I set him free from my heart. I certainly didn't think it fair to torture my heart again for a year or two in duration.

So as you can see, as Bryant and I had really gotten our feelings involved and entangled, yes it happened. He ran like crazy. I wasn't quite sure what was happening as it all went down. All I know is that I had finally met a guy that I actually cared for and now he had chosen to vanish from the relationship. Could it be that he feared what most guys fear the "Big C," as it's so commonly referred to today? Commitment. I really was unprepared to diagnosis the symptoms. I hadn't really encountered this syndrome before with my few past relationships. As far as my college heartbreak, I initially thought that was the classic fear of the Big C, until I had found he had ran straight from me to marry someone else. Then you think well something was wrong with me, evidently. Later to find it was simply another case of the Big R attacking me for the umpteenth time. Leave it to Racism, it always had it out for me.

Nonetheless you know me, I never could just kiss and say good-bye. So I dated other guys as I remorsefully watched Bryant out on dates in the clubs. But hey, I wasn't gonna let it get me quite like it had gotten me before. I had vowed that to myself. And even though we were both dating others, we did stay in touch some; occasionally visiting each other, talking on the phone, or even a letter here or there. (Yeah, I know we lived in the same town, but sometimes a letter just conveys your thoughts in a whole different perspective.)

And a couple months later, Bryant utilized this avenue of letter writing, I guess to continue to confirm to me that commitment was definitely out for him. Though I'm not that dense; I had already gotten the message. So perhaps he was trying to convince himself.

So he writes, "If I were to tell you that I loved you Lynn I would be lying in one respect and in another I would be telling the truth. There are all kinds of love—the love I have for you is a caring kind of love, a love wherein I don't want anything that is of a negative nature to happen to you. It is not, however, not the kind of love that you base a relationship on. I care for you. I miss you when we are apart. But we both know that our relationship is temporary. You have your way to go and I have mine. Just as we were destined to meet and love each other it is also destined that we should part eventually."

Well, I give him credit, he wasn't attempting to string me along. That was a pretty direct we-had-some-good times-and-now *goodbye.* So hey those begging days were over for me. If you want to go, who am I to stop you? It definitely hadn't been the first time and probably wouldn't be the last time. Such are the perils of engaging in the sport of love. It's unequivocally a high-risk game.

Therefore to attempt assurance that I didn't totally demolish my entire emotional and mental state of being hurt too badly this time, I took desperate measures for desperate times. I was getting the heck out of Beaufort and move on with my life. I wasn't leaving anything to chance this time.

Straight away I wrote to the Department of Defense to obtain an application of employment to teach overseas. The further the better. And I filled the 30-page document out and returned it. Yes I wasn't playing around this time. And when they called me to interview with a principal from Germany, I took my little narrow hip (at the time), got in my trusty Toyota Corona, and drove the six hours to Atlanta without a second thought. Unfortunately, they didn't offer me a position. Said I was their youngest applicant and that they preferred someone with more experience. Yeah, yeah, yeah.

In the meantime, I had another iron in the fire as my backup. Always have a plan B, a plan C, and a plan D, if possible. I had applied to the Doctoral Program at the University of South Carolina. All papers were submitted and in order, entrance exams taken and passed, and now it was time to meet with my advisor in Columbia. He attempted to discourage me with citing the drop out and non-completion rates of doctoral candidates, but he was definitely talking to the wrong person. A challenge just puts me up all the more for a battle. So I was all gun ho on beginning my program of study.

I was truly moving on this time. Evidently Bryant knew that too. But as I was moving on, the Marine Corps chose that it was his time to move on as well. And he soon was transferred to California right in the midst of all my searching for my next step. And as my name on the cover may have given it away, that was not a final good-bye to Bryant. After sending more roses, many long distance calls, and just a few weeks of separation, he went from the man who couldn't date just one woman at a time, then to the man that was destined to part from me, and finally to the man who asked for my hand in marriage. Almost a year to the day of our first date. The night of July 27, 1979 to the morning of July 24, 1980. And then to be married a year later on August 18, 1981 when he returned from his next duty station in Okinawa, Japan.

Evidently as the saying goes I had been looking for love in all the wrong places. But I now had found a man that loved me unconditionally. He loved me enough and respected me enough to give me what I had longed for and dreamed of for my future—a family. And had loved me enough to be willing to deal with Racism and whatever consequences that would come as a result of having an interracial marriage and interracial family.

So when Bryant finally worked through dealing with his phobia of commitment, it was such a welcome relief. I would finally get a break from It (that of course being Racism), at least within the confines of my home and the relationship with my husband. There was finally one threshold It could not cross. Race was never a factor for him. And I now had a safety zone.

Afterword

One day while shopping in the commissary, a black family with four young teens passed me by and emphatically whispered to each other, *"She's trying to act B-L-A-C-K!"* At that moment, I was totally engaged in a rather enjoyable and funny-loving conversation with one of my childhood classmates who happened to work in the produce department. And naturally without even thinking about it, I had automatically switched into my childhood language, the heavily-accented dialect of Gullah. (Of course they were total strangers to me. But already in a matter of seconds, my entire person and purpose had been judged and determined. And oh how many times all of us do the same ourselves.) But this penetrating and sting-ing phrase attacked my total being, leaving me totally crushed and devastated. Yes, I've heard this phrase so many times and unfortunately I myself would usu-ally be in agreement with such an accusation, but never had I been the direct recipient of the ridicule meted out by this observation. For when this statement is made by a black person, it's not said in a positive light. It's usually with the intent that "there goes another white person trying to mimic or rob another nugget of blackness."

I've had so many references through my years from well-known and dearly-loved acquaintances, acknowledge their whole-hearted acceptance of me with "Lynn, you know you're black." And I've always declined to accept this well-meant compliment for I felt totally unworthy of its honor. Yes, I'm sure that for the most part I do indeed think and behave more in accordance with the black world than that of the white world. But I haven't paid in the dues of what it actu-ally is to live in this world in black skin, for if I keep my mouth closed long enough, I do believe I can still "pass for white."

But in truth, I should not discredit the honor this compliment represents, but simply respond and acknowledge it with a heart-felt "thank you." A thank you for all that I've received from living within the black world (*not* "taken," but "received" as a gift—hugely important difference to note). Thank you to my community of St. Helena Island for accepting me, including me, and teaching me. I received so very, very much:

- The love of language and dialectical appreciations.

- The absolute love of rhythm & blues, good ole soul music, the funk of the 70's, and the inspiring, soul-stirring and uplifting spirit with which gospel music soothes and sets my soul on fire.

- The simple and yet so essential ability to "dance on beat" (which some folk may take for granted, but trust me there exists a lot of other folk who remain fully intrigued and amazed by the phenomenon).

- My total love of movement to accompany all that good music and the sheer ecstasy of simply dancing 'til the break of dawn.

- The ability to laugh, have fun, and not be downright "too uptight."

- The unconditional love and respect of family ties and family support.

- The utmost appreciation for compassion, service, and just "helping others" under all times, conditions, and situations.

- The ability to "fight" to be successful in spite of anything and anyone who attempts to hold you down.

- The development of inner strength, determination, and confidence in myself.

- A fervent love and need for "down-to-earthness" and just "being and keepin' it real."

For you see, "Once you become black you don't ever go back." Not that I ever wished to, but one particularly restricting reason is that "they" don't want and won't let you back (like I care). And the greatest reason is that you just simply don't have the desire to go back. Being within the black world is such a treasured and special richness. I would *never* choose to trade it or give it up.

Oh, I've suffered some wounds in the constant battles and attacks that our racist society unmercifully unleashes upon so many of us. Racism has certainly engulfed a huge segment of my life. But discrimination along any lines is sometimes almost unbearably difficult. And I definitely have had my share: racial, economic, and religious. And through it all, probably one of the most difficult situations that I haven't handled well at all, is that stigma of many times being left out in "the middle" with no true "home." Whites either "don't get me" or "don't want me" and blacks definitely don't need or want whites in their world.

And certainly I say this as a generalization for there are exceptions to any generalization. For the community I was raised in truly took me in as their own, but in any other avenue traveled from afar, I'm like a fish out of water.

So I've learned to cope with this by further extending and reinforcing a natural ingredient of my personality, the love of being alone. I've truly become a loner for the most part. I've always hung out with my immediate family and usually one or two close friends, and at times in my life it's narrowed as low as one and even sometimes—none.

Thankfully I always had the strength from the precious gift my mother placed within me since a small child, a steadfast love and reliance in God. This stronghold, coupled with the refuge of the Bahá'í Faith to call home always provided a safe haven and cease-fire zone between my two worlds. And the example the people of the Bahá'í community represents has always given me a faith and confidence that these two worlds along with the many other "worlds" of diverse cultures can love, live, work, worship, and play together. The Bahá'í s have applied this divine guidance since its inception for this is the law of God for today, and in adherence to His command then we *must* love, live, work, worship, and play together with all of His children. My prayer is that one day we will all be in "the middle" together.

Yet through all the hills and valleys of my life's sojourn, it's assuredly all been worth the privilege of knowing, understanding, and appreciating two largely different and very unique worlds.

And if I had to choose the course of my life again, one path I know I would not want to be denied is my treasured and priceless journey afforded me of being raised in a black world—through my family, school, and community. So the next time one of my friends tells me, "Lynn, girl, you know you're black," I'll insist on responding with a simple, sincere, and smiling, "Thank you." For I am who I am because of my endless, rich experiences that tribute Blackness. Yes, black is a color, but to me it's more importantly a total state of mind and way of life, in other words a total existence. One that I'm proud to say I've lived and experienced and wouldn't want to ever deny that "That's me."

"Yes! I'm Black and I'm Proud!" I professed, ever so confidently.

APPENDIX

Prayer for Mankind

O Thou Kind Lord! Thou hast created all humanity from the same stock. Thou hast decreed that all shall belong to the same household. In Thy Holy Presence they are all Thy servants, and all mankind are sheltered beneath Thy Tabernacle; all have gathered together at Thy Table of Bounty; all are illumined through the light of Thy Providence.

O God! Thou art kind to all, Thou hast provided for all, dost shelter all, conferrest life upon all. Thou hast endowed each and all with talents and faculties, and all are submerged in the Ocean of Thy Mercy.

O Thou kind Lord! Unite all. Let the religions agree and make the nations one, so that they may see each other as one family and the whole earth as one home. May they all live together in perfect harmony.

O God! Raise aloft the banner of the oneness of mankind.

O God! Establish the Most Great Peace.

Cement Thou, O God, the hearts together.

O Thou kind Father, God! Gladden our hearts through the fragrance of Thy love. Brighten our eyes through the Light of Thy Guidance. Delight our ears with the melody of Thy Word, and shelter us all in the Stronghold of Thy Providence.

Thou art the Mighty and Powerful, Thou art the Forgiving and Thou art the One Who overlooketh the shortcomings of all mankind.

Prayer for America

O Thou kind Lord! This gathering is turning to Thee. These hearts are radiant with Thy love. These minds and spirits are exhilarated by the message of Thy glad-tidings. O God! Let this American democracy become glorious in spiritual degrees even as it has aspired to material degrees, and render this just government victorious. Confirm this revered nation to upraise the standard of the oneness of humanity, to promulgate the Most Great Peace, to become thereby most glorious and praiseworthy among all the nations of the world. O God! This American nation is worthy of Thy favors and is deserving of Thy mercy. Make it precious and near to Thee through Thy bounty and bestowal.

—The Bahá'í Writings

Resource Information

For further information on the Bahá'í World Faith and its work in eliminating racial barriers and the model it provides through its development of communities worldwide living as one human family, please utilize the following contacts:

Website Address: **www.us.bahai.org**
Toll Free Telephone: 1-800-22UNITE

0-595-27466-8

Printed in the United States
963100004B

9 780595 274666